Gender and Change in Developing Countries

Edited by
Kristi Anne Stølen
and Mariken Vaa

SCANDINAVIAN LIBRARY

Stephen R. Graubard (ed.)	Norden – The Passion for Equality
Robert A. Dahl	Democracy, Liberty, and Equality
Øyvind Østerud (ed.)	Studies of War and Peace
S. N. Eisenstadt	European Civilization in a Comparative Perspective
Tove Stang Dahl	Women's Law
Helga Maria Hernes	Welfare State and Woman Power
Charles E. Lindblom	Democracy and Market System
Dag Österberg	Metasociology
Vilhelm Aubert	Continuity and Development
Inga Persson (ed.)	Generating Equality in the Welfare State
Kristi Anne Stølen and Mariken Vaa (eds)	Gender and Change in Developing Countries

Gender and Change in Developing Countries

Edited by
Kristi Anne Stølen
and Mariken Vaa

Norwegian
University Press

Norwegian University Press (Universitetsforlaget AS), 0608 Oslo 6
Distributed world-wide excluding Scandinavia by
Oxford University Press, Walton Street, Oxford OX2 6DP

London   New York   Toronto
Delhi   Bombay   Calcutta   Madras   Karachi
Kuala Lumpur   Singapore   Hong Kong   Tokyo
Nairobi   Dar es Salaam   Cape Town
Melbourne   Auckland

and associated companies in
Beirut   Berlin   Ibadan   Mexico City   Nicosia

© Universitetsforlaget AS 1991

All rights reserved. No part of this publication may be reproduced, stored in a retrieval system, or transmitted, in any form or by any means, electronic, mechanical, photocopying, recording, or otherwise, without the prior permission of Norwegian University Press (Universitetsforlaget AS)

British Library Cataloguing in Publication Data

Gender and change in developing countries.
 I. Stolen, Kristi Anne   II. Vaa, Mariken
 330.917240082

ISBN 82-00-21387-0

Printed in Norway by
Tangen Grafiske senter, Drammen 1991

Contents

Acknowledgements vi
Preface vii
Introduction: Women, gender and social change
Kristi Anne Stølen 1

Part I: Sexuality and Fertility – an Introduction 11
1. Chastity, sexuality and gender perceptions in rural Argentina
   Kristi Anne Stølen 13
2. Revival of female circumcision: a case of neo-traditionalism
   Astrid Nypan 39
3. Economic change, marriage relations and fertility in a rural area of Kenya
   An-Magritt Jensen 67

Part II: Livelihood and Work – an Introduction 91
4. "Wife, today I only had money for pombe". Gender and food: women's bargaining power and agricultural change in a Tanzanian community
   Gerd Holmboe-Ottesen and Margareta Wandel 93
5. Work, livelihoods and family responsibilities in urban poverty
   Mariken Vaa 121
6. What is she up to? Changing identities and values among women workers in Malaysia
   Merete Lie and Ragnhild Lund 147
7. Housewifization of peasant women in Costa Rica?
   Halldis Valestrand 165

Part III: Politics and Institutional Change – an Introduction ... 195
8. The symbolism of gender politics: a case of Malay female leadership
   Ingrid Rudie 197
9. Clans, gender and kilns: examples from a fisheries development project in Sota village, Tanzania
   Siri Gerrard 223
10. Legal reform in Mozambique: equality and emancipation for women through popular justice?
    Nina Berg and Aase Gundersen 247
11. Negotiating gender: the case of the International Labour Organization, ILO
    Ann Therese Lotherington and Anne Britt Flemmen 273
Contributors 309

Editors' Acknowledgements

The realization of this volume owes much to a number of people in addition to the contributors. Of these, one person in particular deserves special thanks for her role in seeing the project through: Ellen S. Aa. Vollebæk, senior executive officer of the Norwegian Research Council for Applied Social Science. At various junctures, she provided moral support and practical assistance both to individual authors and to us as editors which brought us, step by step, towards completion. We also express our gratitude for the encouragement and support we have received from employers and colleagues at the Centre for Development and Environment, University of Oslo and at the Institute for Social Research.

Kristi Anne Stølen and Mariken Vaa

Preface

Women's interests have been a priority goal for Norwegian development aid since the mid-1970s. During the UN Women's Decade (1975–85) it became increasingly clear that if the development process was to benefit ordinary people, women and their interests had to be accorded a primary place in development theory and practice. In 1985 the Norwegian Ministry of Development Cooperation brought to the UN International Nairobi Conference a Strategy for Women in Development Assistance. It was as part of this Strategy that the Ministry launched a five-year research programme on Women and Development. The Norwegian Council for Applied Social Science was asked to administer the programme which was allocated NOK 14.2 million (approximately USD 2.5 million).

Through the research programme on Women and Development, Norwegian development aid authorities confirmed the potential role of research and researchers in development planning and implementation. The overall aim of the programme has been to promote and strengthen national expertise on women and development issues and to make such expertise available to national governmental and non-governmental development agents. The programme invited research efforts and cooperation within three relatively wide areas of study: (a) production, work and economy; (b) politics, power and control; (c) culture, knowledge and conception of life.

During the five years duration of the programme 20 Norwegian researchers from such widely different fields as nutritional science, law and the social sciences have studied the situation of women in a variety of sectors as agriculture, fisheries, the health sector and in industry, and in a number of different countries in Latin America, Africa and Asia. The rich variation in approaches, locations and themes is reflected in this anthology, where major research findings and analytical insights in the broader context of gender, development and change are presented to the international research community.

Research programmes like the present are important not only for the research findings that emerge. Equally essential is the build-up of research experiences and general competence among the researchers financed by the programme. For Norway as a small country with a modest development aid involvement, all the elements of this tripartite consequence of research – the production of knowledge, of individual competence and of international research contacts – are essential. The present anthology is one way of furthering all three. It is also a way to fulfill the overall aim of the research programme on Women and Development, which is to make research competence available to public and private institutions working to promote international development.

The challenging task of distilling individual research contributions to a collective research enterprise has fallen on the two editors, Kristi Anne Stølen and Mariken Vaa. They, as well as the Norwegian Agency for International Development and the Norwegian Research Council for Applied Social Science, are thanked for the opportunity the present anthology provides for researchers and others to enhance their understanding of the complex, yet rewarding field of gender, development and change.

Else Skjønsberg, Chair,
Steering Committee on Women and Development
The Norwegian Research Council for Applied Social Science

Introduction: Women, Gender and Social Change

KRISTI ANNE STØLEN

This collection of articles is the outcome of a research programme covering a broadly defined area of study (ref. Preface). It is characterized by a wide and varied thematic and analytical orientation. The researchers come from different universities and research institutions in Norway. They represent a broad range of disciplines and present material from research in Asia, Africa and Latin America. The papers depict a multitude of contexts, research interests and approaches. This diversity does not facilitate a unified analysis of gender and social change, but on the other hand it does provide a forum for themes and perspectives that have not been given much attention previously, and therefore may enrich the current debate. Some of the researchers have carried out field-work in the same area in different periods, and can now draw conclusions from over a long time span, and make their own comparisons. This is the case of Nypan and Rudie, who started their research in the mid-1960s, and Stølen and Valestrand, who initiated their research in the early 1970s and the mid-1980s respectively.

Most of the contributions analyse processes of change from "below", uncovering strategies of individuals or social groups in various socio-cultural contexts, characterized by rapid market integration. Some are mainly concerned with continuity and change in women and men's behaviour, others with discontinuities at the level of ideas and perceptions of gender, while a few attempt to explore the intersection between the two levels. In what follows, I will address some of the main analytical and theoretical concerns that can be extracted from the reading of this book.

I. Women as Actors of Change

There is now broad agreement among scholars that colonialist and capitalist penetration have restructured Third World societies in a way that has had a deep impact on gender relations, on the nature of the sexual division of labour, and on the kinds of social and political options open to men and women. However, the specific effects of these processes are debated. Some authors have suggested that capitalism combined with Eurocentric ideas about the role and activities proper to women has led to the destruction of women's traditional rights in society and undermined their economic autonomy in relation to men (Boserup, 1970; Pala, 1980; Rogers, 1980; Moore, 1988). This type of "impact analysis" often gives the impression that "things were better before". To this one can respond that it may be wrong to assume that women, for example, had a significant degree of power or autonomy in precapitalist societies. Moreover, it is not necessarily so that capitalist influence leads to the deterioration of women's lives. It may, under certain conditions, as is documented in this volume, offer new opportunities for women which they are able to use for the improvement of their life situation and even to challenge existing discriminatory gender relations and perceptions.

Implicit in the "impact analyses", whether they are concerned with gender or not, is often an assumption that local people are "victims of circumstances", simply "responding" to innovations imposed by others. Studies carried out within both modernization and dependency paradigms have in common that they tend to interpret specific patterns of development/underdevelopment or paths of social change with reference to the intervention of private or public authorities or institutions or to powerful foreigners. They do not pay sufficient attention to the ways in which individuals and groups can contribute and indeed modify patterns of regional and national development.

Lately, development researchers, particularly anthropologists, have called the attention to the variety of responses to similar processes of change (Long, 1977, 1989; Moore, 1988). The variety is attributed to socio-cultural prerequisites that are historically and culturally specific. The relationship between the "local" and the "external" is conceived as a process of interaction rather than one of imposition. This view on social change is associated with an actor-oriented approach. Such an approach assumes that variations in organizational forms and cultural patterns are to a large extent the outcome of the different ways in which social actors organizationally and cognitively deal with problematic situations and accommodate themselves to the interests and "designs for living" of others. Inherent in the concept of social actor is the notion of the human being as an active subject with the capacity to process social experience and to invent ways of coping with life even under extreme forms of coercion. This holds good whether the particular actor is deemed "powerful" or "powerless". Within the limits of their socio-cultural context women and men attempt to solve problems, learn how to intervene in the social events around them and monitor their own actions, as well as observing how others react to their behaviour (Long, 1989, pp. 222–223; Giddens, 1984).

The actor-oriented approach is particularly useful for studying gender and social change. It enables us to appreciate how changes in people's opportunity structures, provoked for example by the introduction of new fish processing technology (Gerrard), by the introduction of new crops (Holmboe-Ottesen, Jensen, Valestrand), or by debt crisis and unemployment (Nypan), are manipulated by particular individuals or groups who pursue economic and social strategies in dealing with their changing environment.

The notion of local women and men as social actors implies that it is difficult or impossible to predict impacts of innovations without a thorough knowledge of the socio-cultural context where the innovation is going to be adopted. In the area of gender studies this means, for example, that there is no predictable relationship between the degree and type of market integration and women's roles in the sexual division of labour. Rather, the division of roles is responsive to a number of conditions, such as the social characteristics of the household and local community, the position of women and men themselves, such as class, the family cycle, kinship position and age, and religion and ideology. Gender studies carried out with such a framework would depict women as active shapers of their lives, whether they exploit new opportunities or resist them, or whether they succeed in their pursuits or not. It is important to emphasize that this view does not imply a disregard of the fact that the constraints on women's actions may be overwhelming and that women are often exploited by or subordinated to men.

The actor-oriented approach does not mean that it is the individual *per se* that is the focus of analysis, but the individual acting in social situations, where the conduct of one influences the conduct of others and vice versa. Thus, even if one focuses on decision-making by the individual woman (or man), this does not imply that their actions can be explained simply by reference to her own dispositions and beliefs. We have to take into account the various social relationships in which she is embedded, both within and outside the family, and not only those present in face-to-face situations, but

also those who are absent but influential both for the action and its outcome.
Social relations and conditions influencing individual behaviour belong to different scale levels. The revival of female circumcision among the Meru of Tanzania (Nypan) can hardly be understood unless one takes into account the economic crisis of the country offering few opportunities for women other than becoming a peasant's wife, with the cultural requirements that this implies. Jensen's study from Kenya explores the relationship between gender and fertility behaviour at the micro level to explain the lack of fertility decline in a region where, according to demographic theories, such decline should have taken place. These examples illustrate how a view of the significance of change from the actor's point of view offers the prospect of relating local level processes to wider regional, national and international processes and thereby not only depicts the microdynamics of social life but also contributes to the understanding of larger scale social structures and processes.

II. Gender Perspective

Most of the studies in this book focus on women, but have been carried out within a gender framework. The concept of "gender" refers to the cultural interpretation of biological differences between men and women. "Sex" and "gender" are concepts that allude, respectively, to the biological differences between men and women and the cultural interpretations of these differences (Moore, 1988). Gender is not a characteristic of a person, something that women have, while men are "men", as many seem to believe (Melhuus, 1988). On the contrary, gender and gender identity are socially constructed through processes of socialization whereby human beings become social persons. Therefore, gender relations or the relationship between women and men should constitute the perspective of analysis when studying women.

What men and women do and how they relate socially is an important aspect of gender. It is also important to grasp the ideas and conceptions that motivate and organize gender roles. Thus, gender entails, on the one hand, men and women's active roles in society, and, on the other, their ideas about "maleness" and "femaleness". What men and women do and how they behave and interact, together with cultural ideas and interpretations of gender differences, constitute a gender system. The concept of gender system implies that the different components of gender are conceived as interrelated and influence each other (Ortner and Whitehead, 1981; Kulick, 1987; Moore, 1988; Stølen, this volume). The gender system is constantly being transformed and recreated as socio-economic and cultural changes take place. Changes may be brought about by new economic circumstances, such as the establishment of foreign enterprises (Lie and Lund), or by the introduction of new agricultural methods or technology (Holmboe-Ottesen and Wandel, Stølen). Transformation of gender relations may also be initiated through legal reforms promoting gender equality, as in Berg and Gundersen's study from Mozambique or through policy reforms, as in the case of the ILO study (Lotherington and Flemmen).

III. Gender at the Interface

Most of the processes of change referred to in this volume can be characterized as social interface situations, social interface being defined as "a critical point of intersection or linkage between different social systems, fields or levels of social order, where structural discontinuities, based upon differences of normative value and social interest, are most likely to be found" (Long, 1989, p. 2). The interface concept implies some kind of face-to-face encounter where the parties involved represent different interests and are backed by different resources. In interface situations discrepancies of social interest, cultural interpretation, knowledge and power are mediated and perpetuated or transformed through interactions and negotiations between specific social actors. Such discrepancies arise in all kinds of social contexts. In a rural village they may, for example, entail struggles between landowners and landless, members of different clans or ethnic groups or between women and men. Discrepancies become particularly evident in situations of development interventions, where external, sometimes expatriate, "agents of change" are present locally (Gerrard). The kind of discontinuities created and negotiated in interface encounters are multifaceted and will vary from one socio-cultural context to another. Here we are particularly concerned with discrepancies in male–female relations.

Since societies are gendered, the way local actors relate to innovations will be gender specific, even when the innovations as such are conceived as "gender neutral" and not directed particularly towards men and women. Berg and Gundersen show, for example, how legal systems based on *de jure* equality may confirm or even aggravate gender inequalities when implemented in gendered contexts. Neither are material innovations – for example, the introduction of new technology – "gender neutral". Technology cannot be understood independently of social contexts, since it is intimately tied to human labour, which is in turn an organized activity. The interesting feature of technology is the way material activities are organized (Melhuus, 1988). In our case it is the way in which the technology intervenes in the sexual division of labour that is particularly relevant. If men dominate the area where technology is going to be used, they will normally be the ones to appropriate it (Stølen, Valestrand). However, new agricultural technology has often been directed towards men, also in cases where women play the main role in agriculture (Holmboe-Ottesen and Wandel). This has to be understood in view of the gender notions held by those who introduce and promote the use of the innovations. They have generally been socialized in a world where farmers are or should be men. In this way both tasks and things are gendered. The introduction of new "things" or "tasks" often creates discontinuities in gender relations.

The articles in this volume are particularly concerned with the production, processing and outcome of gender discontinuities in a variety of situations of social change. The concept of "gender negotiations" is used when referring to the formal or informal, open or secret bargaining coming about between women and men in such situations, regarding what women or men should or should not do or be (Rudie, 1984a).

IV. Continuity and Change in Gender Relations

Cultural ideas about gender do not directly reflect the social and economic positions of women and men (Collier and Rosaldo, 1981; Moore, 1988). Nevertheless, there is a close relationship between what you do, or do not do, and who you are, i.e. between work and gender identity (Melhuus, 1988). Social change is often associated with changes in the conditions of work. If the innovations build on existing gender divisions they may only cement differences that are already there, and not represent a major challenge to dominant gender roles and perceptions. However, certain innovations provoke discontinuities, for example in the prevailing system of sexual division of labour. This is the case in the Muslim community in Malaysia studied by Lie and Lund. Due to the establishment of an industrial plant employing female labour, young women, who were previously protected and controlled, have entered the labour market and to a large extent replaced their fathers as the main income earners of their families. This provoked discontinuities in the meaning of gender, which had to be negotiated and redefined. Women have gained new positions *vis-à-vis* men and this is largely accepted in the local community. However, they do not openly challenge the traditional authority structure, and their identity and value as women still depend on whether or not they conform to traditional values (chastity, marriage and motherhood).

In some cases behavioural changes are strategies to preserve basic elements of lifestyle or traditions, only modified to adjust to new circumstances (Lie and Lund). This seems to be what the political leaders in rural Malaysia attempt to achieve (Rudie). Through the creation of new income-generating activities for rural women, in a situation of rapid market integration, they try to regain gender balance between men and women in the household, characteristic of the now fading "domestic mode of production".

These examples draw attention to the fact that processes of change often contain elements of both a striving for continuity – new ways of behaviour that preserve, or at least are compatible with, "old" gender values – as well as a striving to achieve "new" values. Most of the studies presented here to some extent illustrate this tension between continuity and change, as well as the tension between the level of behaviour and the level of ideas. They depict considerable changes in the roles of men and women and in the relationship between them, which in turn may lead to certain adaptations or modifications in the conceptualization of "maleness" and "femaleness". However, in none of the cases referred to in this book do these modifications seem to challenge the notions of gender as hierarchically structured, which remains a persistent theme throughout. This notion often constitutes what Bourdieu calls implicit meaning, that which is neither articulated nor discussed, but simply taken for granted (Bourdieu, 1977). When social actors are operating within certain social orders, and complying in effect with the rules of the game, the world tends to take on certain seemingly inevitable and "natural" appearances (Ortner and Whitehead, 1981).

Some of the chapters portray situations where people have endured dramatic socio-economic changes, with only minor adaptations or modifications of their perceptions of gender. This is the case of the Argentine farmers (Stølen), of the urban poor in Mali

(Vaa), and of the Costa Rican peasants (Valestrand). These examples show that extensive changes at the level of behaviour may take place without corresponding changes at the level of ideas. In these cases, as in the Malaysian case (Lie and Lund), religion, Catholicism and Islam respectively, through their institutions, ideologies and practices, strongly influence people's lives. These religions are powerful sources of gender doctrines, defining the hierarchical structuring of gender as natural and of a celestial order, and thereby unchangeable (Delaney, 1987). When gender ideologies are rooted in the highly institutionalized "world" religions, which to a large extent "live their own life" highly independent on changes in the "material base", whatever that base might be, they seem to be particularly resistant to change. Thus, as long as the very role of religion is not questioned, both men and women remain caught in a web of dominant gender ideology, which endows women with a subordinate position in relation to men.

However, the fact that women are conceived as subordinate to men may tell us little about prevailing male–female relations, since gender notions rarely reflect the relations accurately. In some of the cases presented here women are represented as more subordinate than they actually are. Holmboe-Ottesen and Wandel show that women may be quite conscious about the discrepancies between representations and "reality"; between how relations should be and how they actually are. A Rukwa woman who knows that she will be beaten up by her husband if she "tries to show that she is strong" performs certain everyday rituals making her husband feel that he is the one who decides, even when this is far from the case.

Sexuality and procreation are crucial elements in the cultural construction of gender. Several chapters focus on sexuality, especially on the relationship between the control of female sexuality and gender identity in situations of socio-economic change (Jensen, Nypan, Stølen). They illustrate how the realization of womanhood, as well as men's social prestige, to a large extent depends on female attributes such as virginity, chastity, fertility or a mutilated clitoris. It has been argued that the fact that female sexuality should be and actually is controlled, while male sexuality need not or even should not be, expresses relations of power between men and women (Ortner, 1981; Shore, 1981). The material presented here confirms this but at the same time it clearly shows that it is not necessarily a type of power forced upon women against their will. Interesting to note is that in situations of socio-economic change when the thinking and doing of gender are negotiated, women agree on, and in some cases even actively strive to maintain, practices that subordinate them to men. This draws attention to the very concept of power.

V. Gender and Power

If gender relations are power relations, what kind of power are we talking about? Power, like gender, is a relational concept; it does not exist outside relations and it is not something that a person simply possesses. Thus, within a gender perspective, the question is not whether women or men have or do not have power, but how power comes about in relationships between them.

For a long time, and especially in women's studies, power has been considered as repressive only. Women were claimed to be victims of the exercise of power by men. Of course, and this should not be forgotten, power in gender relations may be repressive. However, the fact that women often agree with practices that subordinate them, that they resist the exercise of power, and that there often exist friendly relations between women and men, cannot be understood in terms of the exclusively repressive view on power (Halsema, 1991). A view on power as simply repressive conceals the fact that it may also be constructive and enabling (Foucault, 1978). However, one should be careful not to reduce the subjects to simple products of the operation of power. This is not compatible with the notion of human agency and of women and men as active subjects. There can be no absolute control of women by men, regardless of how asymmetric the relationship between them may be. Women will always have "room to manoeuvre" where they can use their creativity. This means that we need a constructive view of power in addition to the repressive one. The material presented in this book depicts a diversity of ways in which women gain or retain room for independent decision-making, for choice, pragmatism and creativity. Few of the chapters address the concept of power directly, but offer important insights for the development of better analytical tools to analyse power relations between the genders.

References

Boserup, E. 1970. *Women's Role in Economic Development*. London: George Allen & Unwin.
Bourdieu, P. 1977. *Outline of a Theory of Practice*. Cambridge Studies in Social Anthropology. Cambridge: Cambridge University Press.

Collier, J. F. and Rosaldo, M. Z. 1981. Politics and Gender in Simple Societies. In S. B. Ortner and H. Whitehead (eds).
Delaney, C. 1987. Seeds of Honor, Fields of Shame. In G. G. Gilmore (ed.).
Etienne, M. and Leacock, E. 1980. *Women and Colonization: Anthropological Perspective.* New York: Praeger.
Foucault, M. 1978. *The History of Sexuality*, Vol. 1. London: Allen Lane.
Giddens, A. 1984. *The Constitution of Society: Outline of the Theory of Structuration.* Cambridge: Polity Press.
Gilmore, G. G. (ed.) 1987. *Honor and Shame and the Unity of the Mediterranean.* Washington: AAA, 22.
Halsema, Ineke van 1991. *Housewives in the Field: Power, Culture and Gender in a South Brazilian Village.* Amsterdam: CEDLA Publications.
Kulick, D. 1987. Hur man blir en riktig mann eller kvinna. In *Från Kön till Genus: Kvinnligt och Manligt i ett Kulturellt Perspektiv.* Stockholm: Carlsons.
Long, N. 1977. *An Introduction to the Sociology of Rural Development.* London: Tavistock Publications.
Long, N. 1989. *Encounters at the Interface.* Wageningen Studies in Sociology 27.
Melhuus, M. 1988. Gender, Culture and Appropriate Technology – A Conceptual Framework. In *Mobilizing Appropriate Technology*. London: Intermediate Technology Publications.
Moore, H. 1988. *Feminism and Anthropology.* Cambridge: Polity Press.
Ortner, S. B. 1981. Gender and Sexuality in Hierarchical Societies: The Case of Polynesia and Some Comparative Implications. In S. B. Ortner and H. Whitehead (eds).
Ortner, S. B. and Whitehead, H. 1981. Introduction: Accounting for Sexual Meaning. In S. Ortner and H. Whitehead (eds).
Ortner, S. B. and Whitehead, H. (eds) 1981. *Sexual Meaning: The Cultural Construction of Gender and Sexuality.* Cambridge: Cambridge University Press.
Pala, A. 1980. Daughters of the Lakes and Rivers: Colonization and Land Rights of the Luo Women. In M. Etienne and E. Leacock (eds).
Rogers, B. 1980. *The Domestication of Women: Discrimination in Developing Societies.* London: Tavistock.
Rosaldo, M. and Lamphere, L. 1974. *Women, Culture and Society.* Stanford: Stanford University Press.
Rudie, J. 1984a. Innledning. In J. Rudie (ed.) 1984b.
Rudie, J. 1984b. *Myk start hard landing.* Oslo: Norwegian University Press.
Shore, B. 1981. Sexuality and Gender in Samoa: Conceptions and Missed Conceptions. In S. B. Ortner and H. Whitehead (eds).

Part I
Sexuality and Fertility – an Introduction

The articles in this section draw attention to the roles of sexuality and reproduction in the cultural construction of gender. Control of female sexuality is uncovered as an important mechanism in the maintenance of women's subordination to men, defended by both men and women.

Sexuality and sexual legitimacy have a dominant place in the gender code of Santa Cecilia discussed by Stølen. A woman's sexual behaviour, her virginity and chastity, to a large extent determine her social value, her attractiveness in the marriage market and her chances of becoming a respectable wife, mother and housewife, which are the most important attributes of womanhood. Interestingly, the sexual behaviour of women is also of crucial importance for the conceptualization of manhood and for the social prestige of men. Stølen discusses how these gender notions regulate and recreate power relations within the family, and in society, over time. She observes a striking continuity in gender notions in spite of dramatic social and economic changes. This is ascribed to the strong position of Catholicism in the area of study.

Among the Meru of Tanzania, analysed by Nypan, gender identity is also closely associated with sexuality. Nypan observed an increase in the number of circumcised women in her area of study during the 1980s compared to the 1960s, when she carried out her first fieldwork in the area. A mutilated clitoris is again becoming an important symbol of womanhood, as it was before independence. Men seem to prefer circumcised women because they are believed to be less passionate and more loyal to their husbands. In the 1960s, the mobilization of educated women (and men) to create "a modern woman", enlightened, economically independent and "sexually hot", led to a dramatic reduction in the number of circumcised women among the Meru, as in other parts of Tanzania. Nypan views the revival of female circumcision as part of a more general revival of ethnic culture and tradition, which she attributes to macro-economic and political changes in Tanzania during the last decade.

In the third article, Jensen examines gender relations in the Bungoma families to explore why there has been no fertility decline in this region of Kenya, despite the transition from a subsistence to a market economy. According to the demographic literature, such a transition is normally associated with a decline in the social utility of children, which in turn leads to a decline in fertility rates. Jensen argues that in situations where women are socially and economically dependent on men for their survival, and men's social prestige is closely associated with the number of children they beget, a decrease in fertility rates is unlikely. Thus, poverty and particularly the weak position of women in Bungoma society intervene in the expected correlation between market integration and fertility decline.

In all three articles gender identity is associated with the control of female sexuality. To become a "real woman" one has to be chaste, circumcised or fertile, and belong to a man. Manhood, on the other hand, is seen as dependent on these female qualities. The fact that female sexuality has to be controlled, and indeed is controlled, expresses power relations between men and women. However, women are not the mere victims of the exercise of power by men. They often agree and even actively strive to maintain the practices that subordinate them. This is particularly striking in the example from Argentina, where women, through gossip, are the main guardians of virginity and chastity. It is also noticeable among the Meru, where young girls themselves take the initiative to become circumcised, often against the will of their mothers, to be more attractive in the marriage market. Similarly, the Bungoma women actively maintain the high level of procreation, in spite of recognizing the advantages of reducing the number of children and having access to the means of doing so, because they fear that their husbands will lose interest in them.

1
Chastity, Sexuality and Gender Perceptions in Rural Argentina

KRISTI ANNE STØLEN

This essay is based on field-work carried out in Santa Cecilia, a rural middle-class community in Argentina.[1] The farmers are descendants of Italian immigrants who arrived from Friuli (northern Italy) in the 1880s, and range from second to fifth generation immigrants. Their settling in Argentina, in an environment that in many ways was different from the rural villages of their "ancestors" in the Italian Alps, required new ways of organizing economic and social life.[2] Since their establishment in the region they have been part of a complex society which has undergone dramatic processes of change during the last century. In Santa Cecilia these changes are primarily associated with the introduction of industrial crops (cotton and sunflower) in the 1930s and the mechanization of agriculture from the 1950s. The introduction of cotton initiated a process of economic growth in the region, which was accelerated with the introduction of labour-saving technologies introduced two decades later. Machinery gradually replaced family labour in agriculture and generated labour surplus in the rural areas, which has led to a massive rural exodus.[3]

At a superficial level, the contemporary way of life in Santa Cecilia seems more similar to what we find on the American prairies than what we associate with traditional rural areas of the Mediterranean. Agricultural production is highly market oriented and mechanized, and people move around in pick-up trucks. The farms are organized in such a way that they can be run by two adults, one man, who is responsible for agriculture, and one woman, who takes care of the home. Ideally they should constitute a nuclear family with three children, of whom at least one is a boy who can secure the continuity of the farm, while the others are expected to find a living elsewhere. The gradual adoption of this "farmer way of life" has, however, not led to a complete rupture with Mediterranean culture. This becomes evident if we look at gender relations. The latter reveal striking similarities with what is reported from the Mediterranean, particularly regarding the importance of female virginity, chastity and domesticity.

This brings us to the interesting, but difficult theoretical question of the interaction between economic, social and cultural factors in the continuity and change of gender relations. In the following discussion gender refers to the cultural interpretations of biological differences between men and women. Gender entails, on the one hand, men's and women's active roles in society, and, on the other, their ideas about maleness and femaleness. What men and women do and how they behave, together with the cultural ideas and interpretations of gender differences, constitute a *gender system*. The concept of gender system implies that the different components of gender are conceived as interrelated (Ortner and Whitehead, 1981b; Kulick, 1987b; Moore, 1988).

The gender system is constantly being transformed and recreated as economic changes take place. The outcome of such transformations will, however, vary according to socio-cultural prerequisites. There is, for example, no predictable relationship between a certain degree and type of market integration and the sexual division of labour. The latter is responsive to a number of variables, such as the social characteristics of the household and the local community, the positions of men and women themselves, such as class, the family cycle, kinship position and age, and religion and ideology. Together these variables constitute the opportunity structure within which individuals or groups of individuals develop new economic and social strategies in dealing with their changing environment. In this perspective people are seen as active shapers of their own reality, not as passive victims of circumstances.

Changes in behaviour do not necessarily lead to changes at the level of ideas. Behavioural changes may also be strategies to preserve basic elements of life-style or traditions, only modified to adjust to new circumstances. Often processes of change contain elements of both a striving for continuity – new ways of behaviour that preserve "old" gender values – and a striving to achieve "new" values (Lie and Lund, this volume). This is the case in Santa Cecilia. Here, I will mainly concentrate on the continuity aspect, the processes by which "old" gender values are adapted to and "survive" in a changing economic and social environment.[4]

Certain ideas and practices are more resistant to change than others. This is the case when values, ideas and practices are shared by all social actors in a given society, and are so self-evident that they are not made explicit, and thus, not questioned (Bourdieu,

1977). In Santa Cecilia certain gender notions and related practice seem to be of this order. One is the association between men and women and public and domestic domains, illustrated by the following popular saying: *"el hombre es de la calle, la mujer de la casa"* (the man belongs to the street, the woman at home). More concretely it implies that a man should be the bread-winner, be responsible for the economic and social welfare of his family members and represent them in the outside world. His wife should be his emotional counterpart in charge of household chores and child care and under his protection. The sphere of social activity associated with males encompasses the sphere predominantly associated with females and is, for that reason, accorded higher value. This is well known from other parts of the world, and the similarities with the Mediterranean are evident (Ortner and Whitehead, 1981a; Gilmore, 1987a).

The high valuation of virginity, chastity and sexual control of women is another area which seems to be particularly resistant to change. As in the Mediterranean sexuality and sexual legitimacy have a dominant place in the gender code. A woman's sexual behaviour determines to a large extent her social value, it is decisive for her attraction in the marriage market and determines her possibilities of becoming a respectable mother and housewife. Female premarital virginity and chastity within marriage, determine to a large extent, the social position of men as husbands, but not as fathers and brothers as seems to be the case in the Mediterranean (Giovannini, 1987). The fact that women must be controlled, while men need not, and indeed should not be, is also an indication of gender as hierarchically structured.

I suggest that these notions of gender difference and hierarchy and the strong concern about sexuality, especially female sexuality, tend to survive the economic transformations because they are deeply rooted in religion, which historically and at present is a powerful source of gender doctrines and a strong shaper of male-female relations and perceptions thereof.

In what follows I will first explore the "Mediterranean connection" by referring to the honour and shame complex as presented in anthropological studies from this region, and to Catholic gender ideology that is extremely powerful both in the Mediterranean and in Santa Cecilia. Then I will point at similarities between Santa Cecilian and Mediterranean gender perceptions, which I believe are rooted in common religious gender doctrines, and to differences that have to be understood with reference to the specific socio-economic conditions of my area of study. Finally, I will discuss continuity and change in gender relations in Santa Cecilia in the light of the dramatic changes that have occurred in the family and household composition, the sexual division of labour, and in marriage and residence patterns since the turn of the century. I suggest that the strong influence of religion is a major factor in understanding why certain ideas about what it means to be a man and a woman "survive" and contribute to maintain the hierarchical structure of gender relations in Santa Cecilia.

I. The Honour and Shame Complex

The emphasis on virginity and female chastity is well known from the anthropological literature on the Mediterranean, where it is presented as a central element in the so-called "honour and shame complex". This has long been regarded as the most unifying cultural theme of Mediterranean societies (Pitt-Rivers, 1961; Perestiany, 1965; Wolf, 1969; Schneider, 1971; Block, 1981; Gilmore, 1987a). It reflects at the same time the public esteem of a person and the sensitivity to public opinion upon which the former depends (Pitt-Rivers, 1965, p. 42).

According to the early writers, honour is a masculine attribute. It is the reward for successful power manoeuvres in which a man's relationship to other men *through women* is the fundamental axis of evaluation. Throughout the Mediterranean region, male honour is said to derive from the struggle to maintain intact the sexual chastity of kinswomen, and this renders male reputation dependent upon female sexual conduct. When males are not successful in this, their prestige in relation to other men is diminished. They lose their honour (Perestiany, 1965; Gilmore, 1987b). Thus, female sexuality is a form of social power that is threatening to men and needs to be controlled by them.

It is interesting to recall that ethnographically speaking women in Mediterranean societies often do not represent property (they are often excluded from inheritance to family patrimony), or labour force. They are first and foremost "domestic". Their social value is associated with an "immaterial resource", virginity/chastity which is given a central role as a kind of "exchange value".

Female sexuality is said to be closely supervised and transferred as part of the family patrimony. At the same time is the female chastity "objectified", i.e. is an object of male seduction. Male reputation is, on the one hand, dependent on the purity and chastity of women, and, on the other, on their capacity to conquer women. The realization of maleness, thus, does not only lead to the "fall" of some women, it also requires control of others (wives, sisters and daughters), who are the potential prey of any and all men at large. If a woman remains at home with her children, her husband feels much more secure than if she should spend her time in places where she will meet men whose reputations depend not on her chastity, but, on the contrary, on their capacity to seduce her. This ambiguity in the definition of masculinity and femininity is reported to be particularly strong in societies with marked class differences like Andalucía and some Latin American contexts (Brandes, 1981; Pescatello, 1973; Stølen, 1987).

Recently, several scholars have criticized the original honour and shame model for being too narrowly focused on sexuality. They argue that moral principles like hospitality, honesty and respect in many contexts overshadow the one associated with sexuality (Herzfeld, 1987; Brandes, 1987; Gilmore, 1987b; Wikan, 1984). What seems to be the controversy in this debate is the *relative* importance of sexuality in the moral evaluative systems. Most scholars seem to agree that premarital virginity and marital chastity remain strong throughout the region in spite of modernization and diversification, and that this emphasis on female chastity constitutes a promising area for comparative investigation (Giovannini, 1987; Gilmore, 1987b).

Delaney argues that one has to examine religious ideas and values in order to understand the particular preoccupation with female sexuality that characterizes Mediterranean cultures. She criticizes the tendency to give "honour and shame" a particular content, as if they were stable and unalterable:

> The mistake has been to interpret the honour code somewhat like a dress code – as a set of rules and regulations – focused on superficial conformity. Instead I propose that it is more like a kind of genetic code – a structure of relations – generative of possibilities (1987, p. 35).

She uses an analogy from biology to illustrate her argument:

> In the way that genetically similar seeds sown in different soils produce phenotypically varied fruits, so do I believe that encoded in the "honour and shame" complex is a specific theory of

sexuality and procreation that produces slightly different permutations in practice, depending on the environment in which it takes root. The key to unlocking the code lies, I suggest, in an examination of sexuality and procreation (1987, p. 35).

Delaney suggests that the importance of sexuality in the "honour and shame complex" is associated with *monogenetic* theories of procreation, i.e. where there is only one principle of generation. This is the case of Judaism, Christianity and Islam. In these religions there is not only one God, but the divinity by and of itself is creativity and potency. Moreover it is defined as masculine. Women are perceived as lacking this power and ability. They may be revered, as in the adoration of Mary, but it is precisely for the absence of potency-generativity. She is revered for her virginal and maternal qualities, for her purity, succour, mercy, self-sacrifice, and as the vehicle through which divinity is made manifest. Monogenetic theories create a symbolic alliance between men and God; men partake of divine power so that their dominance seems natural and ordained in the order of things.

II. Catholic Notions of Maleness and Femaleness

A central core of Christian doctrine is precisely that the world was created by God, a male being, and he did it alone, without a partner. This gives him an unapproachable status above and beyond all holy and secular beings and it creates a symbolic alliance between God and men, which legitimates male dominance and authority.

Historically the Catholic Church has promoted two models of understanding the divine relations. The first is a hierarchical model of feudal relations of servants to lord and king. The Church hierarchy, with the Pope as a leader and the cardinals, bishops, priests and laymen, mediates the relationship between the unapproachable God and the Christian community. This model has now to a large extent been replaced by a nuclear family model: where God is the father, Mary the mother and the Christian community the children. The deity in this family is male and coupled with the feudal model in which God is master and king, it has been suggested that the family model is by association a patriarchal one (Christian, 1972; Skar Lund, 1991).

In contrast to the authoritative God/father, the Church's representation of Mary as the ideal mother emphasizes the attributes of her nearness to the human condition and her willingness to intercede for those who come to her in need. With Christ's resurrection uniting him with the God and divorcing him from humanity, the figure of Mary has become the focus of worship as the truly human element in the holy family. She is the model of Christian virtue, the ideal to which the faithful aspire. The authority of Mary is based on her relationship to Christ, which gives her the contradictory attribute of motherhood and virginity. She represents an ideal which is impossible for the faithful to achieve.

The historical paradox central to Christian attitudes towards women is that it attempted to reinstate women by removing the conditions that stamped them as inferior and kept them in servitude: marriage and motherhood. Women are equal to men in religion although considered *socially* subject to the male. Women who adopt a virginal life (e.g. nuns) will not have to suffer the consequences of the Fall. They will not have a husband to obey or pregnancies to endure. To some extent virginity reverses the Fall. Jerome wrote:

> As long as woman is for birth and children, she is different from man as body is from soul. But when she wishes to serve Christ more than the world, then she will cease to be a woman and will be called a man (Warner, 1976, pp. 72–73).

In the Catholic context, the only female roles accepted by the Church are, first, the one associated with secular marriage and motherhood, which implies the subordination to a husband, and second, the one associated with "celestial marriage", which renders women a certain level of independence at the cost of the renunciation of sexuality and motherhood.

It should be remembered that the Church hierarchy spent several centuries refining the doctrine of the virgin birth and endorsing virginity as the epitome of Christian virtue. Christ could not be the product of an act of passion because sex was associated with the flesh, evil, the Fall and the original sin, and it was particularly identified with the female. For centuries the Church held that procreation was the only justification for sexual intercourse, passionate sexual intercourse was considered sinful.

Delaney argues that monogenesis, patriarchy and mariology are different aspects of the same, an ideology that perpetuates and legitimates male dominance and authority. Power, sex and the sacred are interrelated and seen to be rooted in the verities of biology. According to Delaney, the "truth" of biology in this case is the theory of monotheism (1987).

I find the above insights useful for understanding gender relations in Santa Cecilia. We shall see that they are clearly rooted in a specific theory of sexuality and procreation at the same time as they are adapted to a changing socio-economic environment.

III. The Setting

Santa Cecilia is a "colony" in the north-east of Santa Fe province, where I spent one year in 1973–74 and eight months in 1988. It comprises altogether 34 farms, scattered throughout an area of 20 by 10 km. In the middle of the "colony" there is a small centre comprising the local school, the church, a grocery/bar, a butcher/bar, the police station and a football field. Santa Cecilia is called a "colony" because of its origin; an area of land allocated to a certain number of European settlers who were expected to colonize/cultivate it. A colony is a residential unit defined according to two criteria: neighbourhood and participation in a system of social relations, which includes ceremonial, educational and recreative activities.

The settlers and their descendants are called *colonos* or *gringos* (foreigners), as opposed to *criollos* (natives) who in this area are primarily associated with migrant cotton harvesters.[5] Culturally speaking the farmers constitute an extremely homogeneous group. All of them are devoted Catholics and *gringos* of Friulian origin. The *gringos* consider themselves ethnically and morally superior to the *criollos*. For example, *criollos* live together without being formally married, they do not give much attention to virginity and chastity, and are consequently not considered "good Catholics".

The Church is the most important public institution in the community and the religious festivals, particularly Easter, Christmas and the patron saint fiesta, are considered the major events in community life. The local priests are Italians, members of a congregation called "Maria's servants" (Siervos de Maria), which has a special devotion for the Virgin, but otherwise faithful to the orders of the Church hierarchies. They live in Avellaneda and pay service to a number of colonies. However, the Church is not the only source of catholic gender values. Santa Cecilia is part of a wider society where most institutions are permeated by these values. This is particularly the case of the legal and the educational system, part of the mass media, and the labour market (Weinermann *et al.*, 1983). Criticism of these gender values and practices certainly exists in Argentina, especially among educated urban women, but this has limited impact in the rural areas.

Santa Cecilia is surrounded by other colonies sharing more or less the same ethnic, social and economic characteristics. The colonies are interconnected through kinship ties, and members of different colonies assist in each others' fiestas and sports arrangements. The distance to the nearest town, Avellaneda, is some 25 km. Reconquista, the other urban centre of importance in the area, is located 2 km from Avellaneda. There are close ties between the colonies and these towns. For example, the farmers buy all inputs and most consumer goods in town, where they also sell their produce, and due to rural–urban migration they have close networks of relatives there.

My study covered all the farms in Santa Cecilia. The data collection ranged from day long visits where I participated in "everyday" life on the farms, trying to grasp people's way of living and thinking, to structured questionnaires on particular issues suited for this kind of technique. My informants were men, women and children of different ages, to whom I talked individually or in groups. Being a resident of the "colony" and, during my last period of field-work, a mother of two with my own networks to be followed up, I attended mass, fiestas, marriages, birthday parties and sports arrangements mainly in Santa Cecilia, but also in the neighbouring colonies and in Avellaneda.

IV. Sexuality: Values and Practices

In Santa Cecilia sexuality is no longer only a matter of procreation. The need for sexual expression is recognized as being part of the condition of physical maturity in both men and women. The idea of certain mutual conjugal needs and duties regarding sexual intercourse is accepted, but the sexual needs of men are considered to be more urgent than those of women. This relates to the belief that the sexual urge in the adult female is subject to her control, while that of the adult male is a physical imperative and cannot to the same extent be controlled. A man's sexual needs are "almost incontestable". It is believed that women discharge sexual energy through menstruation, while males accumulate sexual energy which needs to be discharged through intercourse. Women are expected to control their sexual urges, but they are vulnerable; they can be seduced or even violated by sexually voracious men, and therefore, have to be protected and controlled.

In Santa Cecilia as in the Mediterranean societies premarital virginity and marital chastity is highly valued. The struggle for the conservation of female physical intactness is reflected in the socialization of children. Boys and girls are socialized to act out culturally defined personality differences believed to exist in nature. What is considered appropriate behaviour for boys (for example, running, climbing of trees, shouting or loud talking and openness to strangers) is often not acceptable for girls, who are expected to be sweet and neat. If a boy exhibits the latter qualities he is easily suspected of having homosexual inclinations. What is masculine is thus defined in opposition to the feminine. Girls are more protected than boys. Mothers talk about their fear of sexual abuses from adult men as well as from young boys. This fear is especially directed at the *criollo* migrants.[6]

It is believed that in "normal" cases puberty marks the beginning of a woman's sexuality, her own sexual urges as well as her sexual appeal to men. The liberty of movement generally increases with age, but it is controlled. This is not necessarily because the parents do not trust their daughters. Some say that they do, but are still restrictive because "the world is full of men that we cannot trust". Moreover, they want to protect their daughters' reputations. Girls who are roaming around on their own are easy prey for gossip. Boys' sexual maturity is also associated with puberty, but not with similar restrictions. Their liberty of movement increases considerably when they reach adolescence.

It is accepted that young boys and girls should meet and socialize, but under "sound" circumstances, i.e. where one can "keep an eye on the girls". In Santa Cecilia sports and religious events are defined as such. Each community has a mixed volleyball team. They usually practise once a week, and during the summer season they participate in regional tournaments on Sundays. This is a social event where whole families from different communities meet, and young boys and girls are given some space of their own. The patron saint "fiesta" offers similar opportunities. It is arranged once a year on the patron saint day of the different communities throughout the region. The "fiesta" comprises a religious procession and a mass, football and volleyball competitions and ends with a big dance. These events represent legitimate arenas of interaction between adolescent boys and girls, and many of the married couples in Santa Cecilia started and developed their relationships there.

CHASTITY, SEXUALITY AND GENDER IN ARGENTINA

Marriage is no longer a family affair arranged by the heads of families, as was the case among the early immigrants, in which economic considerations were important. It is a matter of individual choice, as long as it takes place within class and ethnic boundaries. In the history of Santa Cecilia only one *gringo* woman has married a *criollo* man. This happened in the 1930s, and was admitted because the husband was culturally a *gringo* since he had been adopted by a farmer family when his mother died soon after his birth.

Ideally, fiancées (*novios*) should not have sexual relations before the wedding ceremony. If they have, but the girl is not pregnant when they marry, their lapse is considered only a minor sin. Sexual intercourse outside formal engagement is, however, strongly condemned and, if it is known, the girl involved is a favourite object of gossip. The same goes for a woman who has given her "treasure" (*tesoro*) to a "fiancé" who later abandoned her. These women are defined as "loose" (*faciles*) and "branded" (*manchadas*), and generally have problems finding a "proper" husband. They will always bear their "brand" (*mancha*), but their social acceptance will depend on how they bear it. If they live a pious life and thereby show penitence, people talk about them with pity. If they lead a "normal" life "as if nothing has happened" (*como si nada hubiera pasado*) they are strongly condemned. I knew of two cases where this happened. Some of my informants referred to them as "detestable" (*asquerosas*). Both of them had migrated to town when they were rather young. There they had met "unreliable" men, they got pregnant, had their babies in town, and stayed with relatives "as if nothing had happened". "Branded" girls seldom participate in public events when they visit their families in Santa Cecilia. When they do, however, they are publicly well treated, "as if nothing had happened". Once they leave, the gossip starts. The girls on their side, well aware of "the rules of the game", do not like to participate in such encounters.

A man's social worth does not depend on his carnal purity. He can be criticized for leading a sexually immoral life, but he has no *manchas*. If he is known as an honest, hard working and "reliable" man (*un hombre serio*), his sexual experience has no influence on his potential for getting married. He is believed to be able to modify his behaviour, and that will suffice.

At the ideal level sexual morality within marriage is not gender specific. Fidelity is a moral value that applies to both men and women. Male adultery is not socially accepted as normal, as is the case in other Latin American and Mediterranean societies (Gilmore, 1987a; Pescatello, 1973; Stølen, 1987). Some women accepted "incidental wantonness" (*calentura pasajera*) in their husbands, leading to an isolated sexual intercourse, normally with a "criollo" woman, while they strongly rejected the idea of prolonged parallel relationships. Others were more strict in their position. They argued for equality of sexual moral standards, i.e. absolute fidelity for men and women, while they recognized the impossibility of fulfilling these standards in cases of "female sexual negligence". A man who betrays a bad wife (one who is not fulfilling her conjugal/sexual duties) is "understood", while the one who betrays a good and devoted wife is strongly condemned. No similar tolerance exists as far as female infidelity is concerned. Women's sexual urge is acknowledged, but a woman who is not able to control her sexuality is not a "good woman" (*buena mujer*). Male sexual negligence or any other circumstances cannot justify female adultery.

V. Gender Division of Roles

In Santa Cecilia womanhood is associated with secular marriage (while celestial marriage, as we saw, implies the abnegation of womanhood). The role of married women can be synthesized in one word: *attention*. A good woman should attend her husband, children, family and visitors within certain culturally defined standards. "To attend and be maintained/to maintain and be attended" (*atender y ser mantenida/mantener y ser atendido*) summarizes the way Santa Cecilians talk about the marital relationship. Female chastity and fidelity are a matter of course in this relationship, and express internalized values of the actors involved. These values are, as we will soon see, embedded in the sexual division of labour which in turn confirms the existing order of things. Direct male control of female chastity then becomes superfluous.

According to the dominant sexual division of labour, it is the husband's responsibility to ensure the material welfare of his wife and children. In the farming context this implies having access to agricultural land, performing planning, cultivation and marketing of agricultural production, and cattle breeding. Domestic work is women's domain, and defined as complementary to agricultural work. The husband controls the means of production – land, technology and know-how – and takes the final decisions regarding investments and use of incomes. He considers himself and is considered by his wife and his community as the head of his household and family unit. This grants him an authority position with respect to women and children. In spite of that women play a crucial role in the family and the community, particularly through the *socialization of children* which is now their exclusive responsibility, through *religious activities* which at the elementary level are primarily taken care of by women, and through *gossip* which is a major mechanism of social control at the community level. Generally, both men and women agree on the content of this division of roles. A farm and home should have both adult male and female members in order to function "properly".

Women who do not have a husband "who can give them advice" (*quién le aconseje*) are pitied. Those who have become widows without having an adult son who is willing to take the husband's economic and social role have sold or rented out their land and joined a relative (preferably a son or daughter) in town. Women are not prepared to run the farm alone.

Similar to what is reported from the Mediterranean, the use of time and space outside the farm is highly gender specific, and so is the use of leisure. In Santa Cecilia women take care of activities related to the welfare of children, i.e. taking them to the doctor, buying their clothes and so on. These are activities carried out in town. Generally, women accompany their husbands when he has some errands to make. Some of the younger women hold driving licences, but they rarely go to town alone. At least they will bring a child. They do not like to go alone because "people start talking".

On Saturday evenings the family members dress up, bundle into their pick-up trucks and go to the centre of the "colony". Women, children and a few men attend the six o'clock mass, while the other men meet in the grocery/bar next door drinking wine, playing cards and chatting. After the mass men and women separate. The men, who have attended mass, join their friends in the bar. The women gather in the sacristy to drink *mate* (local tea) and talk about the latest local events, their children, the sick and the dead and about the other women of the neighbourhood who are not present. The children play in the church backyard. It is during these (and similar) encounters that evaluations of good and bad behaviour are made. The women seldom go to the bar. If they want to buy something from the grocery they enter the back door and are attended by the barman's wife.

Most males return to the bar on Sunday morning, while their wives prepare the "special" Sunday lunch. In the afternoon the family may visit some relatives or they meet at the centre, where males stay in and around the bar while the women and children stay in and around the church, or the males leave with friends while the females stay at home with the children. During visits to relatives men and women often (but not always) form separate groups where the men normally discuss agriculture, sports or politics, while the women talk about some TV programme, their kin, neighbours or children. Many women disapprove of this separation between men and women. They feel that the time and money the husband spends with his friends could be spent on the family. Male friendship is conceived by many women as a threat to family life.

Women's participation in community activities is a prolongation of their domestic roles. Some women are members of the local school and parochial committees, but men have the leading positions and take care of the contacts with the higher organizational levels. Women take care of practical tasks like decorating, preparing food and cleaning when school or church activities are organized. During regular committee meetings men define what should be on the agenda; they chair the meeting, dominate the discussion and, to a large extent, decide the follow-ups. Women must be careful in openly manifesting disagreement; those who do so are criticized for being *mandonas* (trying to take command), which is synonymous with being unfeminine. During public arrangements, for example religious fiestas, men fill the public roles while women stay in the background performing less visible tasks.

Generally speaking, women are more devoted to religion than men. Attendance at mass is higher among women and they consider themselves, and are considered by men, to be the caretakers of religious values in everyday life. However, no women have leading positions in the religious hierarchy. The local laity assisting the parochial priests in performing religious sermons are males and so are the *comulgueros*, five men who have been elected to assist in giving communion. Women are not eligible.

VI. Female Chastity and Social Worth

Mediterranean studies emphasize the dependence of male reputation on female sexual conduct. Men are responsible for the respectability of their women, which is associated with premarital virginity and marital chastity, and their own honour derives in large measure from the way they discharge their responsibility. In the Mediterranean female chastity is said to be a *family* concern. In her paper on female chastity codes and woman as a dominant symbol of Sicilian family, Giovannini argues that in the community of Garre a young women's virginity is viewed as a sign that her family possesses the unity and strength necessary to protect its patrimony from encroachment. In this context, the unmarried women's virginity and the married women's chastity symbolize their family's social worth, it is a *family attribute.* (Giovannini, 1981, 1987). This seems to be the case in other parts of the Mediterranean as well.

In Santa Cecilia a young woman's virginity constitutes a *personal* rather than a *family* attribute in the sense referred to above. It is a "treasure" (*tesoro*) which should be given to the man whom she marries. Loss of virginity diminishes a girl's reputation, her social worth and reduces her possibilities of becoming a respectable wife and mother, which is believed to be the key attribute of womanhood.

Different from the Mediterranean cases referred to above, premarital loss of virginity in Santa Cecilia does not seem to injure the social worth of the girl's family of origin. Families who have experienced *la desgracia* of having a pregnant, unmarried daughter are pitied, but they do not lose respect, if the family members otherwise are living up to acceptable moral standards. "This disgrace can happen to everybody" (*esa desgracia puede tocar a qualquiera*), was a common comment when cases of premarital pregnancy were discussed. However, it is worth noting that even if it is referred to as a *desgracia* for the whole family, the mother is the one who expresses shame and guilt.

In contemporary Santa Cecilia the mother is responsible for the socialization of children, and for giving advice and of controlling their daughters. In the few cases of premarital pregnancy that I registered, the mothers were said to have become depressed and had retired from community life for some time, thus escaping the inevitable gossip. Even if they blamed themselves for having failed as mothers, their strongest feeling seemed to be the pity for their "fallen" daughters. Their husbands did not manifest similar attitudes or feelings. This does not mean that a man's reputation is independent of female sexual behaviour. Female adultery is still considered a tragedy, a cuckold lacks respect: "A man who is not able to keep order in his own home is not worth being respected outside." However, Santa Cecilian husbands do not feel threatened by potential adultery. In the history of the "colony" no case of *gringo* female adultery is known. Considering that most people know "everything" about each other, we may therefore assume that it is quite uncommon. The sexual behaviour of sisters and daughters is not considered to be a male responsibility, even if males play a protective role in relation to them. A man's reputation is not dependent on the sexual conduct of these kinswomen. Female chastity is an indicator of a man's social worth only when the woman involved is his wife. I believe that this difference between Santa Cecilia and the Mediterranean has to do with differences in the social role of the family.

During the first part of the century when agriculture dominated the economic life of the region, both men and women, but particularly the women, had few chances outside the realm of the family farm. Their "destiny", that generally coincided with their desire, was to marry a farmer and become a respectable mother and housewife. During this period marriage was a decision reached between heads of families in which economic considerations were important. Matchmakers played an important role in connecting partners in accordance with the expectations of their parents. Marriage was conceived of in terms of the continuity of the familial enterprise. A person's chances of being thought of as a suitable partner depended on the prestige of his or her family, which, in turn, was highly influenced by the sexual behaviour of the female members. When I first visited Santa Cecilia in the early 1970s it was still common that unmarried daughters stayed with their parents and were inherited with the farm. Mechanized farming and the expansion of the urban labour market combined with access to education has changed this situation. Spinsters are no longer inherited with the farm, they are expected to maintain themselves if they cannot find a suitable man to do it.

VII. Female Chastity and Its Control

In Mediterranean studies it is commonly stated that men control women and that the vigilance of women is transferred from father to husband through marriage. This is no longer so clearly the case in Santa Cecilia. Female sexuality is controlled through internalized norms and values defining womanhood and manhood, and practices which include gender-typed use of time and space, as well as direct surveillance of young girls and unmarried women. Women themselves are to a large extent taking care of the upkeep of these values and practices. Most of them are carefully adapting to traditional standards of behaviour, at the same time they keep an eye on their kinswomen and neighbours.

Young girls and unmarried women are primarily taken care of by their mothers and to some extent their brothers. Previously, when most newly married couples settled on the husband's parents' farm, the parents-in-law took over upon marriage. The house and the immediate surroundings were the mother-in-law's domain. She allocated tasks to be carried out, decided who was going where and when and so on, and her "words were the law" (*su palabra era ley*). The tyranny of the mothers-in-law is a favourite issue of conversation, particularly among the older women.

Nowadays, settlement upon marriage is still virilocal in rural areas, but nuclear families are dominating. The parents-in-law normally retire and move to town when the son takes over the farm. This has not led to a transfer of control to the husband. Due to his work situation, which often takes him away from the house, he is not in a position to keep an eye on his wife. Women are themselves the guardians of virginity and chastity. The main control is embedded in the concept of womanhood which is inextricably related to mothering, child-rearing and domestic work.

The idolized mother is well known from the Mediterranean. The mother is characterized by the physical ability to give and sustain life through her own bodily substance and she represents the security and the continuity of the nuclear family. In fact, "*la mamma is the family*", as Giovannini's Sicilian informant states (1981, p. 416).

In Santa Cecilia *la madre* is also a central figure, and being a mother and a good mother is considered a paramount attribute of womanhood. As soon as a young couple get married they will want and are expected to have children. Three to four children is believed to be the ideal number nowadays, and both men and women desire to have both boys and girls. To have only girls is considered a disgrace, primarily because a boy is needed to secure the continuity of the family farm, but having boys is also believed to be an attribute of manhood. It is associated with strong sperms and potency. Males who have only daughters are objects of jokes and wish to increase the number of children in search of a boy. There is no similar "search" for girl babies, but parents, especially mothers, who have only sons, express their regret at not having a daughter. Daughters represent company and help in domestic chores. However, the strong preference of boy babies that is reported to have existed only a few decades ago has now diminished, probably as a consequence of changes in the relations of production which implied a dramatic reduction in the labour requirements on the farms.

The fear of infertility is great, and if conception is delayed or miscarriages occur, the couple go to great expense, consulting doctors and undergoing medical treatment. In addition, traditional practitioners (*curanderos*) are consulted, and promises are given to saints. Childless couples or couples with only one child are pitied. Spinsters (*solteronas*) and childless women are not considered "real" women and do not feel realized as such. They are pitied by women and objects of jokes by men.

During the last decade some of the younger women have practised modern methods of birth control in spite of it being condemned by the Catholic Church. The say that fertility control is so important to them that they do not confess this practice to the local priests, or they make their confessions to a liberal priest in town who accepts its use. The use of contraceptives is motivated by several factors. The most important one is perhaps the desire to secure the future of the existing children. Today this implies education beyond the primary school level, which is relatively expensive because the children have to stay in town while at school.

Manhood is also associated with marriage and paternity. Bachelors (*solterones*) are pitied because they do not get a son to inherit their property and the domestic services and care that "only women can give", but may enjoy full respect by the community if they fulfil other standards of manhood. It is accepted that a bachelor may live alone and have a sexual life. A spinster should neither live alone nor have a sexual life. We have seen that sexuality has a value in itself; it is partly independent of procreation, but as far as females are concerned, it should be confined to marriage.

Ability as a housewife is another female attribute of great importance and is an indicator of a married woman's prestige and reputation. Women who are not up to accepted standards of housekeeping are objects of gossip. Diligence and hard work are highly valued, while laziness is abhorred for it results in neglect, dirtiness and the disorder of the home. Domestic work, if it is satisfactorily performed, is time consuming and requires almost continuous presence. A good mother and housewife is fully occupied in and around her house, and not exposed to dangers and temptations to which by nature she would be susceptible. Her use of space and time is restricted in terms of the domestic imperative. A teacher and the caretaker of the local primary school, who are the only women who have waged employment in the community, are gossiped about because they are considered not to be living up to accepted standards of domestic work and mothering. Gossip as a control mechanism is well known from other parts of the world (Hirschon, 1981; Melhuus and Borchgrevinck, 1984).

VIII. Continuity and Change in Gender Relations

In Santa Cecilia the parallel between the holy and the secular family is explicitly referred to by the priests as well as by the people themselves. The ideal family is the one where "the husband is the head of his family, as God is the head of the Church". He is authority, protection and advice, he provides material welfare and represents the family in the "outside world". His wife is love, care and mildness, she provides spiritual welfare and domestic attention and is the mediator between the children and the father. This concept of the family coincides with the Catholic notions of gender hierarchy, disseminated by Maria's servants, which assign to women a domestic and subordinate position in relation to men. The gender hierarchy, as well as the sexual division of roles that establishes an equation between male and female and public and domestic domains, thus, appear as of a celestial order, as "ordained in the order of things". I believe that people's faithfulness to Catholicism and the strong position of the Church explains the striking similarities in gender notions and practices that I observed in Santa Cecilia as compared to the Mediterranean. I am thinking particularly of the cultural emphasis on virginity and chastity, the equation between motherhood and womanhood, the equation between male and female and public and domestic domains, and the notion of gender hierarchy. This does not mean, as I have also indicated above, that gender relations and perceptions of gender are fixed and immutable. They are transformed and recreated as people develop new economic and social strategies for coping with their changing environment. To be a mother in contemporary Santa Cecilia is, as we will soon see, quite different from what it was a few decades ago. However, this does not seem to have weakened the emphasis on motherhood in the cultural definition of womanhood. In what follows I will examine more carefully the relationship between continuity and change in the conceptualization of gender in Santa Cecilia with reference to the dramatic socio-economic changes that have taken place in this area since the turn of the century.

The equation between male and female and public and domestic is a persistent fact in Santa Cecilia. Even during the first part of the century when agricultural production was labour intensive and women had a high level of participation, they were defined as domestic and their agricultural work secondary and subsidiary. Their participation varied according to the cyclical changes in size and composition of the household. The temporary lack of accordance between ideals and practice was solved by defining women's agricultural work as *help* given to related males. Independent of its volume, *help* did not qualify for the sharing of incomes or inheritance to land and equipment, which has always been and still is controlled by males.[7] Thus, it did not lead to a questioning of male authority and dominance, which were associated precisely with agricultural work and property rights to land. When agriculture was mechanized in the 1950s, women permanently ceased to work in the fields.

The persistence of the definition of women as domestic does not mean that her role within the domestic sphere is not changing. The volume of housework has been gradually reduced, first through the introduction of piped water and gas cooking, followed by electricity supply, washing machines, fridges and freezers. This change did not, however, either modify the gender typing of housework, or reduce the importance of housework in the cultural definition of womanhood. The reduction in volume has been "compensated" by an increase in the standards of this work. We have seen that women who are not up to accepted standards are objects of gossip.

Women's role as child-bearers has also changed dramatically but without reducing the importance of motherhood as the paramount attribute of womanhood. At the beginning of the century when marriage to a large extent was a family concern and a means of producing children, the prestige of women depended on the number of children she was able to bear. The average number of children around 1920 was 11.4. Around 1950 it had declined to 6.4 (Archetti, 1984, p. 265).[8] Today the ideal number of children is three and the quality of mothering is given attention, not the quantity of childbirths. More than three children means more work and less contact between the mother and each child, which is strongly disapproved of. Moreover, many children means reduced economic possibilities for securing their future.

The fertility decline is associated with changes in the perception of the social role of the child. Before the 1950s children were important for their work utility. The closure of the agricultural frontier, together with the mechanization of agriculture, dramatically reduced the work utility of children. The farmers' sons, who previously married and either stayed on the father's land or bought new land in the area, from now on had to find a future outside the family farm and the rural communities.[9] This process has been gradual. Today the majority of the young people migrate, preferably to one of the nearby rural towns. Old people also settle in town upon retirement. Children are no longer an economic resource, but rather an economic burden.

Through the deliberate decline in fertility women have gradually gained control over their bodies. Among younger women the use of modern contraceptives is replacing coitus interruptus and sexual abstinence which until recently were the only means of birth control. This is in turn associated with certain changes in the concept of sexuality. Today sexual intercourse is not only perceived as a means of procreation as it was only a couple of decades ago (Archetti, 1984, p. 266). Sexual pleasure, if confined to the marriage, is now recognized and accepted as a positive experience in itself, particularly among the younger generation. These changes allow women to be "better mothers and wives" according to the new standards.

Premarital virginity has always been a necessary attribute in order to become a "real woman"; a respectable wife, mother and housewife. During the first part of the century when marriage was a decision reached between the heads of families, in which economic considerations were important, and spinsters were inherited with the farm, the vigilance of virginity was a family affair (Giovannini, 1981). Today when adult unmarried women are expected to fend for themselves and marriage is a question of personal choice, the girl is the one who "loses" her social value if she does not manage to keep her "treasure" intact. Girls are socialized to repress their sexuality and they are looked after by their mothers. Thus, control of female sexuality is also a persistent fact, but today it is more internal than external. While the control of women previously passed from the mother to the mother-in-law, this is now taken care of by the women themselves, through self-control and gossip. Fidelity is no longer dependent upon direct external control.

On the pre-mechanized farm, when the hierarchically organized extended family was the normal pattern, the relative position of women in the household depended on their age. A woman was considered a minor in relation to men of the same generation, but her prestige increased with age and the number of children. A woman with married sons had considerable power in relation to the younger generation, especially the daughters-in-law, who were under her command.

As stated initially, the modern mechanized farm is organized in such a way that it can be run by two adults, one man, who is in charge of agriculture, and one woman who takes care of housework and child care. The "nuclearization" of the farm household has given the young wife stronger influence on household and farm matters. She is no longer submitted to the control and authority of her parents-in-law. She is "the queen" (*la reina*) of the house, monopolizing household matters and child-rearing. Since her husband generally works alone or together with her son her opinions on farm matters, particularly investments, may be heard. Due to increased interdependence between husband and wife, relations of cooperation and confidence are necessary in order for the household and the farm to function properly.

The ideal couple of today is constituted on the basis of romantic love, including both friendship and sexual pleasure. Ideally both men and women should conserve their virginity until marriage, and be faithful to their spouse after that. Even if men do not always meet these ideals, there is no "dual" morality as in other parts of the continent (Melhuus, 1989; Stevens, 1973; Stølen, 1991b).

The existing sexual division of labour is defended both by males and females. Mixing of gender roles, especially when males do what is considered female work, is one of the favourite subjects of jokes and anecdotes, particularly among males. The man is ridiculed as dominated by his lazy wife. His reputation is at stake, but so also is hers, since it is seen as an expression of being a bad wife. However, women are not teased (rather admired) when doing male tasks, for example working in the fields. In this case the husband is characterized as a *pobre tipo* (poor guy) who is not able to cope with what is defined as "a man's duty". The ideal couple is one where man and woman are both friends and lovers and through the division of roles in the family complement each other.

The emotional dependence has been increasingly more important as an articulating force within the family group. The wife/mother has become a symbol of family cohesion, she is adored and idealized. This has certainly improved women's position within the family, but at the same time it reproduces the gender hierarchy. The idealization of marriage and motherhood ties women to the domestic sphere. Males continue their control over the means of production, the process of production and the incomes, as well as their control over the institutions at the community level and also outside the community. Married women are economically and socially dependent. In this way the structure of gender relations is reproduced in spite of the changes.

Notes

1 The field-work carried out in Argentina in 1973–74 and 1988 with financial support from the Norwegian Research Council of Sciences and Humanities (NAVF) and the Norwegian Council for Applied Social Sciences (NORAS). The first period of fieldwork was undertaken jointly by myself and Eduardo Archetti. Thus, part of the data appearing in this chapter is the product of a common effort. I am grateful to Eduardo Archetti, Gerd Holmboe-Ottesen, Signe Howell, Marit Melhuus, Jorun Solheim and for critical comments on earlier drafts of the chapter.
2 The immigrants came from a limited number of villages in the Alps, characterized by rapid demographic growth, and unequal distribution of land, which explain the massive peasant migration from this region during the last part of the nineteenth century (Prost, 1974; Archetti, 1984). In Argentina they were offered state land (min. 36 ha – max. 144 ha.) and other means of production on very favourable terms.
3 For more details on the social and economic organization of Santa Cecilia, see Archetti and Stølen (1975, 1978) and Stølen (1991a).
4 In another essay, "Gender and Agricultural Change in North East Argentina", I discuss the processes of change in more detail (Stølen, 1991a).
5 For more details see Archetti and Stølen (1975) and Melhuus (1987).
6 The sexual morality of *criollos* is considered (by the *gringos*) to be low and their sexual urges not properly controlled. Their children are believed to have "abnormal" sexual urges due to the fact that they sleep in the same room as their parents and are supposed to witness their sexual intercourse.
7 According to Argentine law, men and women have equal rights to inherit their parents' property. The Santa Cecilian farmers have never followed the law, and less so in the past than today. Women have always been excluded from inheritance to land. (For more details see Archetti and Stølen, 1977; Stølen, 1991a.)
8 In his paper "Rural Families and Demographic Behaviour: Some Latin American Analogies", Archetti analyses the changes in the demographic behaviour in Santa Cecilia from the beginning of the century to the mid-1970s (Archetti, 1984).
9 There is no other labour market in the community than the one occupied by the *criollos*. The *gringos* consider this work to be a threat to their dignity.

References

Archetti, E. P. 1984. Rural Families and Demographic Behaviour: Some Latin American Analogies. *Comparative Studies in Society and History*, Vol. 26, No. 2.
Archetti, E. and Stølen, K. A. 1975. *Explotación Familiar y Acumulación de Capital en el Campo Argentino*, Buenos Aires: Siglo XXI.
Archetti, E. and Stølen, K. A. 1977. La Herencia entre los Colonos del Norte de Santa Fe. In Hermitte *et al.* (eds) 1977.
Archetti, E and Stølen, K. A. 1978. Economía Doméstica, Estrategias de Herencia y Acumulación de Capital: La Situación de la Mujer en el Norte de Santa Fe, Argentina. *América Indígena*, Vol. XXXVIII, No. 2, pp. 383–403.
Ardener, S. (ed.) 1978. *Defining Females*. London: Croom Helm.
Asano-Tamanoi, M. 1987. Shame, Family, and State in Catalonia and Japan. In Gilmore (ed.) (1987a).

Bleie, T. *et al.* 1991. *Gender Symbols and Social Practices.* Oxford: Berg Publishers (in press).
Blok, A. 1981. Rams and Billy-Goats: A Key to the Mediterranean Code of Honour. *Man*, Vol. 16, pp. 427–440.
Bourdieu, P. 1977. *Outline of a Theory of Practice.* Cambridge Studies in Social Anthropology. Cambridge: Cambridge University Press.
Bowie, F. and Ardener, S. (eds) 1991. *The Past and Present Impact of Missionary Activities on Women.* Oxford: Berg (in press)
Brandes, S. 1981. Like Wounded Stags: Male Sexual Ideology in an Andalucian Town. In Ortner and Whitehead (eds) (1981a).
Brandes, S. 1987. Reflection on Honor and Shame in the Mediterranean. In Gilmore (ed.), 1987a.
Christian, W. 1972. *Person and God in a Spanish Valley.* London: Seminar Press.
Delaney, C. 1987. Seeds of Honour, Fields of Shame. In Gilmore (ed.) (1987a).
Gilmore, D. D. 1982. Anthropology of the Mediterranean Area. *Annual Reviews in Anthropology*, Vol. 11, 175–205.
Gilmore, D. D. (ed.). 1987a. *Honor and Shame and the Unity of the Mediterranean.* American Anthropological Association, No. 22.
Gilmore, D. D. 1987b. Introduction: The Shame of Dishonor. In Gilmore (ed.), (1987a).
Giovannini, M. J. 1981. Woman: Dominant Symbol within the Cultural System of a Sicilian Town, *Man*, Vol. 16, No. 3, pp. 408–426.
Giovannini, M. J. 1987. Female Chastity Codes in the Circum Mediterranean: Comparative Perspectives. In Gilmore (ed.), 1987a.
Hermitte, E. *et al.* (eds), 1977. *Procesos de Articulación Social.* Buenos Aires: Amorrortu editores.
Herzfeld, M. 1987. As in Your Own House: Hospitality, Ethnography and the Stereotype of Mediterranean Society. In Gilmore (ed.) 1987a.
Hirschon, R. 1978. Open Body, Closed Space: The Transformation of Female Sexuality. In Ardener (ed.), 1978.
Kulick, D. 1987a. *Från Kön till Genus: Kvinnligt och Manligt i ett Kulturellt Perspektiv.* Stockholm: Carlsons.
Kulick, D. 1987b. Hur man blir en riktig mann eller kvinna. In Kulick (ed.) 1987a.
Melhuus, M. 1987. *Peasants, Surpluses and Appropriation. A Case Study of Tobacco-growers from Corrientes, Argentina.* Occasional Papers in Social Anthropology, No. 11, University of Oslo.
Melhuus, M. I Want to Buy Me a Baby! Some Reflections on Gender and Social Change in Modern Society. In Bleie *et al.*, in press.
Melhuus, M. and T. Borchrewinck 1984. Husarbeid: Tidsbinding av kvinner. In Rudie (ed.) (1984).
Moore, H. L. 1988. *Feminism and Anthropology.* Oxford: Polity Press.
Ortner, S. B. and Whitehead, H. (eds.) 1981a. *Sexual Meanings: The Cultural Construction of Gender and Sexuality.* Cambridge: Cambridge University Press.
Ortner, S. B. and Whitehead, H. 1981b. Introduction: Accounting for Sexual Meaning. In Ortner and Whitehead (eds.) (1981a).
Perestiany, J. G. (ed.) 1965. *Honor and Shame: The Values of Mediterranean Society.* London: Weidenfeld & Nicolson.
Pescatello, A. (ed.) 1973. *Male and Female in Latin America.* Pittsburgh: University of Pittsburgh Press.
Pitt-Rivers, J. 1961. *The People of the Sierra.* Chicago: University of Chicago Press.
Pitt-Rivers, J. 1965. Honour and Social Status. In Perestiany (ed.), 1965.
Prost, B. 1974. *Le Frioul-région d'affrontements.* Thèse de Doctorate, Université de Lille.
Rudie, I. (ed.) 1984. *Myk Start, Hard Landing.* Oslo: Universitetsforlaget.
Schneider, J. 1971. Of Vigilance and Virgins: Honour, Shame and Access to Resources in Mediterranean Societies. *Ethnology*, Vol. 10, pp. 1–24.

Skar Lund, S. (in press). Conflicting Cosmologies in Peru's Southern Highlands: Christian and Traditional Views of the Role of Gender. In Bowie, F., Kirkwood, D. and Ardener, S. (eds), *Women and the Mission*. London: Tavistock.

Stevens, E. P. 1973. Marianismo: The Other Face of Machismo in Latin America. In Pescatello (ed.), (1973).

Stølen, K. A. 1987. *A Media Voz: Relaciones de Género en la Sierra Ecuatoriana.* Quito: CEPLAES.

Stølen, K. A. 1991a. Gender and Agricultural Change in North East Argentina, *European Journal of Development Research*, Vol. 3, No. 1, pp. 150–169.

Stølen, K. A. 1991b. Gender, Sexuality and Violence in Ecuador. *Ethnos*, Vol. 56.

Warner, M. 1976. *Alone of All Her Sex: The Myth and the Cult of the Virgin Mary.* London: Weidenfeld & Nicholson.

Weinermann, C. *et al.* 1983. *Del Deber Ser y el Hacer de las Mujeres: Dos Estudios de Caso en Argentina*, Mexico: El Colegio de Mexico/Pispal.

Wikan, U. 1984. Shame and Honour: A Contestable Pair. *Man*, Vol. 19, pp. 635–652.

Wolf, E. 1969. Society and Symbols in Latin Europe and in the Islamic Near East, Some Comparisons. *Anthropology Quarterly*, Vol. 42, pp. 287–301.

2
Revival of Female Circumcision: A Case of Neo-Traditionalism

ASTRID NYPAN

This study is an attempt to understand a resurgence of female genital mutilation among the Meru people who inhabit the foothills of Mt. Meru in north-eastern Tanzania.

The Meru are relatively prosperous compared to the rural population in other parts of Tanzania. This is partly due to incomes from coffee cultivation. It also reflects a willingness to accept innovation and change in agricultural production, social organization and customs in order to improve levels of living (Nypan, 1970a; Nypan and Vaa, 1974a). For instance, from a small beginning of a locally established growers' association, and in conflict with the British, they built up a cooperative union based on primary cooperatives in the villages (Nelson, 1967). The coffee growers voluntarily paid a "tax" on their coffee income on top of public taxes and levies. These funds were used to finance further cooperative development, local roads, grants to university students and a private secondary school.

Clan organization and rules have been adapted to changing circumstances. For instance, a position of clan secretary was created for the clans to make use of young men able to read and write. Furthermore, people have converted to Christianity, marriage customs have changed, and the practice of polygyny is weakened. In the 1960s, it was evident that there had been a considerable decrease in the practice of female genital mutilation. It appeared to be one of the customs which the Meru would in time relinquish entirely. However, according to local sources, there has been an increase in the number of women who undergo circumcision in the 1980s. Although no exact figure can be given as to the magnitude of this increase there are strong indications that it actually takes place. As one local woman said: "It is almost a fashion these days for young girls to become circumcised."

Below, I describe the custom of female circumcision as it appears to have been practised in earlier times and discuss changes which have contributed to its attenuation over time. This is done in order to put the contemporary resurgence in a historical perspective. I shall then be in a position to discuss the conditions contributing to the revival, which amounts to neo-traditionalism, that is a return to a traditional custom, although it has been altered considerably from what the Meru regard as the old or traditional way of practising the custom.[1]

I. Female Genital Mutilation

The term female genital mutilation refers to "traditional practices which consist in cutting away all of, or part of the external female genital organs" (UNESC, 1986, p. 8). The term circumcision is also used in the same general sense. Three main types of mutilation have been delineated, reflecting variations in how much is cut away. There is the removal, or only the pricking of the prepuce of the clitoris, or the removal of part or all of the clitoris, as well as parts of or all of labia minora, and finally, also the removal of labia majora and the stitching together to leave only a small opening for urine and menstrual blood to pass. The most frequently used classification corresponds to these three somewhat variable types: Sunna or circumcision, clitoridectomy or excision, and finally infibulation which is the most drastic form of genital mutilation (UNESC, 1986, p. 9; McLean and Graham, 1985, p. 3, Talle, 1987, pp. 35–36, Koso-Thomas, 1987, p. 16; Kuoba and Muasher, 1985, p. 97; Widstrand, 1964).

Lately several reports have appeared on the practice of female circumcision, or female genital mutilation (McLean and Graham, 1985; Kuoba and Muasher, 1985; UNESC, 1986). Such mutilation has been practised in all continents at some time or another, for instance in ancient Rome and in Tsarist Russia. In England in the nineteenth and twentieth centuries, femal circumcision was practised by surgeons to treat psychological disorders. It is also reported that "until very recently clitoridectomy was performed as a surgical remedy against masturbation in Europe and the US, and this unnecessary genital surgery continues until this day" (McLean and Graham, 1985, p. 6).

Today, the custom is most widely practised in Africa, where it is estimated that part of the female population in 26 countries is circumcised, amounting to about 80 million persons in 1980. In Tanzania, only some of the ethnic groups practise female circumcision, and it is estimated that around 10 per cent of the women are circumcised (Kuoba and Muasher, 1985, p. 99). This practice exists mostly among ethnic groups of the north-eastern part of the country, including the Pare, the Chagga, the Arusha, the Maasai and the Meru.

Female circumcision is now widely recognized as a problem which seriously affects the health of women. Furthermore, the operation is mostly done under highly unsanitary conditions and with unsuitable, if not harmful instruments (UNESC, 1986, pp. 10–12). There may be serious haemorrhage, infections, chronic problems leading to infertility, extensive scar tissue with obstetric as well as psychological complications.

There are objections to female circumcision because it is seen as an extreme example of the general subjugation of women. Even the milder forms with the removal of part of the clitoris will rob a woman of sexual enjoyment.

The glans clitoridis with its specific sensory apparatus is a primary erogenic zone. When it has been reduced to an area of scar tissue, no orgasm can be released by its manipulation (McLean and Graham, 1985, p. 5).

However, the woman is not deprived of her sexual desires.

The opposition to female genital mutilation, internationally as well as nationally, has mainly been motivated by the health risks involved for the women. In Tanzania, the women's organization UWT, wants it abolished, but recognizes that this can only be done over time, through information campaigns. Attempting to prevent it by law is not judged to be effective or even realistic.

1. *Some Conceptual Dimensions*

Female genital mutilation has proved difficult to eradicate. The basis for it is often found in people's religious and cultural values. The cultural definition of womanhood may connect circumcision to the cultural and social identity of women in such a way that important social roles for women cannot be realized by the uncircumcised. Talle argues that circumcision is a necessary premiss for women and men to fulfil their culturally defined roles among the Maasai (1987, p. 39). Clitoridectomy is the treatment which produces or creates women according to their cultural conception. In some cultures, an uncircumcised female is not defined as a woman. So closely may a woman's own feeling of who she is be connected with circumcision that she may characterize the extensive scar tissue after infibulation as "my proper self" (El Sayed, 1982, p. 159). Thus, a woman is a cultural creation and circumcision is normatively obligatory as part of such creation in many cultures. Still, studies show that girls' attitudes prior to circumcision are not always positive and they are subject to considerable social pressure to comply with the custom.

The social structure may limit women's choice if they should want to remain uncircumcised. For example, women may be denied access to resources, such as land in agricultural societies. They may be unable to find a livelihood except through marriage, which again presupposes that they are circumcised. Patrilineal societies often limit women in this way, as land and other resources follow the line of the man or husband.

In order to change the custom of female genital mutilation, it would appear that relatively comprehensive changes in values are needed, as well as structural changes affecting access to resources. This has been observed elsewhere.

> Where the patrilineage has been widely and significantly affected by other changes in the social, political and economic aspects of a society, corresponding changes have been induced in the practice of infibulation (or of its functional equivalents: clitoridectomy and the virginity test) (Hayes, 1975, p. 629).

Several research reports suggest that education contributes to the attenuation of this practice. Those with education are more opposed to femal circumcision than those with little or no schooling (UNESC, 1986, p. 14, Koso-Thomas, 1987, p. 57). However, in spite of increasing education there is still doubt as to whether female circumcision is actually decreasing (McLean and Graham, 1985, p. 6).

We know very little about the mechanisms connecting education and rejection of the custom of female circumcision. It is often assumed that education changes attitudes through increased knowledge and access to information, but this view is surely too simplistic considering the complexity of cultural patterns and cultural gender identities involved. Education may be regarded as a resource. The significance of this resource will depend on the benefits derived from it and the status accorded to education in the culture. However, education may provide women with opportunities for new roles and relationships, creating an impetus for change in women's cultural identity.

There is no knowledge about conditions that encourage a revival of the custom, once it has begun to lose ground. As structural changes and new value orientations may contribute to a decrease in the incidence of female circumcision, it is possible that such factors also provide an impetus for its revival. We may then have a situation where certain elements of the cultural custom are changed, or there is a change in the context of its practice. In this sense there is no return to the original or traditional practice, although it may be perceived as such, but to a neo-traditional pattern.

II. The Meru: Some Aspect of Social Organization

The four villages of this study are situated on the fertile and densely populated foothills of Mt. Meru, also called the coffee belt. It is a smallholder economy based on agriculture and the keeping of a few dairy cows, as well as sheep and goats. Coffee cultivation, often intermixed with several other crops, dominates and accounts for a relatively strong market orientation.

The social organization is based on patrilineal clans. The clans were traditionally the most important political units of Meru society. They still exert influence, as they regulate social matters and resolve conflicts of various kinds. The clans are regarded as the owners of the land, while farmers only have usufruct right. Increasing population density has led to land shortage. There is no new or uncultivated land for young farmers to settle on. The cultivation of a perennial crop such as coffee makes redistribution of land between old and young farmers impracticable. Because of these conditions, the usufruct rights of farmers have become permanent and are transferable to sons or other male relatives. The transfer of land, either by inheritance or exchange, typically occurs according to clan rules and under clan control. Women have no usufruct rights to clan land. In fact, women seldom own any property, be it land, animals, agricultural implements or even durable consumer goods in the household.[2]

In the traditional Meru society women were minors. They have not been able to, and still do not, participate in clan meetings and decisions. Since independence, women have been encouraged by the government and the party to participate in organizations such as the party itself or its women's organization. Participation by women is often sparse and mostly passive.

In the family sphere the ideology of women's equal participation has barely penetrated. A woman is under the authority of a man almost all her life: her father, later perhaps a brother if she is not married yet, or otherwise the husband. It is the duty of a woman to work hard. The husband, as head of the household, supervises her work. His work-load is considerably lighter than hers.

The usual age of marriage has varied somewhat through the years. Since the 1960s women marry between the ages of 18 and 25. In earlier periods they often married a few years after puberty (Puritt, 1970, p. 77). To most Meru women, to get married is not a question of choice, although they may have some say in whom to marry. It is through marriage that they reach adult status. On the whole, it is regarded as unnatural and unacceptable for a woman not to marry, and there are very few unmarried women. A woman without a man is easily suspected of being immoral and sexually loose.

In this society there are few niches for a woman other than marriage unless she is among the few who have been able to get a secondary education. Some educated women work locally in health, education, and community service, but they are all married. Only women who have been able to get relatively well paid jobs and live outside the local society appear to have a real choice of establishing and independent life.

III. The Customary Practice of Female Circumcision

All informants stress that female circumcision is an old custom among their people, and that it was performed as part of the customary wedding ceremony. The circumcision of women thus differs greatly from the circumcision of boys, which was performed in connection with the initiation of young men into an age set. Female circumcision was an individual event, an integrated part of a girl's entry into marriage. Some informants hold the view that the circumcision of the bride constituted the wedding ceremony.

Some time before the wedding, the bride-to-be would visit relatives and neighbours together with some of her friends, announcing the coming wedding and receiving gifts. There were dances for several nights and particularly on the day of the wedding itself. Older women remember this occasion very well. One informant, who was married about 50 years ago, at the age of 15, gives the following description:

> The day of my circumcision was a festive day. We started early. People danced traditional dances and drank a lot of *mbege* (a

local beer brewed from bananas and millet) to my happiness. It was a very special and happy occasion for me when I could dance from morning till afternoon. Then I was taken indoors and circumcised. My fiancé watched as I was circumcised. He was holding me. It is our tradition in Meru that the fiancé should hold the girl around the waist or the shoulders. The best friend of my fiancé was also present.

One anthropological study gives a similar account of a customary wedding in the area. Here, the bride, as she enters the house for circumcision, takes her dress off and

> throws her dress to the bridegroom to demonstrate that she is his. She then sits on a low stool, the bridegroom holds her shoulders or her waist, and she is circumcised.... Of course, there is no question of consummation of the marriage after a clitoridectomy (Puritt, 1977, pp. 130–131).

According to my informants, the bride was secluded after circumcision until the bleeding stopped. For a period of several months she continued to live in her father's home, where the bridegroom was allowed to visit her. She was cared for by her mother and mother-in-law, and served a special porridge, *uru*, made from millet and milk. The older women of the family taught the bride "a number of things about womanhood". At no other time in her life, except at childbirth, would a woman get such care as on this occasion.

Puritt mentions that the Meru performed clitoridectomy, but does not give details. Both the local circumciser, the *nrine*, and several older women insist that "they cut off everything in earlier days". The Meru were for a long period greatly influenced by their neighbours, the Arusha and the Maasai. It would appear, therefore, that at least the whole clitoris and perhaps also parts of the labia minora were removed as has been, and still is, the practice among the Maasai (Talle, 1988, p. 105).

Various reasons are given for this practice. The old *nrine* who was circumcised by her grandmother was told that "this was how women should be". Like many women she also emphasizes that circumcision was necessary in order to show respect for the husband and for his parents.

The Meru believed, and still believe, that women are endowed with extraordinary sexual desires. Women recount that the Meru in the old days said of a daughter when she married and joined her husband that she would be "too hot with him" if she was not circumcised. The implication was that she would have too many children. Furthermore, as an uncircumcised woman would be "too hot" for one man she could not be expected to remain faithful to her husband. The *nrine* herself emphasizes: "Even if the husband is a good lover, the wife will not be satisfied and look for other lovers." If we connect these views to the necessity of showing respect for the husband and his family through circumcision, we see that a woman who refused to be circumcised could easily be suspected of not wanting to be loyal to her husband or his family, but to seek her own pleasures.

My informants state that people also believed that circumcision would increase a woman's fertility and ease her labour during childbirth if the circumcision was done properly.[3] The old *nrine* confirms these beliefs and she adds another consideration: the clitoris is too long. It looks better when a woman is circumcised. She insists that many women have a clitoris that is too long. "It is like a small penis and a woman will not feel well with it." Such reasons for female circumcision are present in other cultures, and the idea of too long a clitoris may be connected with a need to emphasize the cultural conceptions of basic gender differences by also emphasizing the physical difference of men's and women's genitalia.

In summing up the above, we emphasize a few salient features of the old system of female circumcision. Clitoridectomy or excision constituted part of the wedding ceremony or even the wedding of a girl. It emphasized that she reached adult status through marriage to a husband, to whom she was subordinate. The asymmetrical relationship was expressed, among others things, in the throwing of her dress to her husband to show that "she was his". It was also, and still is, expressed in the language. The Meru say that a man marries a woman (active tense), while a woman is taken into marriage by a man (passive tense). This asymmetry may be elaborated through the man's status, as head of the household and his right to land as a male member of the patrilineage and a progenitor of the same.

The occasion of circumcision was made festive, with gifts, dances and the bride received prolonged care and attention from her own and her husband's families. This was dramatically different from her ordinary working life and was not equalled on any occasion, except on that of childbirth.

The respect that a girl should show her husband and his family through circumcision implied a "guarantee" of reduced sexual needs (as it is believed) and ensured that she would be faithful and bear children of the husband's patrilineage. Thus, circumcision can be viewed as an attempt to control the sexuality of the "hot" woman, to emphasize her "femaleness", to reduce risks to her health during childbirth and secure her fertility in the interest of a patrilineal society.

IV. The Process of Change

Discussing recent changes, I consider three periods. The first extends back to a somewhat variable and uncertain time into the 1960s. The second, that of growing opposition, refers mainly to the 1960s and early 1970s. What I call the contemporary period refers to the later part of the 1980s. The distinction between the period of growing opposition and the present does not refer to any particular events or changes in the practice of the custom, but to my two extended periods of field-work in the area in 1967–68 and 1987–89. It is at these points in time that I have been able to make observations and register changes. Most of the data come from my own fieldwork, since there is hardly any information available from other sources on the Meru custom of female circumcision.

1. *Early Changes*

There are two important events which affected the practice of female circumcision up to the 1960s. First, Lutheran missionaries established a mission in the area in 1902 and worked actively to convert people to Christianity. Although the Meru were not eager to convert initially, the number converting to Christianity grew more rapidly in the central coffee belt than in the higher area of Mt. Meru. Informants claim that the missionaries, to begin with, had greater success in converting women than men. Today almost all the inhabitants in this area are Christian.

Over time, Christianity changed the practice of female circumcision in two ways. The first was the introduction of a Christian wedding ceremony. The Christian wedding took place in a church and circumcision had no place in this ceremony. Christian parents would then often arrange for the circumcision of a daughter some time before the wedding. As the influence of Christianity became stronger, some young people, mainly girls, were not circumcised at all (Puritt, 1977, p. 128). Second, according to informants, the missionaries showed little appreciation of many Meru customs, such as dancing, beer drinking, polygyny and circumcision. They regarded them as barbaric and uncivilized practices and tried to persuade the Meru to stop them. Circumcision, however, never disqualified a man or woman from baptism or membership in the church while polygyny has had such consequences in more recent times. In addition, the missionaries conveyed new ideas of proper adult status, for both men and women, in the Christian ritual of Confirmation.

This change in ideas and the attempts of Christian women to escape circumcision at times brought them into conflict with those wanting to preserve their customs. The story of one informant, the daughter of a Christian couple who worked at a local mission station, may illustrate this point. The events took place about 35 years ago. The informant, then a young girl, became engaged to a young man whom her parents found suitable. As the marriage drew closer, the prospective mother-in-law began to insist on circumcision. The informant did not want it. "We were Christians and educated", she says. When she wanted to break off the engagement, her parents warned her. As Christians her parents felt reluctant to contribute to a conflict. Furthermore, they told her that it might be all right for her to be unmarried when they were still alive but difficult when they died and she would be left to fend for herself. Her brothers would not want to take care of her. The informant gave in and was circumcised by a local *nrine* in the house of her mother-in-law. "She cut off everything", she says bitterly. "Then some old women inspected the operation afterwards to see that enough was cut."

The introduction of education represents the second influence towards change in Meru attitudes and practice with regard to female circumcision. Education was first introduced on a small scale by the missionaries in order to enable the local inhabitants to read the Bible. But through the teaching of reading and writing, the missionaries imparted Christian and Western values, including the idea of circumcision as uncivilized. The influence of such ideas grew stronger when the British colonial administration gradually began to expand educational opportunities, particularly after the Second World War. The way in which the informant above tells about the conflict over her circumcision suggests that the Christians and the educated among the Meru tended to set themselves apart as a special category of people who felt above the obligation to observe some of the traditional customs such as female circumcision.

To conclude, by separating the wedding ritual from the circumcision, and thus changing the cultural context of the practice, Christianity provided an opportunity for women to avoid being circumcised and yet achieve the status of married adults. Christianity further contributed to a decrease in the frequency of circumcision by advising against it and by imparting new and mostly Western values for resisting the practice. It appears to have been a slow process. The effect of education may not have been great to begin with but increased as more young people were given the opportunity to go to school, particularly towards the end of the colonial period.

2. Growing Opposition

The 1950s and 1960s were years of important changes in Meru. Both the necessity to fight for their interests against the British colonial administration and the subsequent opportunities offered by independence oriented important sections of the population towards innovation and adaptations to the wider society around them.

In the early 1960s it was estimated that about 50 per cent of the Meru were Christians and that the percentage receiving primary education was slightly higher. The figures would be even higher for the villages in the central coffee belt (Puritt, 1970, p. 74). The proportion of girls attending schools was probably lower. However, in view of the subordinate position of women, the Meru were surprisingly willing to send daughters to school. It was also a relatively prosperous period, due to increased coffee production (Nelson, 1967, p. 135). As schooling opportunities expanded, an increasing number of educated young people aspired to occupations outside agriculture, to participation in a new nation and to a modern style of life as well. "Wa kisasa" or "modern" was an expression used to describe behaviour, housing, methods of cultivation or style of life, and it epitomized both experience of important changes and expectations for the future.

Given the above conditions, it is not surprising that Christian weddings became more frequent and customary weddings increasingly rare. In addition, there were changes in the practice of circumcision. Young men had started to go to hospitals for circumcision instead of undergoing the customary ritual. It was more hygienic, and to some extent regarded as more prestigious to have the operation done in a hospital. An increasing number of girls did not become circumcised. The opposition to circumcision was most pronounced among girls who had received some education. During my field-work in 1967–1968, I met several girls who had successfully avoided being circumcised while in boarding-school, despite pressure from their families. Some of these girls also rejected the idea of marriage and the traditional subordinate role of a woman in the household.

In the mid-1960s a club was formed by some educated young people in the area in order to be able to meet socially and discuss matters of common interest (Puritt, 1970, p. 76). One informant from my most recent field-work had been a member of this club. She says:

> When I was young there were many girls who did not want to get circumcised, especially those with education and even those with just a little schooling. Even men chose not to be circumcised at that time because of Christianity and the influence of education. We had a students' club where all of us in Meru who were in secondary school, in colleges and even in the university participated. We used to meet and talk about how to behave ourselves. Some parents were not happy about our club and our opposition to circumcision. Some parents still wanted their children to be circumcised. Everyone decided not to become circumcised and not to marry anyone who was circumcised. It was a protest. Circumcision is unnatural, it is also unsexy. We wanted to be hot. We wanted a better way of living as husband and wife. We wanted to be closer. I am educated, you know, and my family is also educated and Christian.

Young educated women also had a notion of sex in traditional marriage that made it unattractive to them. As one of them said: "The husband comes and says: Let us do it. Sometimes he will force her. Then he will be finished. It is like among animals".

People frequently emphasized their education when explaining why they feel or act the way they do. Regarding circumcision, women may say, "You know, I am educated. I think circumcision can be done by the uneducated women, yes, they know nothing . . . about sex . . . or such things." To be educated then, meant to young women of the 1960s not only that that they wanted to "be hot". They expressed their expectations of a new role for women different from the traditional one, and emphasized that they had plans for their lives, that they wanted to have good jobs, to work hard and then be well off, although perhaps not rich. Some of the young girls whom I met in the 1960s have managed to get a higher education. Some of them now have children, hold good jobs elsewhere in the country and have stayed unmarried.

However, not only the well educated women stopped being circumcised, but also those with little or no education. It can be assumed, on the basis of interviews with informants who were in their forties during my last field-work, that a considerable number of girls avoided circumcision in this period of growing opposition. The uncircumcised girls appear to have been numerous enough to influence others by serving as examples or role models. For instance, several informants state that they were not circumcised because many of their friends and neighbours were not. Therefore, they felt that they had a choice and could refuse. It is also evident from the interviews that old beliefs in the benefits of circumcision were being challenged. Since uncircumcised friends and neighbours married and had children without any ill-effects during childbirth, other girls lost faith in the belief that circumcision was necessary in order to become married, have children and easy childbirths. We observe a process by which uncircumcised girls, as they become more numerous, influence the behaviour of other girls. The old pattern of female circumcision is no longer dominant, and the deviant pattern of remaining uncircumcised loses its character of deviation.

In summing up, we note that when circumcision was practised during this period, it had increasingly been disassociated from impending marriage. The pressure experienced by some educated girls occurred before they were engaged or intended to marry. Christian weddings had become more frequent and traditional weddings correspondingly rare. It is also likely that some sanitary measures were introduced in line with the changes in the circumcision of boys.

A considerable number of girls, however, remained uncircumcised. They influenced other girls by serving as role models, allaying anxieties over not becoming married and having children. There is indication that some young men also chose not to be circumcised and stopped requiring that girls be circumcised before marriage.

Among the educated girls there was a vision of new roles not available to them in the traditional organization of the family and the local community. Education served to legitimate the right of the educated woman to be "hot" and to expect a different marital relationship with her husband. The women expressed the idea of a new legitimate cultural identity for the adult woman. It was often, but not always, expressed as an identity for the educated woman and was tied to expectations of new opportunities following structural changes which were expected to occur nationally.

3. The Contemporary Scene

At the end of the 1980s virtually all the inhabitants in the villages covered by this study are Christian. Education has expanded further and primary schooling is in principle compulsory. Traditional weddings no longer take place. No informant could remember any such wedding in the villages within the last ten years.[4] One could therefore reasonably expect the practice of female circumcision to have continued to decline. But on the contrary, according to my informants, there has recently been an increase in the practice among girls.

There is no available documentation of the number of girls circumcised these days, nor previously. We have to rely on less precise local sources. One informant, a teacher in primary school, estimated that about 15 per cent of the uneducated and only 5 per cent of the educated girls were circumcised until recently, but she could not provide any estimate for the recent increase. Sometimes people will disagree as to whether there are more cases of female circumcision now than before. This seems to depend on what period of time they use for comparison. Old women often compare the present situation to the days when they were young. Several women, however, insist that the increase is recent, and that it has taken place within the last 5–8 years, although they feel unable to provide any figures.

Mothers constitute one source of information regarding the growing interest of young women in circumcision. Several mothers have noticed this interest in circumcision among their daughters who, they say, talk a lot about being circumcised and discuss it with their friends. I was told that now, girls are often circumcised between the ages of 12 and 17. Some mothers worry because daughters are known to have had the operation secretly without their parents' permission. In one village it is said that "even the pastor's daughter went secretly to the *nrine*. Her parents did not know about it." Yet most parents, who have noticed this interest of young girls in circumcision, believe that their daughters will not go to the *nrine* to be circumcised, or that the *nrine* will not perform the operation without their permission. This is, however, disputed by the neighbours of the *nrine* who confirm that the *nrine* does good business these days. They can observe groups of girls going to her house.

Teachers constitute another source of information regarding the increase in circumcision among young women. Several teachers mention that girls in the last years of primary school these days show considerable interest in circumcision. The girls talk about it in school and many undergo the operation during holidays, after standard six, or even five, but particularly after standard seven, the final year of primary school. Girls who have already been circumcised will recount the event to others in ways that enhances its importance. There is some secrecy about it, perhaps because of the belief that it is forbidden by law and by the Church, and because some parents forbid it.

The old *nrine* in one of the villages confirms that there are more girls coming to her than some years ago. She has more business than she really cares to have. She denies circumcising girls without their parents' permission. With regard to the influence of young men, she states that many girls who come to her do not have boy-friends. Some, however, come because their boy-friends want them to have it done. Others come to be circumcised even if their boy-friends are opposed to circumcision. They come in groups of several girls, each accompanied by a friend or relative. She emphasizes that the operation is different these days: She says:

> In earlier days we used to cut too much because we were ignorant. Some girls lost too much blood. These days we cut less. The custom is good now that we have progressed and are cutting less. I am modern, I have developed (ninaendelea).

She later describes and demonstrates how she spreads the legs of the girl sitting on a chair or stool, uses a new razor blade for every girl, applies methylated spirits to clean the wound, and cuts "just a little", but definitely more than just the skin of the clitoris. "There will not be much bleeding. The girl gets a sanitary napkin and is followed home by the girl-friend or other person who accompanied her."

The young girls themselves claim that these days more girls become circumcised. They say "Ni vizuri", meaning it is good, it is proper, and argue that it is a cultural tradition for girls to get circumcised in Meru. It is also believed that it reduces the sexual urges of a woman, and some girls even feel that "it is a good thing not to feel sexual excitement over boys". They, furthermore, repeat well known traditional beliefs about enhancing fertility and easing childbirth. An argument frequently expressed is that a girl may not find a boy who will want to marry her unless she is circumcised. This appears to be a statement of expectations, perhaps to persuade the yet uncircumcised girls, since the girls are not engaged and there is no impending marriage. As a rule, they do not even have a steady boy-friend.

Among the informants are several well educated girls, but hardly any of them mention their education as a reason why they should not become circumcised. One of the exceptions, who mentions her education, has been subjected to considerable pressure from peers, but still feels that she will not become circumcised as she is educated like her mother, who is also uncircumcised. She will not even marry any young man who wants her to be circumcised. The attitude of her brothers, however, worries her. They would like her to become married, as only then will they feel certain that the parents' land will be inherited by them alone.

The particular story of Magdalena, and her daughter Sara, illustrates some important aspects of the changes taking place. Sara is about 20 years of age and has finished Form IV education. The mother, Magdalena, who is well educated, has not been circumcised and is strongly against circumcision. Magdalena holds the view that an educated young woman should not get circumcised. She tells me that the practice revolts her, particularly when it is a question of educated women. Sara, however, went to the *nrine* to be circumcised without her mother's knowledge about two to three years ago.

Magdalena tells the story as follows:

> I was away from home just for a few days to visit relatives, and when I returned I found that my daughter had been circumcised. She knew I was against it. I was so angry that I cried. You ask me what I said to my daughter. What could I say? I was so disappointed. I did not talk to her. We have not talked about this at all since then. Sara had gone to bed when she returned from the *nrine* and told her younger sister and father that she was ill. But later she had told them to fetch her grandmother. Grandmother then told my husband what was wrong and asked him to slaughter a sheep in the customary way. We served *uru* and invited relatives. We had to observe this custom once she was circumcised. So, on top of everything we also had unwanted expenses. I was so unhappy, and you know, my daughter is educated.

Sara tells me that she went to the *nrine* with some other girls, six of them all together. It was her grandmother who had told her to go. The grandmother had talked to her about the matter of circumcision many times. Sara says:

> At the time I was in school, I refused to become circumcised, even though she told me repeatedly when I came home from school that if I wanted to be a good and proper woman I had to be circumcised. After school, when I stayed at home, my grandmother talked to me so much about it that she persuaded me and I agreed to become circumcised. She gave me money and told me to go to the *nrine*.

In answer to my question about her education and the opinion of her mother, Sara states:

> You know, circumcision is a tradition in Meru and many girls do it these days. We are not like my mother's generation. We are different. My mother's generation was a generation for "akina mama" (feminism, women's affairs). They were strong on that issue. Now grandmothers say "mnapoteza utamaduni" (i.e. you are throwing away, destroying our Meru culture and tradition).

She then goes on to talk about her plans for the future, which are more down to earth than those of her mother. She wants some more education, perhaps to get a secretarial job in the town where she now lives, but she may also obtain access to a plot of land to cultivate and contribute to the income of her husband, who is a wage earner. Sara met this boy after her circumcision. He is not a Meru, and apparently knows nothing about her circumcision and the conflict with her mother.

V. Revival and Neo-Traditionalism

The diverse sources which confirm the increase in circumcision among young girls suggest that a revival is actually taking place, although the magnitude is still uncertain. The revival may generally be moderate, but particularly notable as it occurs among educated girls, a category which was particularly strongly against circumcision in the previous generation.

From the stories of younger girls, teachers and mothers, it is evident that there is informal social pressure in peer groups, among friends and neighbouring girls, both inside and outside of schools.

At times there appears to be proselytizing from those who have already been circumcised. In addition to the influence from peer groups noted above, there is increasing pressure from the old generation of grandmothers, who insist that young girls have an obligation to be circumcised in order to preserve Meru cultural traditions.

With regard to the pattern of neo-traditionalism, we note first that the operation has changed considerably, compared to the traditional excision or clitoridectomy. It has been modernized in the sense that less tissue is cut and some attempts are made to reduce the risk of infection. It is as if the practice has been adapted to some standards of hygiene as well as morals and made less dangerous or objectionable.

Second, it appears that circumcision among young girls is now fully separated from marriage. It is no longer part of a wedding ceremony, nor is it connected with an impending marriage. The age at which the operation is performed has declined. This indicates that circumcision no longer expresses the value of respect shown by a wife to her husband and his family, her subordination as a wife to a particular husband and her "guarantee" of faithfulness to him. The festivities surrounding female circumcision are reduced to the slaughtering of a sheep and the serving of *uru*. The nursing of the circumcised women is considerably curtailed. These arrangements appear to be obligations observed also by relatives who do not approve of the girl's action. Yet circumcision does not confer the status of adult woman on a girl as it did when it was part of, or in preparation for, marriage.

It is clear that the function of the neo-traditional pattern is different – or assumes different motivations and values – from those underlying the traditional custom, although some of the traditional reasons for the practice are voiced by the girls when they justify circumcision. Some even appear to accept the traditional cultural identity of a woman who has reduced her sexual "hotness". Yet such values are taken out of their traditional context, that of the marriage ceremonies. When young girls now decide, or are persuaded to become circumcised, it is as if they expect it to be important among peers, that it will make them more attractive to boys, and eventually will help them to find a husband.

The story of the girl who was persuaded by her grandmother to become circumcised against her mother's will points to another neo-traditional element. The daughter was persuaded by the grandmother's appeal to consider her responsibility for not destroying traditional practices of her people. The appeal concerns not so much values implicit in the custom such as the correct way to achieve adult status, respect for a husband or reduced sexuality, but the inherent value of observing a traditional custom. Such arguments would have failed in the case of the mother who, in fact, opposed such values and wanted to institute new ones in forming her identity as an adult woman.

In the accounts and expressions of the young girls, there is hardly any mention of education as a reason for not becoming circumcised. This is in contrast to the great emphasis on education among girls in the 1960s. We see the clear contrasts between mother and daughter in perceptions of education and the cultural identity of women. The educated mother's opposition to circumcision was, and still is, based on the education that she feels legitimately gives to women a new social and cultural identity. The daughter feels that her generation is different. She may accept a certain status or prestige from being educated, but she, and other girls of her generation, are not as interested in what she calls women's affairs and problems as is her mother's generation. There is no mention of her education as a symbol for any particular cultural identity as a woman, nor is there any notion of a particular life-style or important jobs for her as an educated woman. Education has either no particular meaning for her cultural identity, or a meaning which does not free her from the requirement of being circumcised.

VI. A Tentative Explanation

There may be several possible explanations for the revival of the practice of circumcision of young women. One is that the resurgence is an intergenerational phenomenon where daughters reject mothers' ideals and practices. If so, we have a cyclical change and the present increase might not continue for long. A different explanation, at another level, may be found in the effects of land scarcity and the virtual cessation of the practice of polygyny. Girls may no longer feel assured of getting married as they were when polygyny was practised and land was less scarce. In this situation it might be in the interest of girls to make themselves attractive to young men in the marriage market.

However, because of the observed difference in how education is perceived by the young girls compared to what it meant to their mothers and to the women who were young in the 1960s, I will try to offer a tentative explanation by analysing some changes in education which may be connected to the observed differences between the generations. I will further add to this explanation considerations of changes in the local community which may strengthen this neo-traditional revival of female circumcision. There are indications of a more encompassing neo-traditionalism which entails withdrawal, or disengagement from the national society and a retreat to the local community and its culture.

1. *The Changing Meaning of Education*

In the discussion above I have shown that the altered role of education in the expressions of cultural identity is part of a wider change in the meaning of education for the two generations of women. The question is, are there any changes relating to education itself which may account for the shift in its significance?

Around and after Independence in 1961, young people had very high educational aspirations and expected clear benefits from education, such as jobs that were well paid, prestigious or politically significant in the newly independent nation (Nypan, 1970b, 1971). These expectations included improved living conditions, which amounted to a new style of life. Such aspirations were unrealistic in many cases even in the 1960s, but they were not unusual among young people all over the country, including Meru women.

Since then, educational opportunities have increased considerably. The expansion, especially in primary and even a modest one in secondary schools, has done away with the scarcity of educated people in relation to available jobs. Only a limited number of the young educated people achieve important and well remunerated jobs. Unrealistic aspirations have been adjusted downwards as the scarcity value of education has declined, and so has the status and prestige of moderate education. In addition, the stagnation and even deterioration of the country's economy means that there are in fact still few occuptional opportunities for young people outside agriculture.

The earnings gap between jobs requiring some education, for instance white-collar jobs, and those that do not, has, for historical reasons, been considerable in most developing countries. Soon after independence, the government began to reduce that gap by cutting salaries and fringe benefits for public employees. The gap has been further reduced in the 1980s as economic conditions in the country deteriorated and the government felt unable to maintain the previous levels of income – or even minimum wage levels. Real incomes, even among the best educated, have declined and can no longer provide the level or style of living they used to ensure in the 1960s.

The standards of education itself have also declined. This pertains to the quality of teaching as well as to facilities. Schools fall into disrepair and teaching material, even notebooks, become scarce as the government lacks resources. Young people who now graduate feel that they are less qualified than their predecessors and are told that this is the case.

The economic value and social status of education have declined, although this is not to say that the educated do not have higher status than the uneducated. But education no longer provides the basis for feeling special in the same way it did in the previous generation. Thus, education no longer supplies the potential resources on which the previous generation of women established a new cultural identity for themselves. The revival of female circumcision may be regarded as a result of the weakening of education as a basis for establishing a cultural identity different from the traditional Meru conceptions in which circumcision was regarded as essential. In addition to the declining importance of education one must consider the possible effects of land scarcity and a tighter marriage market. Reduced opportunities for occupations, and an independent life outside the local community which young girls currently experience, occur as young people generally find it difficult to obtain sufficient land locally to establish new households.

2. *The Context of Neo-Traditionalism: Withdrawal from Society to Community*

There are indications that people in the villages no longer are as outwardly oriented as earlier. Local matters and traditional culture are accorded greater importance than they were about 20 years ago. Increasing interest and participation in ethnic affairs indicate a strengthening of Meru culture and social organization. One of the reasons for this situation may be found in a disenchantment with national institutions like the government and the party, resulting in withdrawal of participation from these institutions. Similar phenomena have been observed in other African states: people choose "to cope with the state by distancing themselves from it as a hedge against its instability and declining performance" (Azaraya and Chazan, 1987, p. 108). At times, such withdrawal strengthens the local or ethnic community. For instance, there may be a shift in production away from the market or the use of parallel market. Settlement of disputes and conflicts is increasingly taken out of the administrative channels, and handled according to local mores. Increasing interest in local history and folklore may be symptoms of a more general return to ethnic culture.

The withdrawal observed in Meru may be connected with the general socio-economic deterioration in the country, which in rural areas has been aggravated by an unfavourable government pricing policy for agricultural produce. The real value of prices to farmers for export crops was at the beginning of the 1980s only half of the average level of the beginning of the 1970s (Eriksen, 1987, p. 21). Two political events, however, appear to have contributed more directly and significantly to Meru orientation away from the state.

One such event was the decision by the government and the party to move people in the whole country by force to collective villages (*ujamaa* villages) in 1973–74. This policy was not immediately implemented in Meru. Stories and rumours of how unwisely and carelessly people were moved elsewhere created anxiety as well as hostility towards the government in the Meru areas. People were worried about the consequences of such rigidly planned villages in the midst of their densely cultivated coffee farms. Also, such a rearrangement of people would mean enormous problems in relation to established clan lands. By 1975, it was clear that people in the central areas of the mountain would not be moved to collective villages. However, some of the local people who cultivated additional land on the plains because of land shortage in the mountains lost this land, and their houses there were demolished.

The other event took place in 1976, when the government, with no warning, closed local marketing cooperatives and the cooperative unions and confiscated their property and resources. The assets were taken over by a specially appointed official, locally called the Liquidator, and the coffee was handled by a parastatal organization. It should be remembered that these cooperatives and their union in Meru were originally established and developed by the local farmers themselves. The marketing cooperatives had expanded to include other crops than coffee, and had furnished farmers with various agricultural imputs and credit. Because of good management the union and its leadership was in the early 1970s appointed by the government to organize cooperatives for the whole Arusha region. The success of the local cooperatives and the union was a matter of local pride. The primary cooperatives and the Union were reopened in 1984 by government decree. Most of their previous assets had been lost. Farmers had to start by paying entrance fees and share capital again, and there are more restrictions imposed on their autonomy by government regulations than was previously the case.

These events, as informants state, made people fear the government and the party. People backed away. When discussing villagization (the moving of people to villages), it was explained to me that

> in some places people were all right, but those who lost land and houses were angry. Then after a year or two, the government said that it had not meant to pull down things. It was not the intention to destroy people's properties and the officers concerned had misunderstood. In addition, when the cooperatives were closed, people were not happy. . . . People are tired of hearing this thing now, and then it is changed . . . . that is, they say this now and then it is not as they stated. I think people are more interested in their own matters . . . yes, in their own matters and maybe clan matters; not even village matters, which now is politics and party, but in clan matters.[5] People have begun to think more of Meru and their own way of life.

One official argument for closing the cooperatives in the country was inefficiency and, in some cases, corruption. In their place, the government wanted to establish parastatal marketing organizations. It is at times implied in the way people reason about this event, that this was not the real, or the only reason. There was a feeling that the authorities wanted to curb local organization and communication outside party channels. The cooperatives, no doubt, functioned as channels of communication among farmers, and not only about agricultural matters. These groups probably also served to channel information and protest during the villagization. In Meru there had always been close relationships between the clan organization and the cooperatives (Nypan and Vaa, 1974b). One informant states:

> You know there were outside pressures. . . . There is a way of thinking according to which local or tribal organizations are a

threat to others ... to government and party. But you should resist if you think that government and party is trying to press you down. Now there is no mood for doing things. The mood for initiatives has been cut down. We don't know what will happen next because we have seen what happened the last times when government and party formed policies for this and that.

Other informants add that people who had experience from the cooperatives earlier have other things to do, as many of them now work for the clan organization.

These few examples show that people locally feel some resignation and distrust and are disengaging themselves from government and party, in fact from the state, whose policies and actions may be arbitrary and high-handed. Instead, they turn their attention to local matters and organizations, in particular to the clan. Some informants insist that the clan is now very influential, in spite of the presence of village councils and committees organized by the party. They will talk at length about the councils of all clans, the Mringaringa. The clan has numerous functions such as land allocations, the settlement of disputes and conflict of various kinds, the control in matters of bridewealth and inheritance, and the appointment of guardians for widows and orphans. The Mringaringa functions as the main agency of social control and as the caretaker of Meru values and institutions. It is also interesting to note that people now discuss and reinterpret the historical influence of their neighbours, the Chagga and the Maasai; students at the Theological College in the area reinterpret their local religion in ways which are more consistent with Christianity than missionaries earlier saw it, and they emphasize the general value of their own religion as a guide to behaviour.

This general return to the ethnic culture may revive traditional principles of stratification. Gender is one such principle. At least under conditions of greater emphasis on local values generally, it is likely that adherence to what the Meru regard as the traditional cultural identity of women increases in importance. Appeals to young women to uphold traditional customs like circumcision will carry more weight than before, also for educated girls who no longer find such a firm basis in education for a legitimate alternative cultural identity. It may even be satisfying to young girls to adhere to their particular culture by becoming circumcised. The result may be what one informant described as a fashion, that is, a revival of female circumcision.

VII. Conclusion

The practice of female circumcision has declined considerably over the period of time covered by this analysis. As a custom it has until recently been practised only by a minority of young Meru women. This study supports the claim by local sources that a recent revival has been taking place. The revival may be particularly notable as it occurs also among young educated women who were previously most clearly against the practice and seldom became circumcised.

The revival is not just a return to the old pattern. In spite of the opinion among young girls, that they follow their traditional custom, the many new features indicate that it is a neo-traditional revival. The operation is "modernized" and adapted to contemporary considerations of health, both in terms of how much of the female genitalia is being cut away and in terms of measures of hygiene.

Circumcision is no longer part of the wedding or even a preparation for marriage. It no longer symbolizes, by the ritual of the wedding, the reaching of adult status for a woman through marriage and her subsequent subordination to her husband as head of the household. There are no festivities surrounding the circumcision, and the care of the circumcised woman afterwards is considerably curtailed. When young girls now decide, or are being persuaded, to become circumcised, it is as if they expect it to be important among peers and that it may eventually help them find a husband. In addition, the girls are motivated not only by the cultural values symbolized by the custom, but also by the value of keeping up and continuing a traditional custom in and of itself.

Christianity and education have over the period of time covered in this analysis contributed to the decline in the practice of female circumcision. The influence of education has been considerable until the 1980s, but it no longer appears to have the same influence on young girls at the end of this decade. This change indicates that the role of education in changing customary practices cannot be understood without taking into consideration the meaning of education as an economic and social resource for women. The weakening of education means that it is reduced as a basis for establishing a cultural identity different from the traditional one, of which circumcision was an essential element. This occurs under conditions which strengthen interests in local matters and create a more general revival of ethnic culture and traditions.

Although the revival of female circumcision comprises uneducated as well as educated girls, it is the increase in the latter group that is most remarkable since, in the previous generation, it was in this group that the practice was most clearly rejected earlier. National development has not proved to offer this category of girls the opportunities once expected, including greater independence from local institutions.

Notes

1 The analysis is based on data and general information gathered through several periods of field-work in this area. In 1967 and 1968 I did field-work for eight months on a research project on agricultural development and social organization. Information about the position of women was then provided by informal contacts and conversations, and did not form part of the research project. I also lived for one year in 1974–75 in the main town of the District working in the office of the Regional Development Director.
  The bulk of the data I use in this chapter has been gathered during three periods of field-work of about 12 months altogether from 1987 till 1989 on a research project related to changes in women's living conditions. In this analysis I make use of general observations and participation in local life as well as of a number of informal interviews with women of different ages, in different occupations as well as with a local operator. In addition, I have a large number of informal interviews covering a variety of topics related to women's position in the local community and changes affecting them as well as 600 formal interviews on the more general subjects of the project. The topic of female circumcision and the insistence that it is increasing was brought to my attention by local women themselves. I am indebted, for support and advice, to all colleagues participating in the research programme and in particular to Kristi Anne Stølen, Mariken Vaa, Ragnhild Lund, Gerd Holmboe-Ottosen, An-Magritt Jensen and Margareta Wandel.
2 Some areas on the lower foothills and plains are not controlled by the Meru clans. Here farmers have been able to lease or even buy land for cultivation. Some, but very few women, have acquired such land on loan, as gift or inheritance or even by purchase.
3 The ideas that circumcision reduces sexuality and increases fertility are not regarded as contradictory. Explanations may involve unfortunate consequences for a woman's fertility of having lovers, but strictly speaking, such explanations are not always logical.
4 There are now several ways of getting married: either in church, by registration according to the Marriage Act, and by *fait accompli,* that is elopement with or without church blessing afterwards.
5 Village councils and committees are part of the party organization, which also organises people at the lowest level in every ten houses, the ten-house cell.

References

Azaraya, V. and Chazan, N. 1987. Disengagement from the State in Africa: Reflections on the Experience of Ghana and Guinea, *Society for Comparative Study of Society and History,* Vol. 29, pp. 106–130.

El Sayed Mirghany El Sayed 1982. Reasons and Purposes of Female Circumcision. In Traditional Practices Affecting the Health of Women and Children, *WHO/EMRO: Technical Publication,* Vol. 2, No. 2, pp. 155–160.

Eriksen, T. L. 1987. Tanzania: Et perspektiv på 25 års utvikling. *Forum for utviklingsstudier,* Nos. 1–3, pp. 3–45.

Hayes, R. O. 1975. Female Genital Mutilation, Fertility Control, Women's Roles, and the Patrilineage in Modern Sudan: A Functional Analysis. *American Ethnologist,* Vol. 2, pp. 617–633.

Koso-Thomas, O. 1987. *The Circumcision of Women. A Strategy for Eradication.* London: Zed Books Ltd.

Kuoba, L.J. and Muasher, J. 1985. Female Circumcision in Africa: An Overview. *African Studies Review,* Vol. 28, pp. 90–110.

McLean, S. and Graham, S.E. (eds) 1985. Female Circumcision, Excision and Infibulation. *The Minority Rights Group.* Report No. 47, 2nd rev. ed. London.

Nelson, A. 1967. *The Freemen of Meru.* London: Oxford University Press.

Nypan, A. 1970a. Diffusion of Innovation and Community Leadership. *Acta Sociologica,* Vol. 13, pp. 253–268.

Nypan, A. 1970b. "Tanzanian Youth and Education: Some Aspects of Educational Selection". Working Paper, Institute of Sociology, University of Oslo.

Nypan, A. 1971. Occupational Orientations of Tanzanian Youth. Working Paper. Institute of Sociology, University of Oslo.

Nypan, A. and Vaa, M. 1974a. *Extension Theory and Local Theory – Some Problems of Planned Change.* Report No. 9, Section for Development Studies, Institute of Sociology, University of Oslo.

Nypan, A. and Vaa, M. 1974b. *Leadership, Organizational Structure and Development – Two Meru Villages.* Report No. 4, Section for Development Studies, Institute of Sociology, University of Oslo.

Puritt, P. 1970. *The Meru of Tanzania: A Study of Their Social and Political Organization.* PhD dissertation, University of Illinois, Urbana, Illinois.

Puritt, P. 1977. The Meru of Northeastern Tanzania. In S.F. Moore, and P. Puritt, The Chagga and Meru of Tanzania, *Ethnographic Survey of Africa, East Central Africa,* 18. London: International African Institute.

Talle, A. 1987. Kvinnlig kønsstympning: Ett sätt att skapa kvinnor och män. In D. Kulick (ed.), *Från køn till genus.* Stockholm: Carlsson Förlag.

Talle, A. 1989. *Women at a Loss: Changes in Maasai Pastoralism and Their Effects on Gender Relations.* PhD dissertation, University of Stockholm.

UNESC 1986. *Report of the Working Group on Traditional Practices Affecting the Health of Women and Children:* United Nations Economic and Social Council, Commission on Human Rights. E/CN.4/1986/42.

Widstrand, C. G. 1964. Female Infibulation. *Varia I. Studia Enthographica Upsaliensia,* XX, Uppsala.

3
Economic Change, Marriage Relations and Fertility in a Rural Area of Kenya

AN-MAGRITT JENSEN

When Rose Nafula from Bungoma in Kenya was asked about how many children she would like to have, her answer came without hesitation. She would have children "as long as they get finished from my stomach". So far, nine children had "gotten finished", one of them had later died. Mrs Nafula is 48 years old. Her youngest child, a girl, is one and she is not sure whether this will be her last child.

The population increase in Kenya is among the highest in the world. In spite of social and economic changes and the introduction of family planning programmes, fertility continues to be high. The Kenyan family planning programme has turned out to be among the most costly in the world, and considerable scepticism has been voiced concerning its effectiveness (Bergstrøm, 1983; Sindiga, 1985; World Bank, 1985; Frank and McNicoll, 1987). Recent data suggest that family planning is gaining wider acceptance in Kenya, but this is far from a universal trend (GOK (Government of Kenya), 1989). The focus in this chapter is on a region where such change is not evident: the Western Province. By examining this case, we may shed some light on mechanisms which influence shifts from fairly uncontrolled to more controlled fertility.

There is an extensive literature on the relationship between economic change and fertility levels. A key argument in this work is that areas with pre-industrial economies, dominated by agricultural and labour-intensive production, have high levels of fertility, while societies in which mechanization and a wage labour market gain ground will experience fertility decline (Caldwell, 1982; Simmons, 1985; Mason and Taj, 1987).

The number of children in a family is not usually thought of as a result of planning all the way. Connecting fertility rates at a macro level to fertility behaviour at an individual level may, of course, exaggerate the rationality involved in procreation. Still, it is an underlying conviction in this chapter that despite the uniqueness of each country, cultural specificities and a range of variation between individuals, it is possible to identify a general pattern connecting economy with fertility behaviour.

A change in the perceived value of children to family economy is considered an important factor in explaining the association between economy and fertility (Anker and Knowles, 1983; Mkangi, 1983; Bulatao *et al.*, 1983). It is generally assumed that a cash economy implies a change towards greater individualism and less need for children in daily work. With increasing demand for education, intergenerational transfers reverse direction and the economic and social value of children decreases (O'Brien, 1981; Caldwell, 1982). However, many countries have experienced economic change and the introduction of primary education to children without subsequent decline in fertility. The slowness in the reception of modern family planning illustrates that a shift in the organization of economy is not a sufficient condition for a fertility decline, albeit a necessary one. Against the general assumption of the declining value of children with the transition to a market economy, it is also argued that even though the work utility of children abates, the security function still persists (Archetti, 1984; Cain, 1985; Acsadi *et al.*, 1990). This function remains central when few other mechanisms create old age security. Under conditions of high child mortality, parents avoid limiting the size of their families to ensure that a sufficient number of children survive.

Discussions of children's security functions point to the importance of considering the interpersonal domain of the family when we seek to understand relationships between macro-level phenomena, such as economic change and fertility rates. In this domain, resources are shared, responsibilities are divided and individuals' perceptions of reality are moulded in long-term interdependencies. Family relations have been in the focus of increased attention and in particular the evidence of fathers sharing responsibilities for their offspring as opposed to remaining "free riders": ". . . unburdened by the costs of their procreative activities" (Oppong and Bleek, 1982, p. 30).

In this chapter, a key purpose is to illustrate some possible linkages between societal change and adjustments on the family and individual levels. Two sets of micro-level phenomena are focused on. We first consider changes in marital patterns, especially a trend towards what has been labelled "nucleation". It is assumed that when economic responsibility for children is shared by husband and wife, both of the spouses will recognize the burdens of large families. As a consequence, fertility aspirations decrease, family planning increases, and we expect reduced fertility. On the other hand, if husbands and wives do not share the costs of bringing up children, women "struggle alone" and fertility outcomes are more uncertain.

A second interpersonal phenomenon which shapes fertility attitudes and behaviour is the perception of risks due to mortality. Under uncertain conditions children might constitute the only means of securing old age for women as well as men. Consequently, high fertility persists.

I. Demographic Characteristics

Bungoma District is situated close to the border of Uganda. It is dominated by the ethnic group Luyia, who form the largest cluster of Bantu-speaking peoples in western Kenya. Agriculture is the main economic activity, and cattle have traditionally played an important role in the economy. The major subethnic group is the Bukusu.

Western Province has the highest total fertility rate (8.1) and the lowest prevalence of contraceptive use in Kenya. The annual growth rate was 3.85 in 1979, which is among the highest in the world, and close to the estimated biological maximum. Altogether 64 per cent of the population in Bungoma is below the age of 20 (Central Bureau of Statistics, 1984; GOK, 1989). Since land is equally divided among sons, land fragmentation represents an increasing problem. Population density is 163.9 persons per sq. km, compared to the national average of 27. There is 0.63 ha of arable land per person, which is one of the lowest figures in Kenya (Agatsivat, 1984; GOK, 1984, 1987).

At a national level, Kenya has had remarkable success in reducing child mortality rates. The regional variations, however, are considerable. Child mortality in Bungoma stands at 140, compared to the national average at 87 per thousand (Tostensen and Scott, 1987).

II. Economic Conditions: The Growing Importance of Cash Crops

Residents of Bungoma have a long history as cash crop growers. According to Kituyi (1991) they were among the earliest agitators for African rights in the 1930s, when coffee growing was still reserved for the white settlers. Recently, however, Bungoma has experienced an expansion in the production of cash crops; such as maize, and in particular sugar cane (Kituyi, 1991). At the same time the price fluctuations of sugar cane on the world market have been considerable. The price of sugar was $0.29 a pound in 1979 and had declined to $0.06 in 1986 (Mkangi, 1990).

More than other crops, sugar cane has had a profound impact in the form of increased dependence on a cash economy. While coffee and, later, maize could to some degree be combined with food production, this was not the case for sugar cane. The majority of growers in the area used most of their arable land for the new cash crop, which meant that they had to buy most of their food. This reliance on cash incomes makes the population extremely vulnerable to economic forces beyond their control, such as the ever-decreasing sugar prices on the international market.

When sugar cane was initially introduced, it seemed like a promising route to prosperity. A sugar factory was constructed in the area in 1977. To make space for the factory's sugar fields, a few thousand families had to sell their land and buy new land in neighbouring villages. The first immediate consequence of the construction of the factory, thus, was a higher population density in the surrounding villages. The second consequence was a general expansion of sugar cane cultivation in the area. By the middle of the 1980s, approximately 16,000 farmers had started growing the crop for delivery to the factory. Rather than living in villages dominated by cattle grazing and maize growing, they now became dependent on incomes from sugar cane.

The pioneer farmers earned quite a lot of "flush income". Problems arose when the majority of farmers started to grow sugar cane and the supply exceeded the capacity of the factory. At the same time, the financial situation of the factory deteriorated. During recent years there have been problems with the cutting and transportation of the crop, and the farmers have not been paid. Since sugar cane has a three-year cycle of land use, farmers were trapped in a situation with scarcity of money and food.

At the time of data collection for this study, the sugar fields were ready to be cut, already over-ripened and well into a process of deterioration. The frustration and even desperation of the people was evident.

The change towards increased cash crop cultivation has influenced family patterns in various ways. Cattle are no longer an important component of the local economy. Livestock transactions used to be a time-consuming activity for men. Traditionally, it was "the husband's concern to carry on kinship- and other transactions with his cattle and to exchange fowls for goats and sheep and these again for cattle" (Wagner, 1949, p. 42). Having many children gave prestige to men in such negotiations. The declining importance of livestock reduced a significant male activity and lessened the "objective" need for many children. Cattle herding, which was earlier taken care of by young boys, disappeared as a result of these changes (Kayongo-Male and Walji, 1984). The introduction of cash crops involved a heavier work-load on the part of women. Bungoma was one of the few areas where ploughs were used as early as 1930. The introduction of ploughs made it possible to cultivate larger areas of land, which in turn required increased labour input. In accordance with the sexual division of labour, it was the responsibility of men to clear bush and prepare land, while hand digging, weeding and harvesting were the responsibility of women. The expansion of cash crops also limited the arable land available for the cultivation of subsistence crops. Women had to assume more and more responsibility in agriculture and experienced difficulties in providing the family with sufficient food (Nasimiyu, 1985).

The dependence on cash crops in Bungoma has not led to an improvement in the living conditions of its people. During recent decades, the economic situation of the area has deteriorated. By 1980, Western Province accounted for 12 per cent of the national population, but 25 per cent of the total number of smallholder poverty in the country. The transition from subsistence to cash crops is claimed to be one of the major explanations for decreasing food availability for women and children (Kituyi, 1991). About one third of the children under 5 in this area had symptoms of malnutrition in 1982 (UNICEF, 1985).

III. Gender, Marriage and Parenthood

The Bukusu have been described as a patriarchal group with a weak position of women in marriage. In the case of divorce, mothers have no legal right to the children. A woman's main strategy for strengthening her position was to have many children. The social evaluation of parenthood was high. It affected both the social status of the spouses and their internal relationship. Thus, the presence of children was a crucial factor in the marriage relationship (Wagner, 1949). This description is to a large extent confirmed in a recent study (Berg-Schlosser, 1984). In contrast to this, other studies underline that women in pre-colonial times had rights, in particular to land. These were lost as a result of changes in the land tenure system which started in the 1930s. Individualization of land ownership implied that men got titles while the traditional rights of women were ignored (Nasimiyu, 1985). As this study will show, women are today regaining access to resources which for a long time have been controlled by men.

Education is on the increase. In the sample on which this study is based, almost one third of the older women (over 37 years) have no education, only one tenth of the younger women have not been to school. No women in our sample, however, have education above secondary level. A change also seems to be going on regarding the right of women to own land. According to information obtained at the Land Office in Bungoma an increasing number of women now have title deeds to land. A decade ago, this would have been unheard of.

Women also control what they cultivate in their own gardens. Their produce is for family consumption as well as for sale. In the current study, a majority of women stated that they kept the money they earned from their gardening. However, the sale of produce might threaten food security. Almost half of the women interviewed (45 per cent) said that they did not have enough food for the whole year.

In spite of women's access to education, money and even land, it is difficult to find evidence that gender relations are moving in the direction of equality. Polygamy is a case in point. While polygamous unions are on the decline in Kenya, this does not seem to be the case in Bungoma: "Most of the male adult population is polygamous and pronatalist attitudes are strong in the District" (GOK, 1987). About 40 per cent of the women in Western Province were living in polygamous marriages in 1984, compared to a national average of 25 per cent (Central Bureau of Statistics, 1984, 1986). Similarly, 40 per cent of the women in our sample were living in a polygamous union.

In her study of socio-economic changes in Nandi, also in western Kenya, Smith-Oboler summarizes the consequences for women in this way:

> ... though Nandi society has probably always been economically stratified on the basis of sex, changes stemming from colonial policy, entry into the cash economy, and commodization of

virtually all resources have widened the gap between men and women (Smith-Oboler, 1985, p. 323).

Bukusu women are claimed to have an inferior position in marriage, aggravated during the colonial period. Recent changes have improved individual resources for women, such as education and access to money and property. Still, it is an open question whether the relative position of women in the gender relationship has changed.

IV. Fertility in a Changing Context

Most demographers assume that women in developing countries prefer a lower number of children than men do. At the same time, it is recognized that high fertility, especially many sons, is a channel through which a woman may secure her position. Bearing many children may be the most effective female strategy for achieving short-term as well as long-term security (Mønsted and Walji, 1978; Cain, 1984; Mason and Taj, 1987).

In Bungoma, marriage and children are still the most important means to an acceptable social position for women. Barren women are under high risk of being divorced. Marital breakup for women with children involves leaving the children behind, since they belong to the husband. The emotional relationship between spouses has traditionally had little impact on marriage stability, while a high number of children certainly has been of central importance (Kayongo-Male and Onyango, 1986).

In several studies, it has been concluded that fertility declines when the position of women is based on factors other than child-bearing. The main alternatives identified are women's level of education, income and control over other important resources in society (United Nations, 1985; Krystall, 1986; Safilios-Rothschild and Mburugu, 1986; Sadik, 1988). A question worth asking is whether access to new resources does, indeed, influence fertility, or if other aspects of marital roles need to be considered, such as the degree of co-operation between the spouses.

1. *Methods and Data*

This chapter is based on data collected in Bungoma in 1988 (Jensen and Juma, 1989). The area was selected mostly because of its demographic characteristics, briefly outlined above. A major goal of the study was to explore linkages between population pressure, marital relations and fertility behaviour.

Respondents were selected from three villages. Initial contact was taken with assistant chiefs in each village. They were informed about the project and asked for assistance in summoning women for a public meeting with the researchers. Emphasis was put on the fact that the project should reach women in general, and not specific women, such as members of Women's Groups or certain religious groups. Altogether 240 women turned up at the meetings, and 65 of these were selected through "secret ballot". The interview period lasted for five weeks.

Ten randomly selected men were also interviewed in order to supplement the information provided by the women. In addition, key persons at the community level were interviewed and documentation collected at hospitals, schools and the local administration.

2. *How Many Children? Perceptions and Attitudes among Women and Men*

Information was collected primarily through "focused biographies", following guidelines described in Oppong and Abu (1985). The biographies were based on informal conversations about childbearing, marital relationships, economic activities, child care and nutrition. Each women was visited three times, and the average total interview time was six hours. To secure standard vital information, a questionnaire was filled out in the course of the conversations.

The majority in our sample were of child-bearing age. Only one woman had never been married, and she was the youngest in our sample. Close to 90 per cent of the women were currently married, while the rest were widows or divorced. Respondents' ages ranged from 18 to 78, with 60 per cent of them under the age of 38. The median age at first marriage was 18. Almost two-thirds of the women were married by age 19. At the national level, only 50 per cent are married by this age.

All women, except for the two youngest, had given birth. The highest number of living children for one mother was twelve. Seventy per cent of the women had given birth by age 22. The 65 women had an average of 6.7 births. The average number of living children was 5.6.

Both women and men stated in the interviews that children are the basic purpose of marriage. Without children, the woman would have little security and the man would have low social prestige.

Furthermore, there was consensus between women and men regarding the importance of having many children. Certain cultural obligations must be fulfilled. An equal number of girls and boys was regarded as optimal because of bride price transactions and the renaming of the older generation. To secure the number of surviving children, a family size of six was regarded as a minimum.

The significance of children as security in old age appeared to vary by gender. For women, the children represented economic security as well as persons who could provide personal care if needed. Sons would be living in the area and their wives could provide such care. For men, children first and foremost represented sources of food and shelter. Their daughters would typically have moved to their husbands' homes and would therefore be unavailable for personal care. Since a certain distance is culturally prescribed in men's relationships with daughters-in-law, a son's wife is not expected to provide personal care for her father-in-law. Such care would be the responsibility of the older man's wives. Men would point to the provision of personal care as a reason for having several wives (Maillu, 1988).

When the women were asked if they thought men or women preferred the highest number of children, the majority stated that men wanted more:

> Men prefer a higher number of children than women. The reasons are; he wants it to be known (in the village) that he has a large family. He wants to have several children so that he can be able to get one who is lucky.

One third of the women saw no gender differences regarding the desired family size. They thought both men and women preferred many children:

> Both men and women prefer a high number of children. Men prefer children for prestige and security. Women want them for assistance in domestic work, again in order for their husbands not to marry another wife.

In some cases, husband and wife have discussed and agreed on the number of children. The necessity of having a balance in the number of boys and girls, however, might have overruled such agreement:

> In my case, my husband and I wanted to have the same number of children. There was a misfortune that I gave birth to many boys and fewer girls. My husband decided to marry another wife who can bear him baby girls. It turned out that she gave birth to only baby boys (three). My husband decided to take her for family planning.

Very few women in our sample thought that women wanted more children than men. A common argument among the women who preferred many children was that it would prevent the husband from marrying another wife.

> Women prefer higher number of children than men, especially women in a monogamous marriage. They believe that if they have fewer children the husband will marry other wives to bear him many children.

In essence, women want a high number of children because men want them. The importance of children for the man was related to his role as head of the family's social relations (Kayongo-Male and Walji, 1984; Mønsted, 1977). This role is now in transition. Whether such a change also influences the importance of children to men may depend on how expenses related to children are shared between the spouses. Men do not necessarily have an interest in reducing family size if they do not carry the responsibility for feeding and educating the children, as illustrated here:

> Marriage is not very good on my side. I have had many problems. My husband was struck by a knife by his brother and therefore he is unable to do anything. Even cultivating his shamba he can't. His only work is to drink. That's all. Therefore it's all my business to struggle for the welfare of my children. Feeding them, clothing them, paying for their education. But I can't. I have got a small shamba and I don't have fertilizer. I have no money. Therefore I do not harvest enough to feed my children. But it's God who

protects them, though two have passed away. (Six are left – author's comment).

3. *Marital Relations in Transition: Towards Nucleation?*

The transition from a subsistence and barter economy to a money economy is associated with a process described as "intimization" of the marital relations (Mott, 1981; Caldwell, 1982). This change process has two key aspects. First, family patterns become "nucleated", i.e. young couples become increasingly independent from the older generations. Second, the husband–wife relationship shows higher levels of emotional reciprocity.

Caldwell (1982) and Oppong (1985) both emphasize nucleation of marital relations as a critical link between economic systems and fertility. When the value of children declines, there is motivation to reduce fertility. Altered fertility behaviour, such as the use of modern family planning, necessitates negotiations between spouses. Such negotiations require a certain degree of emotional mutuality in the marital relationship. Furthermore, it is suggested that with increasing mutuality, sexuality between marital partners will become a more central concern, and continuous child-bearing might be seen as problematic. Finally, continuous child-bearing as a potential threat to the wife's health is more likely to be a concern for a caring than for a remote husband.

Oppong (1985) has provided extensive discussion of family changes which are related to fertility decline. Based upon a number of studies in Africa, mainly in Ghana, she points to the importance of "jointness" (togetherness) of the conjugal role relationship in several spheres, such as finances and leisure. Another factor of importance is "closure", i.e. the degree to which the nuclear family functions as a closed unit in financial and housing matters. A high degree of "closure" implies that the nuclear unit (husband, wife and children) is living separately from an extended family, especially the older generation. Physical distance between generations might free couples from cultural restrictions and ease an adaption to new conditions for child-bearing. Degree of "jointness" and "closure" in the nuclear family has been found to be associated with a preference for small families (Oppong and Abu, 1987).

While several demographic theories relate economic change and nucleation of marital relationships, evidence from earlier studies of Bungoma suggests that marital roles may also reveal increasing role segregation. It has been found that a shift towards a cash economy in some cases leads to decreasing responsibility for family welfare on the part of husbands (Kongstad and Mønsted, 1980; Silberschmidt, 1986). In this shift, women are increasingly loaded with work, while

> ... men have become more and more detached from their traditional work and responsibilities, and surplus male labour has been created ... men have become increasingly alienated from the family economy and have drifted into a pattern of sporadic work and drunkenness (Silberschmidt, 1986, p. 11).

Although this description suggests a general pattern of male detachment, it is reasonable to assume that we can also observe marriages characterized by jointness and closure. Central questions in current Bungoma society are how prevalent "nucleated" marriages are, and whether the degree of nucleation is related to fertility behaviour.

Based on the focused biographies obtained in this study, we were able to construct an index of marital relationships. Of special interest was the degree of "jointness" and "closure" in the marriage. The index covers both structural aspects of the respondent's household (e.g. openness to the extended family) and the degree of task sharing and emotional closeness between the spouses. For a full list of criteria used to construct the index, see Appendix 1. The two end-points of a continuum describing marital relationships were named "weak" and "strong". A key goal of the research was to explore if women living in strong marriages prefer smaller families, show greater familiarity with family planning and have fewer children than women in weak marriages.

Among the women in our sample, 30 per cent were living in marriages characterized as strong, in other words high on nucleation. Twenty per cent of the respondents were assigned a low score on the index. The remaining 50 per cent were assigned intermediate scores. Table 1 shows how women with different scores on the marriage relation index are distributed across selected background characteristics, such as age and educational levels of both spouses. As can be seen from the table, younger women have somewhat more (35 per cent) strong relations, compared to older women (29 per cent). However, younger women tend to have intermediate or high scores (approximately 80 per cent). Old women are twice (41 per cent) as likely to have weak marriages, compared to young women (18 per cent). In the case of education, we find a somewhat

Table 1. Marriage relations by age, educational level of woman and husband (percentages)

	Weak (0–5)	Intermediate (6–11)	Strong (12–15)	Total	N
Age					
Under 30 years	18	47	35	100	17
30 to 44 years	13	61	26	100	31
45 to 78 years	41	29	29	99	17
Educ. level, woman					
Less than pri.	18	73	9	100	11
Completed pri.	22	44	34	100	41
Secondary	23	46	31	100	13
Educ. level husb.*					
Less than pri.	67	33	0	100	3
Completed pri.	16	60	24	100	25
Secondary	17	43	39	100	28
Total	20	50	30	100	65

* Nine women did not give information about the educational level of their husband.

clearer pattern. Having completed primary and secondary education increases the likelihood of living in a strong marital relationship. The husband's level of education shows an even stronger trend. Among women whose spouses have secondary-level education, nearly 40 per cent have a high score on the marriage index.

The correspondence between background characteristics and marital relations might be interpreted as an indication of a change taking place. Age, education of the woman and the husband, correspond with the index on marital relations. It is interesting to note that the strongest correlation is found between marital relations and the educational level of the husband.

When discussing the relationship between type of marriage and fertility, one of our central questions is whether it is possible to trace indications of lower fertility among women with high scores on the index of marriage relations, compared to other women.

4. *Fertility Preferences and Behaviour*

We should keep in mind that a high number of children is regarded as an advantage by most people in Bungoma. When asked how many children they would like to have, only five of the respondents in our sample said they would like four children or less. More than 50 per cent stated that they would like to have six children and 40 per cent said they would like to have more than six children.

It is estimated that a completely successful "stop-at-six" policy in Kenya would reduce fertility by 34 per cent (Frank, 1990). It is therefore interesting to note that when the women were asked a more general question about how many children it would be "good for a woman to have", the average number was 5.6 children. We call this the convenient number of children and found a clear correspondence between this and marital relations. While women living in weak marriages tended to give six or more children as a convenient size, the corresponding number given by women in strong marriages was five or less.

Most women in our sample had a clear awareness of the advantages of having a reduced family size and a majority in fact thought that six children would be a convenient size. The main argument was the expense involved in having many children. The idea of controlling fertility, on the other hand, was often confronted with strong perceptions of children as a gift from God, and as such outside human control.

Prevalence of family planning in Bungoma is among the lowest in Kenya. Among the respondents many reasons were given for this. The most commonly available contraceptives were the pill, the IUD (coil) and hormone injections. An important reason given for not using birth control was a fear of side-effects on the women's health or procreative ability. This last factor is especially important in a culture which puts a high value on large families. In our sample, contraceptives were used to terminate child-bearing among women in the upper range of child-bearing age (over 37). Contraceptive use in order to control the spacing and timing of births was highly unusual. Nevertheless, efforts to take active steps towards family planning showed interesting correspondence with the scores on the marriage index.

Information about women's knowledge of and contact with family planning was used to construct a five-point index to measure women's experience with family planning. The index was based on the following items: knowledge of family planning in general, whether they could identify the nearest family planning unit, whether they had visited such a unit within the last year or previously, and the husband's attitudes towards family planning.

As Table 2 shows, there is a clear association between marriage

Table 2. Experience with family planning (index) by type of marriage relations (percentages)

Marriage relations	Family planning experience			Total	N
	Low	Intermediate	High		
Weak	64	22	14	100	14
Intermediate	50	25	25	100	32
Strong	42	5	53	100	19
Total	51	18	31	100	65

relations and experience with family planning. Women in strong marriages were more likely (53 per cent) than women in weak marriages (14 per cent) to have extensive exposure to family planning.

The strong association between marriage relations and family planning experience is an indication of the important role the attitude of the husband may play in family planning issues. Traditionally, men in Bungoma are supposed to take the initiative in matters of birth control. Most in our sample were positive towards the idea of family planning, but they also expressed conflicts described in an earlier study by Silberschmidt (1986):

> ...men seem to be in a deep dilemma, where they are caught between cultural norms and traditions on the one side and their rationality – especially the economic one – on the other side ... what do men do when traditions say one thing and the rationality another? (pp. 55–56).

The variety of statements made by men interviewed in our study reflects the tensions captured in the above quotation: "These days there are no universal reasons for many children"; "A man should have as many as 20 children, or even more. Depending on his capability." Among the nine current users of contraceptives in our sample, co-operation from the husband seemed central and they were mainly found in the group with high scores on the marriage index.

Eighty per cent of our respondents were familiar with modern family planning and the majority recognized the advantages of smaller families. Our data, however, show no clear link between marriage relations and experience of family planning on the one hand, and reduction of fertility on the other hand. In fact, women who reported the most extensive contact with family planning (scores of 5 on the index) where the ones who had the highest number of children.

If we seek to examine the relationship between family size and marriage relations, age complicates the issues. As was mentioned earlier, younger women were more likely to have marriages which were characterized as strong. These same women are, of course, also still of child-bearing age. In Table 3, the average numbers of live births are compared, for women under and over the age of 45, across types of marital relations. As we see, women of child-bearing age who live in strong marital unions have had fewer (5.4) births than their peers in weak marriages (6.2). On the other hand, they have more children than women with an intermediate score on the index of marriage relations. Among women who are past child-bearing age, we also find lowest fertility among women with an intermediate score on the index of marriage relations. Since the sample mainly consisted of women in their child-bearing age, we should be careful about drawing strong conclusions about the fertility pattern of women over 45 years.

Table 3 reveals no systematic association between marriage relations and fertility. It is, however, worth noting that the strongest reduction in fertility, comparing across the age groups, is found among women living in strong marriages. This might indicate a long-term change in fertility.

Our discussion so far has provided glimpses of how traditional customs and values, economic change and emerging marital patterns might shape fertility attitudes and child-bearing. As we have seen, some marriages have moved towards nucleation, while others are characterized by decreased responsibility for family welfare on the part of the husband. The connections between a cash economy, marital relations and fertility in Bungoma are complex and do not reveal clear patterns of association which have been predicted in past work. One factor which may fundamentally affect the phenomena under discussion here is child mortality.

Table 3. Average number of births, by women's age and type of marriage relations

	Under 45	45 and over
Weak	6.2	6.7
Intermediate	4.9	5.2
Strong	5.4	9.4

5. Child Mortality

The 65 women in our sample had given birth to a total of 436 children, out of whom 71 had died. More than half the women had experienced the loss of at least one child. The maximum number of children lost by one woman was eight.

We find a clear relationship between type of marital relationship and child mortality. Women living in strong marriages had lost fewer children than was the case for women living in weak marriages. While 64 per cent of the women in weak marriages had lost a child, 47 per cent in strong marriages had had this experience. Every second woman in weak marriages had lost two children or more, compared to every seventh in strong marriages.

Table 4 displays a strong reverse association between the average number of children lost by the index of marriage relations. Women living in strong marriages have lost a considerably lower number of children, compared to other women. This association is also consistent when dividing the sample by age. As expected, women over 45 have lost more children than younger women. The reverse association between children lost and weak and strong marriages is as strong for older women as it is for younger, while the intermediate groups shows a different pattern. The evidence suggests that the nature of marital roles and relationships may indeed affect child mortality. It remains to be seen if women in strong marriages, who have lost fewer children than their peers in weak marital unions, will end up with lower total fertility. As we saw in Table 3, up to the point of the interview, they had a somewhat lower average number of births (5.4) than women in weak marriages (6.2).

As mentioned in the introduction, Kenya has had a decline in child mortality on a national level, but Bungoma does not fit this pattern. Several authors ask when the decrease in child mortality is sufficient to reach a "threshold level" necessary to reduce fertility

Table 4. Average number of children who have died, by women's age and type of marrige relations

Marriage relations:	All	Under 45	45 and over
Weak	1.6	1.2	2.0
Intermediate	1.2	1.0	2.5
Strong	0.6	0.4	1.2

(e.g. Johnston and Meyer, 1976). The "threshold level" theory assumes that there is not a linear relationship between mortality and fertility. The mortality level has to be low enough that people are not reminded through their own or their neighbour's experience that there is a risk of losing children, before a reduction in fertility can be expected. Such a low level has not yet been reached in Bungoma.

A strong link between child health and fertility belongs to the major findings of the World Fertility Survey, in which Kenya participated (Cochrane et al., 1990). The correspondence between scores on our index of marriage and child mortality indicates that factors at the interpersonal level may constitute an important factor in the understanding of changing fertility behaviour.

V. Discussions and Conclusions

Kenya has been undergoing a transition from subsistence to market economy during recent decades. During the same period many resources and much attention have been given to family planning programmes. However, despite the presence of these crucial elements associated with a demographic transition, Kenya still has one of the most rapidly growing populations in the world. This apparent contradiction motivated us to explore the validity of theories of demographic transition, and to identify mediating factors at the micro level, influencing the expected linkages between economic change and demographic behaviour.

Bungoma was selected for study since there is no trace of fertility decline despite the economic transition. Two sets of micro-level phenomena were discussed, marriage relations and child mortality. We found that a change in the value of children is perceived and reacted upon, particularly among couples who are living in strong marriages. A high degree of nucleation characterized by shared responsibilities was associated with positive attitudes towards reduced family size and acquaintance with family planning. However, even though it may be concluded that family planning was known, and available to these women, it was not used. A common attitude when asked was that one should be careful before interfering with the plans of God, since nobody could say how many children would be taken away. This observation draws attention to the next set of micro-level phenomena in focus, namely the prevalence of child mortality as a factor intervening between economic change and fertility decline. We suggest that Bungoma has not yet reached a "threshold level" in child mortality to witness reduced fertility. Close to every third woman in our sample had lost two or more children. Thus, even though the benefits of smaller families are recognized, parents in Bungoma cannot expect children to reach adulthood and serve as sources of support and care for them in old age.

Bungoma is among the areas in Kenya where land scarcity represents an ever-increasing problem. The traditional way of life, with sons inheriting a part of the parents' land, is increasingly more difficult to maintain. Most women as well as men in our study were not able to provide sufficient land for their sons. This, in turn, had implication for the emphasis which was put on education. Parents who could not provide their sons with sufficient land could struggle to give them some education. Education represents a substitute for land at the same time as it is the main factor turning children into a cost for the family. Education, thus, has two opposite implications for fertility. The first is that the family will be burdened with increased costs of having many children. The second is that educating children represents an alternative way of securing old age for the parents when too little land is available. If the parents succeed in educating at least one child, they may hope that this child in the future will get a job and be able to provide for them. Through education, children still represent security for their parents.

Most people in Bungoma make great sacrifices in order to educate their children. As a planned investment in future security, however, education involves considerable risks. The educational ladder is high and steep, and success also depends on factors outside the control of individual students and parents. However, the possibility of giving birth to a "genius", the one child who is able "to make it", is in principle open to everybody. Through children, even poor people might "pick luck", and the more children, the more chances. As Cain (1985, p. 115) comments, "the harsher the environment of risk, the more likely that parents will overshoot goals just to be on the safe side".

In this way, poverty intervenes in the expected relationship between a cash economy and fertility decline. The fact that parents have no other security in old age than what children can provide represents a barrier against reducing fertility. Bungoma has experienced increases in poverty and malnutrition, which in turn have resulted in high child mortality. Thus, many of the families in our study do indeed experience harsh environments of risk.

It is important to note, however, that the data presented here also offer some ground for optimism. Among women of child-bearing age, having a strong marital relationship with shared responsibilities greatly reduces the risk of losing children. How emerging marital patterns will affect these women's total fertility remains to be seen, but it seems reasonable to expect that a decreasing number of them will continue to bear children "as long as they get finished from the stomach", the way Mrs Nafula does.

Note

I want to thank Gunhild Hagestad for valuable comments and advice on this chapter.

References

Agatsivat, J. L. 1984. Land Use in Bungoma District. In *Technical Report* No. 100. Nairobi: Kenya Rangeland Ecological Monitoring Unit (KREMU).

Anker, R. 1985. Problems of Interpretation and Specification in Analysing Fertility Differentials: Illustrated with Kenyan Survey Data. In Farooq and Simmons (eds) (1985), pp. 277–311.

Anker, R. and Knowles, J. C. 1983. *Fertility Determinants in Developing Countries: A Case Study of Kenya*. Liege: International Labour Organization, Ordina Editions.

Acsadi, G. T. F., Johnson-Acsadi, G. and Bulatao, R. A. 1990. *Population Growth and Reproduction in Sub-Saharan Africa. Technical Analyses of Fertility and Its Consequences*. A World Bank Symposium. Washington, DC: World Bank.

Acsadi, T. T. F. and Johnson-Acsadi, G. 1990. Demand for Children and for Childspacing. In Acsadi *et al.* (1990), pp. 155–185.

Archetti, E. 1984. Rural Families and Demographic Behaviour: Some Latin American Analogies. *Comparative Studies in Society and History*, Vol. 26, No. 2 (April).

Berg-Schlosser, D. 1984. *Tradition and Change in Kenya. A Comparative Analysis of Seven Major Ethnic Groups*. Paderborn: International Gegenwart, Ferdinand Schønigh.

Bergstrøm, S. 1983. *Familjplanering i U-land. Om barns värde, barnbegränsning och barnlöshet i Tredje världen*. Stockholm.

Bulatao, R. A. and Lee, R. D. with Hollerbach, P. E. and Bongaarts, J. (eds) 1983. *Determinants of Fertility in Developing Countries*. Vol. 1: *Supply and Demand for Children*. New York: Academic Press.

Cain, M. 1984. Women's Status and Fertility in Developing Countries. Son Preference and Economic Security. In *World Bank Staff Working Papers, No. 682, Population and Development Studies*, No. 7. Washington, DC.

Cain, M. 1985. Fertility as Adjustment to Risk. In A. S. Rossi (ed.), *Gender and the Life Course*. Aldine Publ. Co.

Caldwell, J. C. (ed.) 1977. *The Persistence of High Fertility. Population Prospects in the Third World*. Dept of Demography, Australian National University, Canberra.

Caldwell, J. C. 1981. The Mechanisms of Demographic Change in Historical Perspective. *Population Studies*, Vol. XXXV, No. 1, pp. 5–27.

Caldwell, J. C. 1982. *Theory of Fertility Decline*. London: Academic Press.

Central Bureau of Statistics 1984. *Kenya Contraceptive Prevalence Survey*, First Report. Nairobi.

Central Bureau of Statistics 1986. *Kenya Contraceptive Prevalence Survey*, Provincial Report. Nairobi.
Cochrane, S. H., Sai, F. T. and Nassim, J. 1990. The Development of Population and Family Planning Policies. In Acsadie *et al.* (1990), pp. 144–154.
Farooq, G. M. and Simmons, G. B. (eds) 1985. *Fertility in Developing Countries. An Economic Perspective on Research and Policy Issues*. London: Macmillan.
Frank, O. 1990. The Demand for Fertility Control. In Acsadi *et al.* (1990), pp. 186–198.
Frank, O. and McNicoll, G. 1987. An Interpretation of Fertility and Population Policy in Kenya. *Population and Development Review*, Vol. 13, No. 2, pp. 209–243.
Government of Kenya 1984. *Bungoma District Development Plan 1984–88*. Nairobi: Ministry of Finance and Planning.
Government of Kenya 1987. *5 year Development Plan (1984–1989)*. Ministry of Health Chapter – Bungoma District.
Government of Kenya 1988. *Bungoma District Development Plan 1988–1992*. Nairobi: Ministry of Finance and Planning.
Government of Kenya 1989. *Kenya Demographic and Health Survey 1989*. Nairobi: National Council for Population and Development, Ministry of Home Affairs and National Heritage.
Government of Kenya and World Bank 1987. *Population III. Project Proposals 1987/88–1991*, Part One. Nairobi.
Jensen, A. M. and Juma, M. N. 1989. *Women, Childbearing and Nutrition. A Case Study from Bungoma, Kenya*. Oslo: NIBR-Report No. 16.
Johnston, B. F. and Meyer, A. J. 1976. *Nutrition, Health and Population in Strategies for Rural Development*. Nairobi: Discussion Paper No. 238, Institute for Development Studies.
Kayongo-Male, D. and Onyango, P. 1986. *The Sociology of the African Family*. London and New York: Longman.
Kayongo-Male, D. and Walji, P. 1984. *Children at Work in Kenya*. Nairobi: Oxford University Press.
Kituyi, M. 1991. *Variables in Peasant Security: Preliminary Findings from Western Kenya*. Bergen: Chr. Michelsens Institute, forthcoming Working Paper.
Kongstad, P. and Mønsted, M. 1980. *Family, Labour and Trade in Western Kenya*. Uppsala: Scandinavian Institute of African Studies.
Krystall, A. 1986. Situation Analysis of Children and Women in Kenya. Section 1. In *The Roles and Situation of Women*. Central Bureau of Statistics and UNICEF, Kenya.
Leibenstein, H. 1981. Economic Decision Theory and Human Fertility Behaviour: A Speculative Essay. *Population and Development Review*, Vol. 7, No. 3, pp. 380–400.
Maillu, G. W. 1988. *Our Kind of Polygamy*. Kenya: Heineman.
Mason, K. O. 1985. *The Status of Women. A Review of its Relationship to Fertility and Mortality*. Rockefeller Foundation.
Mason, K. O. and Taj, A. M. 1987. *Gender Differences in Reproductive Goals in Developing Countries*. Research Report No. 105, Population Studies Center, University of Michigan.
Mkangi, G. C. 1983. *The Social Cost of Small Families and Land Reform. A Case Study of the Wataita of Kenya*. Oxford: Pergamon Press.
Mkangi, K. 1990. *Debt Crisis. The African Perspective*. Nairobi: An ACLCA publication.
Mott, S. H. 1981. Westernization as a Framework for Analyzing Contraceptive Behaviour in Kenya. Paper presented at annual meeting of the American Sociological Association, 24–28 August, Toronto, Canada.
Mønsted, M. 1977. The Changing Division of Labour within Rural Families in Kenya. In Caldwell (ed.) (1977), pp. 259–312.

Mønsted, M. and Walji, P. 1978. *Demographic Analysis of East Africa. A Sociological Interpretation*. Uppsala: Scandinavian Institute of African Studies.

Nasimiyu, R. 1985. Women in the Colonial Economy of Bungoma: Role of Women in Agriculture, 1902–1960. In Were (ed.) (1985).

O'Brien, M. 1981. *The Politics of Reproduction*. Boston: Routledge & Kegan Paul.

Oppong, C, 1985. Some Aspects of Anthropological Contributions. In Farooq and Simmons (eds) (1985), pp. 240–274.

Oppong, C. and Abu, K. 1985. *A Handbook for Data Collection and Analysis of Seven Roles and Statuses of Women*. Geneva: ILO.

Oppong, C. and Abu, K. 1987. *Seven Roles of Women: Impact of Education, Migration and Employment on Ghanaian Mothers*. Geneva: Women, Work and Development, No. 13, ILO.

Oppong, C. and Bleek, W. 1982. Economic Models and Having Children: Some Evidence from Kwahu, Ghana. *Africa*, Vol. 52, No. 4, pp. 1–32.

Rossi, A. S. (ed.) 1985. *Gender and the Life Course*. New York: Aldine Publishing Company.

Sadik, N. 1988. *The State of World Population*. New York: United Nations Population Fund.

Safilios-Rothschild, C. and Mburugu, E. K. 1986. *Women's Income and Fertility in Rural Kenya*. Nairobi: Working Paper No. 441, Institute for Development Studies.

Silberschmidt, M. 1986. *Studies on the Local Context of Birth Control in Kisii District*. Kenya: Report to SIDA.

Simmons, G. B. 1985. Theories of Fertility. In Farooq and Simmons (eds), (1985), pp. 20–66.

Sindiga, I. 1985. The Persistence of High Fertility in Kenya. *Social Science and Medicine*, Vol. 20, No. 1, pp. 71–84.

Smith-Oboler, R. 1985. *Women, Power and Economic Change. The Nandi of Kenya*. Stanford, Calif.: Stanford University Press.

Tostensen, A. and Scott, J. G. 1987. *Kenya. Country Study and Norwegian Aid Review*. Norway: Chr. Michelsens Institute.

UNICEF 1985. *Social Statistics Bulletin. A Publication of Eastern and Southern Africa Region Offices*, Vol. 8, No. 1, Nairobi.

United Nations 1985. Women's Employment and Fertility. A Comparative Analysis of World Fertility Survey – Results for 38 Developing Countries. *Department of International Economic and Social Affairs/Population Studies*, No. 96.

Wagner, G. 1949. *The Bantu of North Kavirondo*, Vol. 1. London: Oxford University Press.

Were, G. S. (ed.) 1985. *Women and Development in Africa*. Nairobi: Gideon S. Were Press.

World Bank 1985. *Population Change and Economic Development*. Reprinted from *World Development Report 1984*, Oxford University Press.

Appendix 1

Index on Family Relations

The index was developed in order to distinguish families with a high degree of nucleation from families with a low degree of nucleation. The profile is based upon 20 criteria:

	Per cent who met each criterion
1. Only one wife	57
2. The wife knows the income of her husband	35
3. The spouses share household expenses	65
4. The family does not support an extended family (adult relatives, siblings) – except for parents with money	48
5. Either husband, or both, pay school fees for children	54
6. Either husband, or both, pay for school uniforms for children	46
7. Husband contributes to the household with food, furniture, other expenses, or there is an "even contribution" between the spouses	48
8. All children have the same father	82
9. The husband does not have children with other women	40
10. The spouses have some daily work together	59
11. The spouses have some shared leisure	23
12. The wife states that "happiness" is very important to the marriage	65
13. The husband does some household work	12
14. The husband participates in household work at a frequency of "occasionally" or "daily"	6
15. The husband is the "main domestic assistance" to the wife	12
16. The husband is the "second main domestic assistance" to the wife	6
17. The family has no adult co-residents from an extended family (they may have children)	82
18. The husband is in the home "regularly" or "always"	79
19. The husband, if not living in the household, visits the home regularly	23
20. The husband participates (or did) in child care	57

The index contains 20 points. The highest score obtained in our sample was 15. Women were characterized as living in a marriage with weak degree of togetherness when they obtained 5 scores or less, intermediate between 6 and 11 scores and strong marriages between 12 and 15 scores.

Part II
Livelihood and Work – an Introduction

This section deals with livelihoods in a variety of situations of socio-economic change where the existing sexual division of labour and responsibilities is altered and provokes formal or informal debates about what women and men may or may not do or be. They cover different socio-economic contexts characterized by rapid market integration.

In the Rukwa case, analysed by Holmboe-Ottesen and Wandel, debates are explicit and often centre around food and feeding. Because of changes in the natural resource base in the region, men's traditional areas of productive activity have disappeared while there has been a concomitant up-grading of agriculture, previously the domain of women. In the context of a steadily growing market integration this seems to provoke increased strain on household resources and conflicts between spouses. Holmboe-Ottesen and Wandel focus on conflicts over food – or feeding – drawing attention to the fact that men and women often have different priorities. Analysing conflicts between spouses, they attempt to identify changes in power relations and decision-making within the household and the possible implications for household food security and child nutritional status.

Men's withdrawal from their role as providers is observed by Vaa in her study of urban poor in Bamako, Mali. Women have become ultimately responsible for feeding the members of the household. This is in contrast to earlier practice and the Islamic gender norms, according to which men should provide for their families. Contrasting with what is observed from Rukwa, men's abdication from economic responsibility does not seem to have diminished their authority at home. The Bamako men, cultivating their social networks as members of power hierarchies outside the household, maintain their dominant position in relation to women despite their economic marginalization.

Lie and Lund examine changes in gender relations brought about by the employment of young girls in export-oriented industry in a

Muslim rural community in Malaysia. In superseding their fathers as the main income providers, these factory girls have attained a position where they can negotiate their status and authority *vis-à-vis* men. Their new role as "agents of change" challenges the existing image of women and poses new dilemmas. Lie and Lund show how the different local actors deal with these dilemmas in a way that minimizes the threat to existing gender relations, characterized by ideas of male supremacy combined with the image of the pious woman.

As distinct from the above, changes in the sexual division of labour in Coto Sur, Costa Rica, do not seem to challenge existing ideas about male and female roles and how men and women should behave. The introduction of the African palm, currently taking place in this area, has led to a considerable increase in the level of income of peasant households. A reorganization of farm work is taking place, by which men are becoming the providers and women the mothers and housewives, a sexual division of labour that was not achievable in the poor subsistence economy. Women in Coto Sur aspire to become mothers and housewives, and the centre of the home. This is deeply rooted in their catholic-influenced culture. Valestrand challenges Mies' thesis of the worldwide "housewifization process", for reducing women to victims of circumstances. The fact that there are housewives in various parts of the world does not imply that being a housewife means the same thing cross-culturally, Valestrand argues.

The articles in this section show that women are taking over areas of responsibility and gaining influence over new fields of life, but without challenging existing gender hierarchies. Similar to what was conveyed in the articles in the first section, it seems that despite important changes in gender relations, women remain caught in a web of dominant gender ideology, whether rooted in Catholicism or Islam, which endows women with a subordinate position in the gender hierarchy.

4

"Wife, Today I Only Had Money for Pombe"

Gender and Food: Women's Bargaining Power and Agricultural Change in a Tanzanian Community

GERD HOLMBOE-OTTESEN AND MARGARETA WANDEL[1]

I. Introduction

In most societies husband and wife have disputes or conflicts that are more or less serious in nature, ranging from relatively peaceful discussions to physical fights and sometimes wife beating. In Rukwa, Tanzania, where the material for this chapter was collected, such conflicts often revolve around food. A typical situation giving rise to conflict is when the husband comes home at mealtimes to find that his wife has not prepared food for him. This conflict and the way it may be solved was described by one of the village leaders as follows:

> The man becomes angry. The dispute that follows is usually by words, but if the woman tries to show that she is strong, either by the way she is talking or by beginning to fight, the husband may beat her up. If this behaviour of the wife is repeated, the husband may bring the dispute to the attention of the village elders. The advice from the elders in this case is usually that the woman should go and cook for the husband. If she still refuses, they will advise her again. The second time around she will usually obey. Such behaviour on the part of the wife would be considered a reason for divorce. However, the elders usually handle these disputes so well that they do not have such a consequence.

This short example illustrates that conflicts over food – or feeding – are a recognized area of dispute, and it draws attention to the fact that men and women often have different priorities. It also sheds light on gender roles and the underlying perceptions of male and female in this society. In general these roles and perceptions are closely tied to food, due to the fact that a large part of people's, especially women's, preoccupations and daily activities are geared towards the procurement and handling of food.

Our intention in this chapter is to use conflicts around food as an entry point to discuss how gender relations, particularly regarding men's and women's say in decision-making processes, affect the production, distribution and consumption of food in the household. We would argue that an understanding of these processes is essential to the study of determinants of household food security and child nutrition. It has been argued that the more command women have over household resources the better for the household food supply and nutritional situation. The reason is that women, more than men, are likely to favour the basic food needs in the household above other needs; thus, if women have enough say they will not jeopardize the household food security if it can in any way be avoided (Katona-Apte, 1983; Tinker, 1979; Holmboe-Ottesen *et al.*, 1989).

Women's command over resources that are important in the procurement of food is to a large extent dependent on their ability to influence decisions regarding allocation and use of these resources. In describing the decision-making processes and conflicts, we will use the concept of "bargaining power". Women's bargaining power may be understood as women's ability to *influence* decisions in the household, independent of their authority to exercise direct power. It is thus not synonymous with "decision-making power", which signifies the power to make decisions on one's own account, i.e. to have "the final say". Bargaining implies some form of cooperation in which the parties involved would have some utility tied to it (Elster, 1989). "Bargaining power" has accordingly been defined as a form of power which usually presupposes that the partners involved have something to offer in return for what they obtain (Bülow, 1991). In Rukwa, for example, we observed that women in their bargaining take advantage of husbands' dependency on their labour in food production in attempts to influence decisions.

Many researchers have mentioned the study of decision-making processes as an important approach to analysing the food and nutritional situation in the household. However, empirical studies examining this aspect of gender relations are scant and give little information as to the dynamics of such processes. The reasons are in part that this subject is methodologically difficult and time demanding to study, and besides there seems to be no agreement on what are the most relevant variables for investigation (Safilios-Rotschild, 1980).

The study reported here[2] is part of a larger project aimed at investigating women's role in food-related activities and the implications for the food and nutritional situation in the household, especially with regard to changes associated with development interventions in the agricultural sector. Its focus is on gender dynamics related to the allocation and use of household resources, such as labour, income and food, and underlying factors such as cultural norms for gender behaviour and perceptions of male and female within these areas of activity.

By using conflicts around food and food-related activities as an entry point for discussing decision-making processes, the differences in priorities and perceptions among the sexes become more clearly revealed. Conflicts can be expected to occur when the cultural norms for gender behaviour are violated by men as well as women. However, conflicts may also arise due to the ambiguity inherent in the cultural conceptions of gender roles, whereby the role expectations in one "arena" of social life are in contradiction with others in different arenas. For instance, being good housewives and mothers is often in contradiction with the role of women as effective producers or procurers of food. In Rukwa women have such a double role in production and reproduction (Mascarenhas, 1983). As the above example illustrates, women may give priority to activities other than cooking and feeding (such as production). Likewise, we shall see that men's responsibilities towards their families sometimes stand in sharp contrast to what is associated with being "real men".

In the following we shall discuss the conflicts around food and food-related activities and attempt to relate these to role expectations and the underlying perceptions of male and female. We will then explore how these perceptions influence women's bargaining power *vis-à-vis* men and their opportunities to fulfil their role as mothers, housewives and procurers of food. Finally, we describe how processes set in motion by development efforts have influenced women's bargaining power, and discuss implications for household food security and child nutritional status. The terms "food" and "food-related activities" are here used in a wide sense, including, in addition to meals and meal preparation, all activities related to procurement and handling of food.

It should be noted that the use of conflicts as an entry point in the presentation of this material will necessarily presuppose a focus on the extreme household situations. This approach will therefore tend to expose those men who are considered to be the more "difficult" among the ones studied. Thus, the picture drawn of men and couple relationships may have a negative bias, and is not truly representative of the situation in the study area. However, we believe that the conflicts reflect underlying problem areas not limited just to the cases presented. Therefore, an analysis of the way conflicts are handled in the household will shed light on the prevailing gender ideology and power relations, as well as help explain how social change processes may affect gender behaviour around food.

II. The Study Area

1. *Socio-economic Pattern and Gender Division of Labour*

The study was conducted in two villages on the Ufipa plateau, which is situated between Lake Tanganyika in the west and Lake Rukwa in the east. It is a mountainous area with a median altitude of about 1,800 metres. The area, which was almost completely wooded 20 years ago, is today mostly covered with grassland interspersed with trees. The rainfall is unimodal, amounting to about 1,200 mm a year. However, during the dry season most farmers still have access to water for irrigation from mountain brooks and springs.

The population is ethnically homogeneous, mostly Fipas, a bantu-speaking tribe. The tribe is patrilinear and patrilocal. The majority are Christians; mostly Roman Catholics. Monogamous and nuclear-based families are the most common forms of household set-up. Usually other members of the patrilineal kin live in separate dwellings and form separate production and consumption units. Only 10 per cent of the households in the study area are polygamous (polygynous), usually not containing more than two wives. Polygamy has become less common, probably due to the influence of Christianity. However, extramarital relationships are quite frequent. It is common to have children outside marriage, arrangements which entail few responsibilities for the men.

The household economy is based on subsistence agriculture, although the use of cash has increased considerably over the last 20 years. Due to deforestation and subsequent disappearance of game, people are presently almost entirely dependent on agriculture. At the same time there has been a gradual increase in hybrid maize production, partly at the expense of millet, and partly by expansion of the areas under cultivation. The introduction of the ox plough in the 1950s, the government drive to increase food crop production in the 1970s, and the introduction of modern cultivation techniques especially suited for maize, have all contributed to the increase of maize production in the area. Today maize is both the major subsistence crop and the main source of cash.

These changes in production pattern have affected the gender division of labour in agriculture. Earlier the women were farmers and the men hunters. Women cultivated millet (the main staple food), local maize (in small quantities) and beans. They did all the agricultural tasks alone, except the first clearing and preparation of land, for which they received help from the men. The men have become increasingly involved in agriculture, particularly maize production. While weeding and harvesting were traditionally women's work, men now participate in these activities, except in the case of millet and ground-nuts, which are still considered "women's crops".

The majority of households keep cattle. This represents a way to store wealth. Cattle are mainly used in ceremonial exchanges and as draught power. Meat and milk production is therefore very low. Many households keep a few goats and chickens, used mostly for household consumption, but only on rare occasions. Except for chickens, animal husbandry is exclusively a male task.

2. *Women's Legal Position*

Women's legal position is still far from the principle of equal rights for women laid down in Tanzania's new constitution. The disparity is particularly evident with regard to women's marital position, property rights and custody of children. The Marriage Act of 1971 proclaims the principles of, among other things: (a) equality of spouses to matrimonial property acquired through joint effort; (b) prohibition of corporal punishment by husbands. However, the impact of the Marriage Act is still limited. Women are not well informed about their rights, since the laws are not widely known and not available in their vernacular language. Moreover, property and savings are usually registered in the husband's name, and in the case of divorce the woman may receive little or nothing (Havnevik et al., 1988).

The parliamentary law, however, has provisions that allow the practice of the old customary laws. The option to choose between the different legal systems usually works in favour of customary law. According to the Marriage Act, custody of children after divorce should be determined by both parents. However, the customary law proclaims that the man or his clan has the right to all children conceived in the course of his marriage. In reality this means that the husband or his relatives are given custody of the children in the case of a divorce (Government of Tanzania/UNICEF, 1985). According to both legal systems, women are at a disadvantage regarding land inheritance not only as daughters compared to sons, but also as widows, who are not eligible to inherit the land from their husbands (Government of Tanzania/UNICEF, 1985).

In the community studied there is still enough available land for cultivation. A single or divorced woman with children, originating from the community, is therefore given usufruct rights to a piece of land by her male relatives. This piece of land is usually smaller than is allotted to couples. However, a woman who has grown up in another village and who becomes divorced usually has no other choice but to move back to her natal village. The only property she is allowed to bring with her are her clothes, cooking pots and her hand hoe. She may be allowed temporary custody of her small children for practical reasons, pertaining to breast-feeding and care. However, they are considered to belong to the father, and after 7 years of age they are often taken from the mother and moved to the father's house.

III. Conflicts Concerning Food and Food-related Activities

The most common disagreements between husband and wife pertaining to food were related to different priorities concerning the *allocation of time and labour*, the *use of productive land* and *the use of food and cash*. The following gives a description of these conflicts and the circumstances under which they arise.

1. *Allocation of Time and Labour in Food Production*

Conflicts originating with women's failure to have a meal ready on time often occur in the labour-intensive season, when women are working long days in the fields. Due to the urgency of the work and long distance to walk, women may decide to return home later than the regular mealtime. Men would usually accept such a priority, either because they are working together with their wives or because they recognize the benefit of their wives investing time in production. However, as the earlier example showed, men may get upset if they do not receive what is considered a very basic service from women.

Another source of conflict would be when the husband feels that his wife does not work enough in the fields, but puts other activities first.

> Early morning Hugo[3] asks when Telesia is planning to go to the fields. She tells him that she is not going today, she will go to the church for bible lessons to prepare for Easter. The husband then complains that she is going late to the field every day, and he says he is sure that she will not be able to finish weeding the field. Telesia says: "Even you work less hard than you could. So it is not good that you complain about me, both of us are late." After some time Telesia went to the field, but Hugo stayed home the whole day.

As is evident from this example, women may also complain about the labour contribution of their husbands. Men may promise to do their share in the fields, but they may drop out at the last moment, or make their workdays short. Many leave the fields in the middle of the day to drink pombe (beer) in the local bar.

> Lusia says that her relationship with the husband is filled with conflicts, mainly because he is lazy. He refuses to work in the fields. When they have a dispute over this, it often ends with silence. Sometimes they do not talk to each other for a whole week.

> Lazaro and Salome have a big maize field of three acres. Salome is going to the field to weed every day, except Sundays. The field is 2½ hours' walk from the house. She usually leaves at 7 in the morning and returns between 2 and 4 in the afternoon. It takes 1 month to weed the field. This is done twice during the cultivation season. In addition she has to weed the ground-nut field which takes two weeks. Lazaro is helping her to weed in the maize field, but only twice a week. He leaves the house at 6 in the morning and returns at 11 a.m. Salome thinks she does not get enough help in weeding from Lazaro, but she has not tried to raise this issue with him, because she thinks it would not help.

2. Use of Productive Land

The men generally show a great interest in increasing the surplus production. Due to the limited productivity of the land and the lack of funds to buy fertilizer, an increase of the area under cultivation is the only way of increasing production. Their wives do not always agree to such plans of expansion:

> In the evening Chales and Saudina discuss plans for cultivation. Chales suggests they make a larger maize field next year. Saudina disagrees, saying it will be too much work for her to weed. After some discussion she is able to convince Chales that her capacity is stretched to the limit, and they agree that the field they have is enough for them.

Husband and wife may also have vested interests in producing different crops:

> Divinus has been cultivating a field where he produces onions for sale. He wants Leokadia to come and weed it for him. Leokadia refuses and argues that she has to finish weeding the maize field first, so as to secure food for the household. The discussion ends in a physical fight.

A woman may want to produce crops, such as millet and groundnuts, to get cash which she can control. The most important of these crops is millet, which is used for beer brewing, an economic activity that is controlled by women. The cash rendered by selling beer would be handled by women.

3. Use of Food Crops and Cash

After harvest the main part of the staple food crops, such as maize, millet and beans, is stored for household consumption. All adults know how much of these crops their households will need until the next harvest. What is considered surplus produce is usually sold immediately. The money is used to pay back loans and to buy agricultural inputs and household necessities as well as other consumption items, such as beer. The problem arises later in the season when all the money has been spent. Food from the household stores may then be sold to obtain more money, thus putting the household food security in jeopardy:

> Velidiana says she becomes very angry when Helmani wants to sell so much of the food crops that they do not have enough for their own use. They do not usually fight, but they will go to his parents and ask them for their judgement.

> John has come home from the pombe bar. Sophia is clearly showing her disapproval. She starts complaining about his drinking and that he is using more money than they can afford. She is pointing to his practice of taking food from the household stocks to obtain money for drinking beer. He argues: "You, a woman, do not understand economics. My economic dispositions are in fact very sound and may yield more money. In addition to sale of maize I earn money on the production of tomatoes and onions. Although I drink for part of my earnings, I also use the extra income to buy fish in another village, which I in turn sell for a profit in the village."
> Later in the evening he tells her that he does not want to eat ugali (porridge) and beans which she is planning to prepare. He says he wants meat or fish. She says: "Why didn't you buy meat and fish at the market, if that is what you want?" He says: "Wife, today I only had money for pombe, not for fish or meat."

Even though both men and women are interested in production to earn cash, women tend to give first priority to the subsistence needs of the family, while men are more likely to emphasize other more dubious needs, as the examples show. This fact may in itself give rise to disagreement on how the food crops should be used. This type of conflict was the most common disagreement registered during the field study. Men who use the cash on beer have less to spend on household necessities and are less likely to fulfil their responsibility to buy clothing, kerosene, school uniforms and books, and agricultural inputs.

Women have little control of the cash that their husbands earn. Many women complained that they had no idea of how much money their husbands received for the sale of maize, beans, fruits and vegetables grown for sale. When men are in need of cash and have exhausted their own opportunities to generate cash, they can demand assistance from their wives. The women may earn cash through activities such as beer brewing or sale of ground-nuts. Although women "control" these cash-generating resources, it is difficult for them to refuse their husband's request for money.

IV. Local Perceptions of Male and Female

In order to understand the factors and processes influencing women's and men's views and priorities, exposed through the conflicts, it is necessary to look more closely at local socio-cultural norms governing the behaviour of men and women as well as the underlying perceptions and ideas of male and female. We will shed light on these factors by focusing on work, within both the productive and the reproductive sphere of activities. Work will here be discussed as suggested by Moore (1988):

> It is not just a matter of what people do . . . it will also include the conditions under which work is performed and its perceived social value within the given cultural context.

Thus, work not only has a practical, but also a symbolic dimension. The symbolic meaning of work is closely tied to personal identity: What you do, or do not do, may say something about who you are. Hence, work is an important factor in shaping male and female identity (Melhuus, 1988).

In Rukwa, women's identity seems first and foremost tied to their role as mothers and housewives, in which their moral obligation is to prepare food and make sure that all members of the household get their rightful share. Since women are active in agricultural production of food, their identity is also tied to this work. However, as we shall see, their moral obligation to secure food for household consumption is closely tied to their caring role. A women who fails to live up to this obligation is considered a "bad" woman and is socially condemned. Therefore, the quality of women's reproductive work and care is an important determinant of their social esteem. Any obstacle that may prevent women from fulfilling this role may be seen as a threat, not only by husbands, but also by the women themselves.

Men's traditional role was tied to hunting and may have contributed to shaping male identity in the past. Since very few men are involved in this activity at present, they have lost an important domain for their social esteem. However, the introduction of "modern" technology related to hybrid maize (the use of the plough and agro-chemicals) and the orientation towards the market have provided entry points for male participation in agriculture distinct from women's role. By defining their role in agriculture as "farm managers", in charge of planning and resource allocations in cultivation, men have "created" work appropriate for themselves. Socializing with other men is also an important source of confirmation of their identity. It is important for the male image to participate in discussions wherever men gather, e.g. in beer bars and in the shade under a tree or in formal village meetings.

Gender identity is to a certain extent based on the negation of activities related to the opposite sex. In the Fipa society a "man" may not cook, he may not feed and dress children, which are defined as female tasks. Likewise, a "woman" may not plough and she may not engage in activities which require "intelligence", such as the operation of machines, e.g. the maize mill. A negative attitude to women in management positions is also in part a reflection of this view. However, there are many indications that it is more difficult for men than for women to transgress the prescribed fields of activity.

Table 1 indicates what tasks women and men usually perform, what they seldom do – but can do without social condemnation – and what they cannot do under any circumstances. The table is based on the responses of wife and husband jointly about the division of labour within the household. Women and girls do housework, while men and boys look after the cattle and do construction and repair work. Women and men, girls and boys are all involved in agricultural activities. Interestingly, both men and women stated that most of the agricultural work is shared equally between them. However, more in-depth interviews and observations indicated that these answers overestimate men's labour contribution in agricultural tasks (for instance in weeding). Table 1 shows, however, the current pattern of how the division of labour is perceived. Thus, the findings may be interpreted in the direction that men may share agricultural work equally with women concerning the crops where men have their cultural and economic interests (such as hybrid maize and beans), without damaging their male image.

The tendency for both men and women to overestimate men's contribution to work tasks where women have the main responsibility and men only give "assistance" to their wives is a phenomenon that has been registered in very different cultures. For instance, studies on time allocation in Norwegian households showed the

Table 1. Division of labour: Who does the work?[1]

Activities	Women	Girls	Men	Boys
Food-supporting activities				
Collect water	3	1	0	(+)
Collect/split firewood	2	1	2	1
Make fire	3	1	(+)	(+)
Taking maize to mill	3	2	0	(+)
Housework				
Prepare/cook food	3	1	0	(+)
Tidying/cleaning	3	2	0	0
Child care	3	1	0	0
Washing clothes, mending	3	1	(+)	(+)
Sweeping yard	2	2	(+)	(+)
Animal husbandry				
Watching/feeding cattle	0	0	2	2
Slaughtering animals	(+)	0	(4)	(+)
Agricultural work				
Land preparation, seeding, manuring, weeding, harvesting	2	1	2	1
Ploughing	0	0	2	1
Hoeing	2	1	2	2
Put pesticides	2	(+)	3	(+)
Transporting from fields	1	(+)	3	1
Threshing	3	1	1	0
Keeping seeds	4	(+)	0	0
Income-generating activities				
Making charcoal for sale	0	0	4	0
Brew beer	4	(+)	0	0
Fishing/(hunting)	(+)	2	3	1
Buying/selling				
Selling crops	(+)	0	3	(+)
Keep money	2	0	2	0
Going to shop	2	1	2	(+)
Building/maintenance				
Making bricks	(+)	(+)	3	1
Building/repair	0	0	3	(+)
Collecting timber				
Plaster/paint walls	3	1	0	0
Medical care				
Child med. care	4	(+)	(+)	0
Collect/prep. trad. medicine	2	0	2	0
Other				
Adult education	3	0	1	0

[1] Code: 4 = does all work; 3 = does most of the work; 2 = does a substantial part of the work; 1 = does only a small part of the work; (+) = does the work occasionally; 0 = never does the work

same tendency to overestimate men's sharing of household work (Haavind, 1984).

Even though men help more in agricultural tasks now than before, women still carry the main burden of work. The following quotation was overheard when a husband and wife were working in the field:

> "You know my wife, I am just helping you with this work. It is not my work. Actually my time is just to rest. So when you see me here at the field you should just be happy. I can choose whichever time I want to go back and you should not complain about me. I have already helped you enough." They continue weeding for a while. After less than an hour he says: "You are not forcing me to work. I am going back home." He took his hoe and left. Later, the wife returns home to cook. After eating, the husband went to the pombe bar and the wife resumed weeding in a field closer to the house.

Men's role as "farm managers" defines the limits to their actual labour contribution in the various agricultural tasks. It is inconceivable to establish an arrangement whereby the woman in principle could stay at home, doing housework while her husband is weeding in the field. As a norm, the "upper limit" for men's participation seems to be an equal share of the work. The example below shows that this man's behaviour is at, or beyond, the limit for what is considered proper conduct of a man:

> Philbert helps Rose with the weeding every day, even when she is not going to the field with him. He starts off to the field at 6 in the morning, while she is leaving home later, because she has a small child to take care of first. They usually return home together. Rose is aware of the fact that she is getting more help from her husband than most women in the village. She says some people are laughing at her husband because he is doing more weeding than her.

In order to get some idea of the prevailing gender ideology in married relationships, women were asked about what qualities a "good husband" should have, and men about the qualities of a "good wife". Interestingly, both men and women put up "hard working/industrious" as the most important quality for a spouse. In other respects the answers differed, women estimated highly a husband who "does not beat his wife" and "does not drink too much" and one who "looks after/cares for wife and children". Men valued other qualities in a wife, such as "be respectful to husband" and "give husband many children" and "do what she is doing well". Thus, higher standards are set for women's performance than for men's. By using negations of unwanted qualities, women seem to be content with men that are not "too bad", while men want women who are "the best".

Food and eating are often strong symbols for sense of community, setting of bounds, as well as hostility (Borchgrevink, 1987). This is because food is often used to express fundamental human feelings, such as respect, love and care, as well as the opposite. A change in food behaviour may therefore be interpreted as a change in the relationship between husband and wife. In Rukwa food was used in many instances to signal the power hierarchy between the sexes. For instance, husbands expect their women to show respect, i.e. show deference. There are many ways of showing "respect". Greeting the husband with a smiling face, not talking back in the case of an argument, refraining from showing too much "strength", are ways of indicating respect. Respect is also demonstrated through the cooking and serving of food, which are regarded as services to the husband. Therefore, when a wife does not have the food ready on time, the husband may interpret this as a strong signal of lack of respect or love, or as a threat to withdrawal of such emotions. Men may in certain instances demonstrate their superiority by demanding service or care from their wives outside regular hours.

> Agnes tells that Paskali often comes home drunk from the bar. "At such times he will ask where the food is. Then he asks me to come and wash his hands before he eats. He has the idea that a loving wife should do this to her husband. If I do not have food ready or do not want to come and wash his hands, he beats me."

Women seem to get their sense of worth confirmed more through *work* than anything else. Our data on time allocation, from both observations and recall interviews, showed that women were engaged in all sorts of activities all day, while men spent more time drinking, talking and resting. In addition, when the women were asked what they would do if they had more time, or what they did when they were not working so hard in the field, they seldom mentioned resting/relaxing as an alternative. Most women would mention activities such as more housework and handicrafts as being those in which they wanted to spend more time. Women's wish always to be busy must be interpreted on the background of the gender ideology existing in the area.

The data indicate that women, more than men, are dependent on living up to the idealized picture portrayed by the other spouse. A woman may be eager to do this, because it is also the picture of mother, nurturer and food procurer with which she confirms her identity. However, a contributory factor may also be that there is a constant threat of negative sanctions, such as physical violence and even divorce, if she does not live up to her husband's expectations. Since a woman's legal position is still weak, and she may lose most of her assets, including her children in the case of divorce, she will usually put down a great deal of effort to avoid this.

The idealized picture of men as portrayed by the women does not include the socializing behaviour. Such behaviour, usually accompanied by beer drinking, is important in confirming maleness. Thus, a man's picture of himself as a man may be different from a woman's picture of him as a good husband. In addition, a man does not fear the same sanctions as women do, when not living up to the other spouse's expectations. He may, therefore feel more free to indulge in activities such as beer drinking, which may in turn give rise to conflicts between the spouses.

V. Decision-making Processes

1. *Bargaining and Control of Resources*

In a questionnaire survey husbands and wives were asked separately about decision-making in relation to different tasks/activities (see Table 2). These activities were assumed to influence directly or indirectly the food and nutritional situation in the household. The most consistent feature is that wives seldom make any decisions alone. Most decisions are taken either by husband and wife jointly or by the husband alone. There was a high degree of correspondence between husbands' and wives' answers, except in a few cases. However, there seemed to be a slight tendency for women to think that decisions were taken jointly, while men were of the opinion that they were taking the decisions alone.

It is interesting to note that the decision to buy food is seldom taken by women alone. As indicated by Table 2, this decision is taken by wife and husband together. In reality this means that

Table 2. Who Decides? Decision-making related to selected activities*

	Decision taken by:					
	Wife's answer			Husband's answer		
Activity	h %	w %	b %	h %	w %	b %
Preparing land	29	19	52	30	5	65
Crops grown	45	10	45	38	10	52
When to plant	53	6	41	50	0	50
When to harvest	27	9	64	20	0	80
How to cultivate	64	5	32	95	0	5
What to sell	43	7	50	53	0	47
What to cook	0	95	5	0	95	5
When to cook	0	100	0	5	95	0
What to eat	0	81	19	5	63	31
To make beer	5	90	5	6	83	11
To buy food	23	9	68	60	10	30
To buy soap	10	10	80	24	10	66
To buy clothes	30	5	65	40	0	60
To buy livestock	48	0	52	30	0	70
To slaughter pig/goat	58	0	42	37	5	58
Children's schooling	59	0	41	60	0	40
Children's medical treatment	18	27	55	10	5	85

h = husband, w = wife, b = both husband and wife
Sample size: n = 22
* Because of variation in the number of responses, the figures are given in percentages to render comparable results.

women usually have to obtain their husbands' permission before anything is bought. Thus, women are placed in a difficult position: they are responsible for cooking and serving the food, but they are not able to buy food without consulting their husbands. This is all the more necessary since men usually keep the money. The following story illustrates this problem:

> The salt was finished and I did not have any money to buy some. As I knew that my husband was drinking pombe in the bar, I decided to go there and ask for money. When I reached the bar and told him about the problem he got very upset with me for not having chosen a better time to ask, and he told me to go to hell. I

thought it was important, as my husband would get very upset to get food without salt when he would come home after drinking. The men have just small reasons for beating their wives, especially if they are drunk. And I just wanted to avoid that.

Men seem to make decisions alone more often in activities related to cultivation, particularly in regard to cultivation methods and use of inputs (i.e. how to cultivate) than in other food-related activities. Women participate more in the decision concerning how much of the produce to sell. About half of the husbands as well as the wives reported that they were taking this decision together, while the other halves were of the opinion that the husbands take this decision alone.

There are important nuances which are not reflected in the answers given in Table 2. Our in-depth interviews show a great deal of variation, even in households where most decisions are stated to be taken jointly. In some of these households men in practice took all the decisions, even though the women were consulted. In a few households women took the final decisions alone. In general, women's ability to make decisions on their own would, among other things, depend on the type of crop involved. As expressed by a key informant:

> Usually the men make all the decisions concerning cultivation, but nowadays they will often consult their wives first. They take these decisions because they are the leaders of the household. It is the men who decide how the maize should be planted. Even millet cultivation is decided by the men. However, women usually take the decisions concerning ground-nuts and green vegetables (minor crops).

A woman's status relative to her husband was also important for her bargaining power and her ability to make decisions alone. It was, for instance, noted that in households where women had relatively high education, they had more bargaining power and had more say in decision-making than in households where women had little or no schooling.

Even though the authority to make decisions officially rests with the men, women may find ways to have their views accepted. This would among other things depend on their smartness and ability to find arguments that the husband could accept.

In the evening, after working together the whole day in the field, Adamu and Josephina are discussing plans for cultivation. Josephina suggest that they should enlarge the maize field next year so that they can earn some more money. Adamu does not agree. He suggests they make a large millet field. Josephina disagrees and argues that extending the millet field will give her much more work than if the maize field is extended. In the end both of them agree that the best thing to do would be to extend the maize field.

According to Willis (1989) the Fipa women have a strong standing compared to their counterparts in other East African tribes, such as the Bemba. In the 1960s Willis found that decisions were usually taken on the basis of discussions in the household, but that the man had the final say. This seems still to be the general rule, though it entails that the women, despite their relatively good position, have a subordinate position in decision making.

However, the importance of women's ability to bargain in disputes with their men should not be overlooked. When a husband demands more assistance in the fields, the woman may point to her limited capacity to supply labour and argue that other important tasks may not be done if his will prevails. By the force of the argument she may also be able to convince her husband that his use of money may jeopardize the food security in the household or the satisfaction of other essential needs. In such disagreements women often have the support of the existing norms or moral codes in the community. She may raise the problem with parents-in-law, or with village authorities to get the necessary backing for her views. If she is "right" and he is "wrong" according to these norms, it will be easier for her to push her views through. Hence, the social norms governing the behaviour of men and women are important determinants of the bargaining power of women.

2. *Decision-making and Socio-economic Change*

Even though the development processes aimed at improvement of women's position in Tanzania have been slow and sometimes fraught with failure, there has been a definite change in the life of women in some aspects. This is probably best seen in regard to education. The socialist policy of the Tanzanian Government has opened up for better education for both boys and girls (Government of Tanzania/UNICEF, 1985). As a result, the educational "gap" between men and women is closing in the area studied, as elsewhere in Tanzania. Whereas few of the older women had any schooling and were illiterate, most of the younger women have had some schooling. In addition, adult education classes for women are given on a regular basis in the area.

Furthermore, the Government has launched information campaigns through the mass media about women's issues and equal rights for women. The establishment of a local branch of the national women's organizations (UWT) under the auspices of the local party (CCM) offices has made it possible to bring women's issues to the attention of people at the grassroots level.

Changes in the socio-economic conditions in the project area have to a large extent occurred as a result of development efforts within the agricultural sector. Although agricultural production is still mostly concentrated on food crops, it is no longer exclusively oriented towards subsistence – but also towards marketing. This transition is the result of the increased use of modern technology implements (such as hybrid seeds, fertilizers and pesticides), which has entailed an increased need for cash. The need for cash has been met by increased production. At the same time, the better access to markets has opened up the opportunities for increased consumption of all sorts of goods, thus furthering the need for surplus production for cash.

Many of our informants expressed the opinion that there are more conflicts between husband and wife nowadays than before. Although there are no available historical data to support this notion, other findings from our study point in the same direction. If this is so, it may indicate that the developmental processes have led to changes in the underlying factors governing decision-making and gender relations in the household. We will especially point to two possible explanations for the increase in gender conflicts:

1. The socio-economic change has led to an increase in women's bargaining power, thus leaving more "space" for women to bring up controversial issues with men.
2. The change processes have created more pressure on household labour and resources, thus exposing more clearly the gender differences in priorities and expectations.

These explanations are not mutually exclusive. On the contrary, these processes may in fact reinforce each other. The relevance of the *first explanation* is illustrated by several statements made by both women and men:

> In the old days men decided everything. The women did not have any power at all to make decisions. This has changed very much. Now both women and men decide on household matters and matters of cultivation. (Edwina, born around 1910)
>
> In the old days they never discussed anything in the family. The men decided everything. There has been a change in this matter. Nowadays the man will usually tell his wife about his ideas and then they discuss. (Edinata, born around 1905)

The men had the same view:

> The men used to take all the decisions concerning cultivation, but nowadays they will often consult their wives first. (Malius, a middle-aged model farmer.)
>
> ...Today women think more of themselves than they used to do... (Zenohi, about 80 years)

The improvements in women's social status have been slow and women are still non-assertive, i.e. due to fear of physical punishment and divorce. However, in spite of this, most women feel that there has been a definite change. Better education and a slowly awakening awareness of their rights may have given the women the psychological strength and the moral backing to start to push their views *vis-à-vis* their men. In fact the men were complaining about this situation:

> Deusi is inviting two neighbours to share his food while he and his wife are taking a break to rest from field-work. While they are eating the men start to talk about how life has changed lately. They say: "These days men have a much more difficult time than earlier. The women have become more demanding. They voice so many more needs, they even want nice clothing and jewellery." They conclude that it is difficult for a man to have more than one wife if he should be able to meet all these needs.

The second explanation points to the linkages between changes in the resource situation and decision-making processes in the household. There are several indications that also support this explanation. The first indication concerns our finding that there are variations in household food availability according to degree of integration into the market. Although the two study villages are similar in many respects, such as access to land, production pattern, socio-cultural and ecological aspects, one village is more integrated into the market than the other. The more market-oriented one is characterized by a greater internal cash flow, and there is a better access to markets both within and outside the village. In the other village people rely to a greater extent on the traditional system of bartering and have less access to outside markets. Despite the high degree of similarity, a marked difference was found in the household food security situation in the two villages. Even in an agricultural year when the average harvest of the major food crops, maize and beans, was almost the same in the two villages, the more market-oriented village ran out of household food stocks faster than the other village (Wandel and Holmboe-Ottesen, 1991). It was more common in this village for the men to take from these food reserves in order to obtain money, and use the cash to buy non-food items and beer.

In addition, our interviews and observations indicated a clear tendency of more conflicts between men and women in the more market-oriented village. The increased need for cash leads, sooner or later, to a situation where the food stocks run so low that men's and women's divergent priorities concerning these stocks will be in conflict. In order to meet their obligations as food providers of the family, thus living up to their ideal as "good wives", the women feel forced to fight their husband's decision to sell from the food stocks. As we have seen, women are not always successful in such attempts. However, many women, by force of their arguments alone, are able to get their men to change their minds.

Commercialization of agricultural production leads not only to pressure on household food stocks, but also to constraints on women's labour. Larger areas are cultivated, resulting in more work for women in the fields, particularly in weeding. The larger work load in the field forces women to make priorities within their area of responsibility. Housework, child care and feeding, as well as cooking, are activities that receive less attention when women are busy in the fields. This, in turn, exposes women to the criticism of being "bad women" and to husbands' anger for not having food ready when they expect it.

On the other hand, the increased acreage put under cultivation has opened up greater involvement in agricultural activities for men, even in weeding, which used to be entirely a "women's task". The following explanation made by one of our informants regarding why they were not engaged in weeding was typical for many of the men we interviewed:

> The men are taking part in weeding now, because this has become necessary after we started cultivating big fields. If the men are not helping, the women will not be able to finish in time. Then the weeds will grow large before they are removed and the yields will be less. . . . Men are able to help in weeding because now maize is cultivated in rows, and not broadcasted as earlier. They can help when maize and beans are cultivated separately [which is the modern way of cultivation – our remark], and not intercropped. This is because men are using a bigger hoe than women, and with that they cannot weed with a small space in between the plants [which is the case when broadcasting or intercropping is practised – our remark].

The fact that men have become engaged in weeding, the most heavy and time-consuming task in the field, opens up the possibility for women of negotiating with their husbands about their labour contribution:

> Edwina says that she always has to ask her husband to come along to the field to help her weed, otherwise he will not go, even though he does not have any other work to do.

> Fortunata says that last year Didasi hardly helped her with the weeding at all. This year she asked him to help her more with the weeding than he did last year, and he is now doing that.

The wives may argue with their husbands for all the benefits entailed if they get help, both in terms of higher production and in terms of more time for cooking and other household tasks. The fact that the women are nowadays able to ask for more help from their husbands in weeding, and sometimes get it, indicates that women have increased their bargaining power.

VI. Implications for Household Food Availability and Nutrition

Our findings support the notion that the more command women have over household resources (including food, cash and labour), the greater their chance of securing adequate food supply and nutritional well-being in the household. The reason is that women more than men tend to favour basic food needs above other needs in the household. Similar results have come from studies elsewhere in Tanzania (Tobisson, 1980; Mascarenhas, 1983), and from other countries in Africa (Skjønsberg, 1981; Kumar, 1985; Bério, 1984). In fact, this gender-specific pattern seems also to be common in other developing regions (Holmboe-Ottesen *et al.*, 1989).

The extent to which women have command over household resources relevant to food depends mainly on two factors: first, on women's direct access to these resources, and second, on their ability to influence decisions concerning the allocation and use of them (i.e. their bargaining power). In this community, women's direct access to food resources is limited to what is left to be stored in the household granaries after the surplus from the harvest has been sold. From this time women are faced with the problem of trying to prevent their husbands from selling food from the household stores. In addition, women have direct access to cash from their own income-earning activities, which for most of them is limited to beer brewing and sales of small quantities of ground-nuts. However, since men can demand a share of these earnings, women's control over these resources depends on their bargaining power *vis-à-vis* their husbands.

The processes of change in Rukwa have, by changing women's situation, influenced the food and nutritional situation in the household both positively and negatively. As mentioned earlier, there are many indications that women's bargaining power has increased as a consequence of the Tanzanian policy on education and women's issues. It can therefore be expected that nowadays women stand a greater chance of influencing the decisions where men still have the final say. This is particularly important with regard to sale of food stocks, and the way in which cash is used.

The increased bargaining power of women may also have been important in men's partaking in field-work, especially in weeding. This may be one factor that has led to increased yields, and thus augmented the opportunity of securing food for the household all year around.

One possible effect of men's increased involvement in agricultural work could be to relieve women of some of the time constraints they encounter in providing adequate nutrition to the family. One could perhaps expect that when men involve themselves more in production, women could work less in the fields, and thus have more time to spend on cooking and on child care. When women are busy working in the field, they are not able to cook proper meals and children are fed less often (Wandel and Holmboe-Ottesen, 1989). However, data on time use showed that women who have husbands who are highly active in the fields have to work more than women who have husbands who contribute much less in this respect (Holmboe-Ottesen and Wandel, 1991). As pointed out earlier, this is due to the fact that women are considered to be the main ones responsible for this work, while men in their role as "farm managers" are just "helping out" in the field. An industrious man thus requires a wife who works at least as hard as he does.

The nutritional status among children was found to be markedly worse in the more market-oriented village. Children were found to be fed less often during the day and this discrepancy was particularly pronounced in the pre-harvest season when food is short and women have a high work-load. Analyses of the data revealed that there were many reasons for this difference (Wandel and Holmboe-Ottesen, 1991). However, a main factor was found to be the lower food security in the households in the market-oriented village.

Market integration has thus led to a squeeze on the food resources in this community, which in turn has had adverse consequences for child feeding and nutrition. Similar findings have been obtained from other studies (Biswas, 1979; Dewey, 1981, 1990). On the other hand, the modernization of agriculture which has been part and parcel of the market-integration process has increased production and thus improved the potential for better food security and nutrition. It can therefore be argued that there is no inherent negative aspect of commercialization of agriculture in terms of food and nutritional effects (Pinstrup-Andersen, 1985). It is more a matter of household priorities in terms of allocation of labour and the use of food and cash.

When discussing the implications of market integration for the food and nutritional situation in the study area, it is important to draw attention to the change in beer drinking habits which has occurred concomitantly. Beer, earlier offered seasonally on special occasions, has now become highly commercialized. Due to surplus production of grains in many households and the preference for cash earning activities, beer is available every day, the whole year around. Since the social life at the beer bars is held in high esteem, especially by men, there is a great temptation to spend substantial amounts of their time and money this way, even at the expense of household food security. It is important to emphasize that men do not get their "maleness" confirmed by excessive drinking. However, it can be assumed that many men have been caught in an evil circle, from which alcoholism becomes a likely outcome of this type of socialization among men.

Women have also been active in this change of drinking habits. They have a vested interest in increased beer production, since they have a larger control over money earned this way than over production of the main crops, such as maize. However, none of the women wanted their husbands to be large consumers of their own products, since that would mean more hardships for themselves, in terms of violence as well as a deterioration of the household food situation.

In order to secure a more positive nutritional outcome in the area it will be necessary to promote development efforts that come to grips with these negative trends. The foundation needs to be laid for a larger fraction of the men to become "good husbands", i.e. drinking less and helping their wives in the fields, and for nutrition to be given higher priority by both men and women.

Notes

1 We wish to acknowledge the helpful contribution of Elisabeth Fürst and Siri Gerrard to an earlier version of this chapter. In particular we want to thank Marit Melhuus, who spent quite some time and effort in helping us restructure and sharpen our arguments in this chapter. We are also especially indebted to the two editors, Kristi Anne Stølen and Mariken Vaa, who guided us safely through the lengthy process of writing.
2 The field research included both qualitative and quantitative data. This chapter is based mainly on the qualitative data from interviews with women and men, single or in groups, as well as participant observation and notes from discussions between villagers in the fields and at home. For a more thorough description of research design and methods, readers are referred to Holmboe-Ottesen and Wandel (1991) and Wandel and Holmboe-Ottesen (1991).
3 All names used in the examples are fictitious, but names commonly found in the Fipa society.

References

Bério, A. J. 1984. The Use of Time Allocation Data in Developing Countries: From Influencing Development Policies to Estimating Energy Requirements. Paper delivered at International Research Group on Time Budgets and Social Activities, Helsinki, August. Rome: FAO.
Biswas, M. R. 1979. Nutrition and Agricultural Development in Africa. *International Journal of Environmental Studies*, Vol. 13, No. 3, pp. 207–217.

Biswas, M. R. and Pinstrup-Andersen, P. (eds) 1985. *Nutrition and Development.* Oxford: Oxford University Press.

Borchgrevink, T. 1987. *Kjærlighetens Diktatur; Kjønn, Arbeidsdeling og Modernitet.* MA Thesis, Department of Social Anthropology, University of Oslo.

Bülow, D. von 1991. Male Domination and Female Power: A Discussion of Women's Bargaining Power and Gender Struggle. In *Proceedings from Nordic Symposium "Gender and Social Change in Developing Countries" Granavolden, Norway 11–14 October 1990.* University of Oslo: Centre for Development and Environment (SUM).

Carroll, C. R., Vandermeer, J. H. and Rosset, P. (eds) 1990. *Agroecology.* New York: McGraw-Hill.

Dewey, K. G. 19891. Nutritional Consequences of the Transformation from subsistence to Commercial Agriculture in Tabasco, Mexico. *Human Ecology,* Vol. 9, No. 2, pp. 151–187.

Dewey, K. G. 1990. Nutrition and Agricultural Change. In: Carroll *et al.* (eds) (1990).

Elster, J. 1989. *Nuts and Bolts,* Chapter XIV: "Bargaining". Cambridge: Cambridge University Press.

Gamser, M. S. (ed.) 1988. *Mobilizing Appropriate Technology.* London: Intermediate Technology Publications Ltd.

Government of the United Republic of Tanzania and United Children's Fund 1985. *Analysis of the Situation of Children and Women.* Dar es Salaam, Tanzania: UNICEF.

Haavind, H. 1984. Love and Power in Marriage. In Holter, (ed.) (1984), pp. 136–168.

Havnevik, K., Kjærby, F., Meena, R., Skarstein, R. and Vuorela, U. 1988. *Tanzania Country Study and Norwegian Aid Review.* Centre for Development Studies, University of Bergen.

Holmboe-Ottesen, G. and Wandel, M. 1991. Men's Contribution to the Food And Nutritional Situation in the Tanzanian Household. *Ecology of Food and Nutrition,* Vol. 26, No. 1, 83–96.

Holmboe-Ottesen, G., Mascarenhas, O. and Wandel, M. 1989. *Women's Role in Food Chain Activities and the Implications for Nutrition.* Geneva: ACC/SCN State-of-the-art Series, Nutrition Policy Discussion Paper No. 4. United Nations Administrative Committee on Coordination – Subcommittee on Nutrition, c/o WHO.

Holter, H. (ed.) 1984. *Patriarchy in a Welfare Society.* Oslo: Oslo University Press.

Katona-Apte, J. 1983. A Socio-cultural Perspective on the Significance of Sex Roles in Agriculture. In *Nutritional Impact of Agricultural Projects.* Papers and proceedings of a workshop held by the UN ACC, Subcommittee on Nutrition. Geneva: UN-ACC/SCN, c/o WHO, pp. 28–43.

Kumar, S. K. 1985. Women's Agricultural Work in a Subsistence-oriented Economy: Its Role in Production, Food Consumption and Nutrition. *IFPRI Working Paper,* International Food Policy Research Institute, Washington, DC.

Mascarenhas, O. 1983. Implications of Constraints in Women's Control and Utilization of Resources for the Food and Nutritional Status of Their Families. Paper presented at the TFNC/UNICEF Workshop on "Hunger and Society" in Tanzania, December. UNICEF, Dar es Salaam.

Melhuus, M. 1988. Gender, Culture and Appropriate Technology – A Conceptual Framework. In Gamser, (ed.) (1988).

Moore, H. L. 1988. *Feminism and Anthropology.* Cambridge: Polity Press.

Pinstrup-Andersen, P. 1985. The Impact of Export Crop Production on Human Nutrition. In Biswas and Pinstrup-Andersen (eds).

Safilios-Rotschild, C. 1980. The Role of the Family: A Neglected Aspect of Poverty. In *Implementing Programmes of Human Development.* Washington, DC: World Bank Staff Working Paper, No. 403, World Bank.

Skjønsberg, E. 1981. The Kefa Records: Everyday Life among Women and Men in a Zambian Village. *Third World Seminar publications*, No. 21, Centre for Development and Environment (SUM), University of Oslo, Norway.

Tinker, Irene 1979. *New Technologies for Food Chain Activities: The Imperative of Equity for Women*. Washington, DC: Office of Women in Development, USAID.

Tobisson, E. 1980. *Women, Food and Nutrition in Nyamurigura Village, Mara Region, Tanzania*. A report presented to the Tanzania Food and Nutrition Centre (TFNC). Dar es Salaam: TFNC.

Wandel, M. and Holmboe-Ottesen, G. 1989. Maternal Work, Resource Allocation and Child Nutrition in Relation to Men's Contribution. *Proceedings of the 14th International Congress of Nutrition*. Seoul: Korean Nutrition Society, c/o Department of Foods and Nutrition, Ewha Womans University.

Wandel, M. and Holmboe-Ottesen, G. 1991. Child Malnutrition and Development Processes in Two Tanzanian Villages (accepted for publication in *Health Policy and Planning*).

Willis, R. 1981. *A State in the Making: Myth, History and Social Transformation in pre-colonial Ufipa*. Bloomington: Indiana University Press.

5
Work, Livelihoods and Family Responsibilities in Urban Poverty

MARIKEN VAA

The poorest countries in Africa have for several decades witnessed rapid urban growth, both through in-migration to the cities and through the high rates of natural increase of the young urban populations. Since the late 1960s, an alarming reduction of living standards has also occurred. The cost of urban living has increased, wages have declined and wage work in itself has become harder to find. Urban poverty is not only widespread but increasing (Amis, 1989). One certain consequence of these trends is that a growing number of urban households have to find ways of supplementing wages by other forms of income earning, or find their livelihood outside formal employment altogether. Thus, the distinction between the formal and the informal sector is breaking down. At the same time, the gap between urban and rural incomes has narrowed, but this apparently has not led to a decrease in rural–urban migration. Rather, households and individuals pursue what has been labelled "interactive survival strategies", exploiting both rural and urban niches (Jamal and Weeks, 1988).

When substantial segments of a population begin to face severe poverty, one would also expect changes in norms and behaviour relating to rights and duties between people. More specifically, when day-to-day survival becomes a challenge, it is to be expected that both the culturally prescribed division of labour between the genders, and norms regarding men's and women's responsibilities for supporting their families, are modified, if not at the ideological level, at least in practice.

Against a general background of rapid urbanization and subsequent pauperization, two themes are explored in this chapter: how new urbanites come to rely on livelihoods outside wage employment, and new divisions of responsibility between men and women in looking after their families. The report is based mainly on material from Bamako, Mali. The presentation draws both on published research and available documentation as well as data from a study undertaken in one particular neighbourhood in Bamako.[1] The questions in focus are what non-wage livelihoods are available, how they are exploited by men and women living in various degrees of urban poverty, and how gender-based divisions of responsibilities in households are modified as a consequence of the various constraints and possibilities encountered.

First, the concept of livelihoods is introduced, and linked to self-employment and social networks in the urban informal sector. Then some background information on Mali, including recent trends in economic development and urbanization, is provided. Some salient features of gender relations in Mali are presented, focusing on the division of work and in providing for dependants. Case material from the Bamako settlement is then presented, and some implications of new economic responsibilities for women as well as men's withdrawal from their role as providers are proposed.

I. Some Key Concepts: Livelihoods, Networks and the Urban Informal Sector

There is a growing consensus among students of peripheral economies that conventional definitions of work, employment, enterprise and income neither capture the economic circumstances of the very poor in general nor the nature of women's participation in the economy and their contribution to household, community and national income. Instead, the concept of livelihood is proposed. It is defined as comprising: "the activities pursued by individuals and households to increase levels of wealth and of stocks and flows of food, cash and other resources to provide for subsistence and security against impoverishment" (Chambers, 1985, p. 85; *World Development*, 1989, p. 1140). A livelihood system thus refers to the mix of individual and household strategies that mobilize available resources and opportunities. These strategies include not only involvement in the labour market, but a range of economic activities such as saving, borrowing, and innovation and adaptation in consumption and production, as well as social activities like associating with kin, friends and protectors, joining and forming organizations and so on. Individuals as well as households adjust the mix according to season and personal circumstances, be they resources or constraints. Livelihood systems are by definition and necessity dynamic (Grown and Sebstad, 1989, p. 941). The concept not only links different components of analysis in the economic sphere, but also captures underlying relationships within the household and between household members and external actors.

The concept of livelihood underlines the intermingling of social and economic strategies. The activities that produce livelihoods must be constantly sustained and improved on in order to ensure survival and a minimum of security. A wider and more complex range of interpersonal relationships is drawn on than that at a workplace. Livelihoods are by definition tied up to the personal relationships or networks in which each individual is involved. Seen in isolation, some of the income-generating activities of the poor make little economic sense, for example in terms of remuneration per time unit. It should be borne in mind, however, that when people exert themselves for negligible economic rewards, they may at the same time be engaged in intricate relationships where not only goods and services are exchanged, but where new possibilities of patronage are explored. Time and energy spent in maintaining one's social network can be likened to putting cash in a savings account (Lloyd, 1982, p. 74).

Increasing numbers of men, women and children in Third World economies make their livelihood in so-called informal activities. The labels "formal/informal" gained wide currency in the early 1970s, as the International Labour Office adopted this terminology in its various city case-studies under the World Employment Programme. According to this usage, the formal sector consists of enumerated, large-scale, capital-intensive firms, while the informal sector is seen as composed of the unenumerated self-employed. One of the most widely used definitions stems from the ILO report on Kenya, where the informal sector is characterized by ease of entry, reliance on indigenous resources, family ownership of enterprises, small scale of operations, labour-intensive and adapted technology, skill acquired outside the formal school system and unregulated and competitive markets (ILO, 1972, p. 6).

This two-sector classification has engendered so much discussion and criticism that many revisions and refinements have been suggested.[2] To review all the arguments presented is outside the scope of this presentation. One of the most frequently voiced criticisms is that to classify economic activities into two categories is not only a gross oversimplification, but tends to ignore the interconnections among various types of activities. Furthermore, many activities have some of the characteristics of the formal sector and some of the informal ones. Entrance into some activities may be far from easy, but dependent on means to acquire modern, imported and quite capital-intensive technology. Not all incomes in the informal sector are low, illegal activities may be organized on a rather large scale, markets may be monopolistic and so on.

In fact, activities labelled informal seem to have only negative attributes in common.

> The informal economy... is a process of income-generation characterized by one central feature; it is unregulated by the institutions of society, in a legal and social environment in which similar activities are regulated (Castells and Portes, 1989, p. 12).

Not only is the work performed unenumerated in official statistics, but the "firms" or "enterprises" are not registered, and written contracts are rare. When people are hired, labour legislation is ignored, and if taxes are paid, taxable income is not based on written accounts. When the term "the informal sector" is used here, it is not due to its analytical rigour, but simply because it provides a label for something that otherwise could only be referred to by rather cumbersome wording.

Women who find their income in the informal sector are in many countries not counted among the "economically active". Official censuses and economic surveys tend to take into account "primary activity" only, and classify married women as housewives unless they are full-time employees in the formal sector. Yet special studies of the gender composition of the work-force in the informal sector in developing countries show that more women than men are involved, and that most of them are found at the lowest end of the income distribution. There is certainly some variation both between and within countries as to what tasks are defined as men's and women's, or which are open to both. But regardless of cultural diversity, women everywhere often combine their work as housewives and mothers with income-generating activities performed in their own homes, such as artisanal work or taking in washing, sewing or industrial piece-work. Or they may be unpaid family workers, helping their husband, father, brothers or other relatives in their enterprise. This work is often highly integrated with their domestic activities, and the line between unpaid family work and housework is often difficult to draw.

As was the case of working women in the industrial world only a few decades ago, women in Third World cities today are typically found in commercial, service and casual work. Very young women are overwhelmingly in domestic service, and the pay they receive may be symbolic only. Recent case-studies from settings as different as Nairobi and Mexico City indicate that the skills poor women sell are often the same as those they are also expected to practise in their homes. Both in the domestic realm and in the market, women provide food, child care, domestic services, companionship and sex (Nelson, 1979, Arizpe, 1977). The boundary between women's unpaid domestic labour and the paid labour they perform is often tenuous.

II. Mali: The Country and the City

According to official statistics, Mali is an extremely poor country. It occupies among the lowest ranks in the world both on such economic measures as GNP per capita and on development indicators such as life expectancy, infant mortality and school attendance (UNDP, 1990). With the economic decline that Mali shares with most of sub-Saharan Africa, differentials in access to resources and in monetary incomes are important and probably increasing, within both urban and rural communities. But the country has a prestigious past and a rich cultural heritage. Mali is today a multi-ethnic society, Islamized over the last 1,000 years. Most ethnic groups were historically divided into a hierarchy of nobles, free men, people of caste and slaves. The importance of these status groups in present-day Malian urban society is uncertain and contested, but it seems reasonable that the ubiquity of patron–client relationships partly reflects this historical heritage.

Mali was until recently among the least urbanized countries in the least urbanized region in the world. When the first nation-wide census was undertaken in 1976, only 11 per cent of the population lived in agglomerations of 5,000 inhabitants or more, as against 24 per cent in 1987. Bamako, the capital, is by far the largest. During the first half of this century, the town grew at a moderate pace, and its population was only 76,000 in 1958 (Gugler and Flanagan, 1978, p. 41). In the next 30 years, it grew ninefold. In 1987, the total resident population was enumerated at close to 650,000, which gives an overall annual growth rate of 4.2 per cent since 1976 (BCR, 1987, p. 59). In-migration and natural increase are estimated to have contributed equal shares of this growth.

The population increase is unevenly distributed in different parts of town. Illegal or unauthorized settlements are estimated to have absorbed 45 per cent of Bamako's population growth between 1976 and 1986. Bamako is divided into six communes,[3] and three communes where the newer unauthorized settlements are located had annual growth rates from 10 to 14 per cent, compared to rates of 1 to 5 per cent in older parts of town (DNSI, 1986, p. 20). Migrants to the city settle primarily in the peripheral, unauthorized settlements.

Censuses and surveys of employment and income count only "principal activity", which does not capture the diversification of activities pursued, nor the extent of unremunerated family labour. But some indication of the nature of the urban economy is nevertheless given by the fact that no less than 68 per cent of the economically active were in 1983 found to derive their principal activity from the so-called non-structured or informal sector, and in trade and other services rather than in manufacturing (PUM, 1984). Although far from all engaged here are poor, *employment* in the informal sector is typically characterized by wages far below the legal minimum, if paid at all. Real levels of unemployment are also disguised by unpaid or only intermittently paid work in the informal sector.

In the modern or formal sector, the state is still the largest employer, but salaries are low, and with the exception of the police and the armed forces, employees are frequently paid after several months' delay. A job in the public sector is attractive less for its salary than for the legal and illegal fringe benefits it offers, which range from subsidized cereals, transport allowances and the like to receiving gifts for services rendered, exacting payment for bending regulations, "making arrangements" and so on. The state apparatus provides supports to numerically important segments of the population through kinship networks and personalized patron–client relationships, and has been likened to the system of pillage and redistribution which was the basis of pre-colonial political structures (Amselle, 1985, 1987, Lambert de Frondeville, 1987).

III. Gender Relations

The literature on gender relations in Malian society is scant. Older ethnographic accounts often limited themselves to depicting normative aspects of maleness and femaleness among the upper strata in tribal societies, and provided little evidence as to the importance of these normative systems in the lives of the majority of men and women. More recent works deal with various aspects of the position of women.[4] Of these, only a few are based on data from urban Mali

(ISH, 1984; Lambert de Frondeville, 1987; Wéry, 1987; Rondeau, 1989). The following presentation is based on a variety of sources, both written works and discussions with colleagues and informants. It is by necessity rather tentative on a number of points, and possibly overgeneralizing on others. For general background as well as key concepts, it draws on various contributions in Oppong's collections of 1983 and 1987.

The majority of Bamako's adult urban population was born in the countryside, or their parents were, and ties to kin and area of origin remain strong. Rules governing marriage, descent and the organization of work in traditional rural society are often mentioned in accounting for present-day attitudes and practice. We shall therefore start with a brief review of some central characteristics of rural social organization. The agricultural and agro-pastoralist societies of southern Mali, comprising the majority of the country's population, were traditionally patrilineal and patrilocal gerontocracies, which entailed not only a segregation of the genders, but relegated women to a subordinate position. A marriage was a contract between lineages and was confirmed by the transfer of bride wealth from the man's lineage to that of the woman. If she became a widow, she was given in marriage to a younger brother of the deceased. A woman was valued for her labour as well as for the children that she produced. Women were guests in their husband's lineage, they had property rights neither in their affinal family nor in their family of origin once bride wealth had been paid. Their material assets depended on what they personally managed to accumulate.

As in other West African societies, parenthood was and still is the most valued of all adult statuses, for both genders:

> There is first of all the principle ... that no one is a complete person until he or she marries and achieves parenthood.(...). Secondly there is the deeply ingrained idea that normal men and women should continue to beget and bear children throughout their fecund years (Fortes, 1978, p. 141).

Children become lineage descendants of the men, and provide support in old age for both parents.

The strength of kinship ties and the importance of marriage persist, both in town and countryside. Except for the nomadic populations in the north, polygyny was and still is widespread and shows signs of increasing, in both urban and rural areas. Age differences between men and women on first marriage are still considerable (Kaufmann *et al.*, 1988). In the villages, the basic residential unit is with some exceptions the extended household, consisting of an elder with his wives and his married sons and their families. In the cities, there may be a trend towards nuclearization of families, but this may be more of necessity than preference, since nuclear units are found primarily in the poorer, peripheral settlements, not in the better-off, more settled neighbourhoods (UNICEF, 1989, p. 115).

In the ideal-type rural society, division of work and responsibilities are to a large extent based on gender complementarity. Certain agricultural activities are construed as specifically male or female, while others may be carried out by both genders. Men typically are in charge of preparing fields for cultivation and building and repairing houses, as well as performing specified handicrafts. Women prepare food, fetch water and fuel, bring up children and look after the sick. In addition, they do a larger part of the agricultural work on family and communal fields, and also have their own personal gardens. They may be involved in small-scale marketing of agricultural surplus and of handicraft products. Men are expected to provide the staple foods – rice, maize or millet – while women provide the sauces to go with the cereals. This they do from the produce of their vegetable gardens, from gathering wild plants and fruits and from ingredients bought in the market from their own earnings. However, rural women often have more extensive responsibilities for feeding their families, especially during the periods of the year when the men's granaries are empty (Rondeau, 1987). A woman is in theory allowed to accumulate personal assets through production and marketing, but only as long as she does not neglect her obligations to the household. Her wealth is used primarily for social rather than purely personal ends; apart from clothing herself, she may use it to take care of her children's needs, to prepare trousseaux for her daughters, for obligatory gifts to kin and neighbours, and to help out if the household falls on hard times. Women are ultimately responsible for feeding children. Their lives are filled with numerous pregnancies and a heavy load of agricultural and domestic work, but there is also scope for independent entrepreneurial activities.

Despite differences among ethnic groups, and between urban and rural society, stratification by gender and age is still pervasive. Men and women also live to a large extent separate lives. Post-independence legislation proclaims the equality of men and women in most areas, but observers stress how traditional norms of segregation and power differentials still govern relations between the genders in most social fields (Lambert de Frondeville, 1987, p. 96). The extensive economic responsibilities that many urban women carry do not appear to have remodelled the stereotypes of what is intrinsically male and female. Men's reputation is tied up with that of the kin group and the communal, while women are first and foremost evaluated as wives, homemakers and mothers. A woman not only owes her husband deference and submission, but she is also to some extent maker or undoer of his reputation. A man's successes or failures are often explained by reference to his wife. Women's position is thus characterized by ambiguity, subordination and responsibility at the same time (Diallo, 1988).

IV. Gender-based Responsibilities in Urban Households

In the cities, where the provision of basic necessities such as shelter, clothes, food and fuel have been monetized, men's and women's productive tasks are no longer complementary. While Islamic norms enjoin a man to provide for his wife and children (Boye *et al.*, 1987, p. 60), many urban men fail to do so. It is then up to the woman to "look after her own needs and those of her children, since the husband's salary – if there is one – is not sufficient to cover housing, food, clothing, medical expenses, school fees etc for the whole family" (Keita, 1981, p. 47). But there is also the notion that a woman's earnings are her own to dispose of. As reported in numerous studies from urban West Africa, household incomes are not necessarily pooled to be used for whatever needs arise. A husband's income is normally kept secret from his wife, so is hers from him, and each spouse covers a defined set of expenses, often borrowing from each other (Le Cour Grandmaison, 1979; Pittin, 1987). This form of contract between husband and wife, where men and women have separate economies, may be seen as a modification of the gender-based division of work and responsibilities prevailing in rural societies. The urban economy was initially based on male wage labour, and only rarely was women's work recognized as part of the monetized economy. The norms regarding urban men as sole providers for their families spring from these historical circumstances.

But there are no studies to support the notion that urban women were ever economically inactive, and did not perceive themselves as needing money for themselves, or for the family, for that matter.

The early African urban studies rarely looked into this, however. If dealing with women's work, this early literature tended to portray urban, economically active women as single, or on their own, and confine them to petty trade, prostitution, beer-brewing and so on (Little, 1973). In his study of Bamako in the mid-1960s, Meillassoux does not deal with the division of responsibilities within households. According to him, urban women were provided for, but they might need money for various social obligations. Participation in rotating saving-societies was one of the few possibilities they had of generating some cash – in contrast to rural women, whose role in production and marketing gave them access to money (Meillassoux, 1965, 1968). On the other hand, Meillassoux also mentions the fact that the wives of recent migrants to Bamako might work as cooks for African families, presumably out of economic necessity. But he does not give the impression that poverty was widespread in Bamako of the 1960s, as it is today.

Whatever the prescriptions of Islam, it is now probably the case that the majority of urban husbands do not manage to provide fully for their families. Among the better off, the norm and to some extent the practice seems to be that a husband should be responsible for lodgings, children's tuition and monthly supplies of cereals and fuel, and a daily "prix du condiment", i.e. money for vegetables, spices and meat or fish to go with the cereals. The women may also expect new clothing for themselves and their children for major religious holidays. Through saving societies and miscellaneous trading activities, a woman may raise money for obligatory gifts at weddings and baptisms, for contributions to her family of origin, funds for investing in jewellery for herself and gifts to her children, which may be seen as an investment in the future security in case of divorce (*Jamana*, 1985). But for most of the urban households, the reality is very different. The cost of living in Bamako, compared to the extremely low level of wages and the high level of unemployment, means that husbands often do not manage to raise money to buy staples every month, nor do they always provide the necessary cash for daily food purchases. As in rural society, it is up to the women to ensure that the family has something to eat (UNICEF, 1989). The majority of working women probably seek incomes in specific niches of the informal sector, but there are as yet no representative surveys of this, only scattered case-studies (Wéry, 1987; Rondeau, 1989; Vaa, 1989). The various studies conducted by ILO on Bamako's informal economy did not include trade and other services, nor the production and sale of street foods (Sidibé,

1982). So while undisputably active women are highly visible in the streets and markets of the city, their economic role is very poorly documented.

V. Bankoni: a Bamako Settlement

The data for the case-studies presented below were collected during 1987 and 1988 in a subsection of one of the larger unauthorized settlements in Bamako. It is called Bankoni and situated a few kilometres outside the city centre. In the early 1960s, Bankoni was a collection of hamlets housing a few families. By 1987, according to the census taken that year, more than 50,000 people lived there. The population of Bankoni is very mixed, ethnically, economically and in geographical origin. Some well-to-do merchants, middle-class employees and successful entrepreneurs live here, as well as wage workers in industry and transport. But many men are unemployed, and the majority of households are poor, even by Bamako standards. Comparing conditions in the late 1980s to what was reported in a housing study undertaken in the late 1970s (Sarr, 1983), it is evident that both housing standards and the level of living in general have deteriorated. Many buildings are in disrepair and the number of occupants per room has gone up, while incomes have gone down.

As in most other parts of town, dwelling units in Bankoni are grouped in compounds (in French, "concession" or "parcelle"), which consist of a walled-in courtyard leading to rooms with separate entrances around all or most sides, and only one entrance from the street. Compounds vary greatly in size; some are vast with only a few residents, while others are narrow strips between two rows of rooms, sometimes with several lodgers to each room. Amenities are few, there is no electricity, and while most compounds have their own well, water quality is variable and many have to buy drinking water by the bucket for at least part of the year.

Compounds are rarely inhabited by one household only. In Malian statistics, households are defined as groups of related or not-related co-residents who recognize the authority of a common household head (BCR, 1988, p. v). This covers a multitude of forms. Households may for instance consist of a husband with several wives and children, or of a monogamous couple with their children. Such units often have one or more members of the grandparental generation residing with them. Some resemble the typical rural extended household, where the head of the household is an elder with his wives who live together with some of his sons and their wives and children, as well as close or distant relatives. Or households may consist of single persons, both men and women, who sometimes pool part of their resources with other individuals for a shorter or longer period. Whatever their basic organizational principle, households vary in size and composition over the year. In the dry season, which is a slack period in agriculture, the compounds swell with visitors and job-seekers.

Data for the present study were collected through formal interviews, more informal discussions, and participation in daily life and more festive events in the community. A sample of 30 women was selected for lengthy interviews about their family situation, migration history, social and family contact with home area and in Bamako, economic activities and responsibilities, and so on. The selection of respondents started with a key informant who also served as interpreter. The sample consisted of all adult women resident in her compound, at least one woman from each of the compounds in the same block, and some of her closest friends and relatives who lived nearby.

VI. Working Women in Bankoni

Of the 30 women interviewed, only one had never married. Three were engaged and two were widowed. Twenty were married, while four were divorced and temporarily single. Only three of the women pursued no income-earning activities. One of them was very old and now provided for by her children, but had earlier been engaged in trading spices. The other two were young housewives with small children, whose husbands were traders, and the only men in the sample to provide fully for their families. Their wives hoped to take up some trade later, if their husbands would allow it and provide them with funds for getting started. Seven of the currently married women were without any support from male income at the time of the study, while the others had husbands whose incomes were either insufficient or very irregular.

The trades, productive or salaried work taken up by the women were all typically female occupations. Of the four women in wage work, two were young girls who had come to Bamako to work as housemaids. They both stayed with relatives but had their meals with their employer, where they worked a 12–14 hour day. They earned only 3,500–5,000 FCA per month (70–100 FrF), and planned to bring all their earnings back to their families. The other two working for wages were the only ones in this sample who had regular jobs at wage levels comparable to that of men in the formal sector. One worked as a cook with an expatriate family, the other had for several years worked as a cook and cleaner, or as a "boy" as it is called in Mali, at a dam construction site some distance from Bamako. At the time of my last field visit, she was home on temporary leave. She was divorced and lived in her brother's compound with her daughter and mother. Most of her earnings went to a common fund to feed 15 people.

The traders were all unlicensed. Some of them now and then went on trading trips to other West African countries where they sold Malian handicrafts and brought back industrial goods. This, however, required fairly substantial capital outlays. They rarely managed to keep a revolving fund intact, so each trip depended on their ability to raise credit or on gifts received from relatives or benefactors. Their earnings and trading activities were sporadic. The others were involved in selling from door-to-door or at the local market, some also sold goods from their own compounds. There was, however, an interesting difference between those who traded in everyday consumption goods sold in small quantities, such as charcoal, spices and vegetables, and locally made soap, and those who dealt in goods which were not everyday necessities and where the price per item was higher, such as ready-made children's clothes or industrially printed lengths of cloth for women's garments. The first group never made any windfalls; their earnings, as far as it was possible to calculate them, were small and they sometimes incurred losses, but they usually managed to stay in business on a regular basis. The second group might have a brisk trade now and then, for instance in the weeks preceding a religious holiday, when everybody who could afford to bought new clothes. But as with the long distance traders, their business was sporadic and depended on their ability to raise funds to buy stock for each trading episode.

The 12 women who were involved in production also sold what they made. They fell into two distinct categories: they were either engaged in producing goods at low cost per unit for which there was a day-to-day demand, or they produced more costly items where profit per unit might be higher, but where demand was less certain. The first processed food and sold snacks or ready-made dishes or they made soap from ground-nuts. Some mixed ingredients for incense which they sold in small portions from their house. Those who sold street foods in particular had long working days and small profit margins. When prices of inputs went up they might sell at a loss for several days before they dared to raise their own prices. They were all dependent on credit from their suppliers to stay in business.

The others were in various types of cloth trade. Some did traditional embroidery on lengths of cloth used for ceremonial gifts, others made hand-sewn layettes or machine-sewn modern clothes for adults and children, and a couple were dyers. Their wares were neither luxury items nor day-to-day necessities. They complained of money being tighter and their business dwindling. Most only made things on command now; they could not afford to buy inputs if they were not assured of selling what they produced. Their customers were either from the neighbourhood or friends or relatives of neighbours. Like the traders who dealt in industrial clothes, they were expected to give credit, and were obliged to weigh the risk of giving credit versus insisting on cash payment. If their creditors failed to pay, they would lose their own outlays. But demanding cash involved the danger of displeasing those friends and acquaintances who had found them their customers.

All the women interviewed complained in various ways that money worries were a permanent feature of their lives. But there were major differences in what kinds of expenses they lacked money for, depending on how poor they were. The two young housewives who pursued no income-earning activities themselves said they would have liked to be able to send regular contributions to their mothers, but seemed to have no worries about day-to-day expenses. The hardest off were those women who, with the help of their daughters, were the sole providers of their families. They might work long hours on producing and selling day-to-day necessities while lacking money to prepare proper meals. If you asked them about their health, one answer that frequently cropped up was: "I am suffering from the malady of poverty".

Several of the women who were engaged in episodic trading ventures complained about lack of funds to stay in business on a more regular basis. If unmarried, they usually turned over most of their profits to their mothers, and part of their proceeds also went to cover debts already incurred. But they rarely had to go without meals, even in periods when they had no income. For them, trade was not something they did for a living, it was rather seen as a lottery that occasional gifts and loans enabled them to participate in. What profits they might make were diverted into channels for fulfilling social obligations, which made accumulation very difficult. While friendships and family ties were important assets, both on a day-to-day basis and for raising funds for trading episodes, redistribution normally took primacy over accumulation. Commerce usually both started and ended with intense social activities, such as exchange of gifts and visits, circulation of goods and of people among different households of the same kin group and among friends.

VII. Households in Different Circumstances

A closer look at three cases will illustrate various aspects of the conditions under which urban households live, and the strategies they pursue. These three households differ along a number of dimensions. They are all poor, but in various degrees. The poorest own their house, while the others have the two other typical housing arrangements: rented accommodation or free board with relatives. They are in different stages of the domestic cycle; in one household the couple have completed their reproductive career, with grown-up children as well as young ones. Another couple have six children ranging from teenagers to babies, but many years of reproductive age ahead of them, while the third have just started having children. The division of responsibilities between husband and wife, and the household's dependence on other family members, differ: the oldest household manages precariously on what the wife, assisted by teenage daughters, earns in petty production, with occasional help from adult children. In the second household the husband gets a regular wage, but this is not sufficient to make ends meet and keep the family together. Three children are being brought up by grandparents in the countryside, and the town wage has to be supplemented by the wife's daily trade and more occasional extra earnings by both husband and wife. The third couple seem to be the best off despite very irregular earnings, since they are able to draw on support from the husband's family, both for shelter and for their day-to-day living.

1. *Isolation in Poverty*

The household consists of Adama (55) and his wife Sadio (48) and their six children. The oldest is 22, and the youngest just six years old. Sadio has an adult son from a previous marriage who visits now and then, but he lives most of the time with relatives in his father's village, working the land. After the harvest, he brings a sack of millet as a gift to his mother. Adama has a second wife who lives in the same compound with a foster daughter, but the two wives are on bad terms and rarely cook for each other or otherwise pool resources. Adama owns the compound and this provision of housing is his only contribution to the upkeep of his families. His wives provided him with meals on alternate days. The compound is fairly large, but some of the structures are crumbling. There is no all-year well, and water is fetched, usually by the younger children, at a public well about half a kilometre away. Adama is retired, but has no pension. He spends his mornings at his old place of work where people now and then give him money gifts "out of respect for his age", and the afternoons at the local mosque. Sadio complains that if he has any money, he gives it to his second wife rather than to her.

Sadio's eldest daughter is a trader who goes to Abidjan for several months at a time to sell Mauritanian and Malian tie-dye cloth and buy industrial goods such as costume jewellery, handbags and printed fabrics which she sells to friends and acquaintances in Bamako. She may send money to her mother during her absences and give her a lump sum on her return if she has anything left after having repaid debts incurred to buy stock. Sadio tries to reserve these contributions for school fees. She comes from a family of Muslim scholars and wants her children to attend the Medersa, the Franco-Arabic school. Sadio used to be a successful trader with her own stall at the central market in Bamako, where she sold cola nuts and cloth. But she lost all her stock and capital in a robbery, and was left with a large debt. With the help of two teenage daughters, she now ekes out an income from preparing and selling a dish based on mutton heads and vegetables. The profits are low and irregular and it is not unusual that the only family meal is the unsold mutton dish. The preparation of the dish is hard work, and both dirty and time-consuming. When Sadio fell ill, Adama sent for a nephew from his home village to take over the production, while the daughter took care of the selling. The daughters now and then receive cast-off clothes from a slightly better off female relative, but apart from her, the family has no benefactors to rely on. Both Adama and Sadio have kinsfolk in Bamako, but they rarely see them. Sadio says they are not welcome because they are too poor to bring the expected gifts. Both Adama and Sadio are very religious, and although Adama's economic contribution is negligible, his authority is never questioned.

2. A Regular Wage is Not Sufficient

Mamadou (35) and Amy (29) have six children, the oldest 13 and the youngest a toddler. They rent two small rooms in a compound where all the other residents are lodgers. The three eldest children have been sent back to stay with Mamadou's parents in his home village. He works as a messenger at an industrial plant, and earns probably 25,000 CFA a month (500 FrF). In addition, he gets a monthly sack of rice at a subsidized price. He pays the rent and gives Amy a small daily sum of money for firewood and the ingredients for the sauce to go with the rice. But this needs to be supplemented by Amy's earnings, which she gets from petty trade. Clothes for herself and the children are usually paid for by her.

Amy's trade is very diversified; she buys home-made soap from a nearby producer which she sells partly from her house or door to door, and partly through a woman friend who sells bundles of firewood. She also buys ground-nuts which she grinds at the miller's and resells in small portions. A neighbour has just started to make knitted baby's bonnets and socks, and Amy finds customers for her for a commission. Amy does not know how much her husband's monthly wage is, nor does she know how much she makes herself, since her turnover is very varied. She just made a windfall because a friend of her husband commissioned her to sell lengths of cloth in the weeks before the Tabaski feast, when demand is very brisk. She finds both her suppliers and her customers through her network of neighbours and friends. Her earnings are dependent on her industriousness and business acumen, but also on her sociability and her reputation for being trustworthy.

Amy and Mamadou now and then earn some extra money by singing at weddings and baptisms. They both belong to the griot caste, the entertainers and messengers of traditional society. As youngsters they were both apprenticed to older relatives in their home village to learn the skills of the trade. There is no fixed price for these appearances, as griots are paid through contributions from the guests at celebrations, whose praise they sing. But at a wedding in her home village some weeks previously, Amy received as much as 10,000 CFA for performing. However, when going home on visits, one is expected to bring presents, so trips like this also entail expenses.

The couple belong to the local chapter of the association of migrants from their home region, whose approximately 50 members meet twice a month and contribute 200 CFA to a fund used for helping members in need, and for weddings and baptisms. Both Amy and Mamadou have siblings in Bamako whom they see fairly regularly. The family is poor but not desperate. They have proper meals every day and are able to fulfil social obligations of hospitality and gift-giving. But they can not afford to rent more spacious accommodation, nor to have all their children living with them. The reasons presented for the three eldest staying with their grandparents is not lack of means, however, but simply that this is where they belong. When asked whether she ever thought of practising family planning, Amy laughs and says that this is for her husband to decide. Mamadou says he is seriously considering sending Amy to the Planned Parenthood office; to have six children at the age of 35 is a considerable burden, and he does not want to produce beggars.

3. *Family Support*

The third household consists of a young couple, Awa (22) and Bourama (27) and their two children, five and three years old. They both come from a small town a couple of hours' travel from Bamako. They live in a large compound owned by Bourama's eldest brother, who spends part of his time looking after his tailor shop in the home town, but also travels back and forth selling grain in Bamako. This brother also has a fairly stable monthly income from letting rooms in his Bankoni compound. He charges no rent to Awa and Bourama, who look after the compound when he is away. Bourama works with a friend who has a workshop where he repairs and sells second-hand mopeds. He is self-employed, and his work days and his earnings are very irregular. Lacking capital, he is dependent on having found a customer each time he buys a wrecked bike to be repaired. He probably spends as much time chasing bikes and potential customers as on repair work.

Awa earns a little money from doing traditional embroidery, but demand is very uncertain, so she now only does this work after having found a customer. She also sells necklaces made by a sister-in-law from glass and ceramic pearls. If she sells on credit and manages to recoup the money, the profit per item may be quite considerable. Now and then she also gets a batch of cloth lengths to sell on commission for an itinerant wholesaler. As with the necklaces, her profit is dependent on her ability to assess risk in giving credit. Her earnings supplement what Bourama gives her for daily expenses, and go to pay debts she has incurred and for clothes and gifts to her mother.

When Bourama is short of money he is always able to borrow from his brother, repaying him each time Bourama sells a bicycle. This arrangement is not a commercial one, since the sums transferred either way are not kept track of. It is the eldest brother's duty to look after the younger one and his family, as it is the younger brother's duty to give his earnings to the elder for redistribution. At his level of economic operation, this adherence to custom is clearly beneficial to Bourama. In exchange, both Awa and Bourama pay deference to him in everyday interaction as well as on decisions in family matters, such as when to bring their son of five home to be circumcised.

The couple belong to the local association of migrants from their home town, which seems to be purely social in purpose. There is no fixed membership fee, but members contribute to celebrations of marriage, births and festivals in their home town. Awa and Bourama complain about constant money worries, but theirs is more a cash flow problem than actual need. Neither one has ever experienced having to go without meals. On the contrary, they can afford to be hospitable and they frequently invite more hard-up friends to eat with them. Their friendships and social contacts stretch well beyond the local neighbourhood.

These three households illustrate degrees of urban poverty. Sadio occasionally receives some help from her grown-up children, but the family's day-to-day living depends on what she and her young daughters manage to earn. Her husband has more or less abdicated from material responsibility; however, he has used his authority to send for a young relative and put him to women's work. The loss of status the family has experienced because of Sadio's misfortune has a very material side to it. Since they no longer can afford to fulfil social obligations, such as bringing gifts on family visits, their kin network in town cannot be counted on for help. Whatever help they can get from kin has to come from the rural end of their families, who provide grain after the harvest and manpower for productive work.

This is an example of a reversal in the flow of resources between town and country, where the poorest segments of the urban population actually receive help from rural kin and not vice versa. The flow from town to country has been amply documented (van Westen and Klute, 1986). Amy and Mamadou are also partly dependent on the rural end of their families. Their town earnings are not sufficient to keep all their children with them. They cultivate strong ties to their home region through their participation in the migrants' association, also a form of insurance against misfortune. Their involvement in this club also helps them get singing commissions to supplement Mamadou's wage. To obtain such commissions they need a wide network of acquaintances to spread information about their skills and availability. Amy's petty trade also necessitates well-developed social skills, to get information about bargains and about possibilities for credit and to locate potential customers.

The intensity of town and country contacts is also documented in Awa's and Bourama's circumstances. They have a very advantageous arrangement with the husband's elder brother, who successfully exploits economic niches in the urban–rural interface. At the same time, he honours the norms of responsibility prescribed by his seniority. Through his material support, Awa and Bourama are not only living fairly well, but they are in a position to build up and maintain a social capital to be exploited in their own economic activities.

Women's economic enterprises, and for many their household viability, depend on the ability to draw on networks of kin and friends. But support is not an automatic response to need. Social relations need to be constantly renewed through visits, gifts and displays of respect. This possibly excludes people in downward spirals of poverty from benefiting both from immediate assistance and the more long range redistribution of assets. One important mechanism of redistribution is the obligation to display generosity whenever good fortune occurs. Because of the prestige that old age carries, the old may benefit from distributive flows without reciprocating. For others, the joint obligations of generosity and reciprocity may constitute obstacles to financing business ventures that can be kept afloat and expand. While poverty is shameful, so is stinginess on the part of the more fortunate. Gift-giving is at one and the same time morally prescribed and used strategically, but at least in small businesses it precludes long-term rational-strategic behaviour.

VIII. Changing Gender Relations?

In studies of urban poverty, it is often stressed that one dominant feature of survival strategies is maximum diversification of income-earning and social activities. In Bankoni, it seemed that women more often than men resorted to a wide variation of activities in order to earn money and secure household survival. Few of the unemployed men used their time to seek other work than what they were trained for, although relatively well paid casual construction work might be available. Perhaps this expresses social taboos linked to social hierarchy: in traditional rural society, only slaves or those who acknowledge slave descent are free to do any type of work (Grosz-Ngaté, 1988). While there certainly are also taboos regarding what type of work women can do, a wide range of activities is open to them in producing and selling food and other daily consumer items.

Being ultimately responsible for feeding the household, many women have very long working days, and the poorer they are, the longer. Both self-employed men and those who are wage workers have much shorter working days than women. A large proportion of Bankoni men also have a lot of enforced leisure either through unemployment or through early retirement. So while poverty may be an equalizer in status among women, it does not equalize ways time is spent, nor the division of work between men and women.

The way poverty is shouldered differently by men and women has led to a widening gap between the normative and the actual. Men should provide for their families, but in many cases they fail to do so. Not all seem to exert themselves to find work and money. Resentment was rarely expressed against husbands for not earning money; this was accepted as no fault of their own. Norms were broken without there being any relevant sanctions in operation.

Men's abdication of economic responsibility does not seem to have diminished their authority in the home. They may be economically marginalized, but the ideology of their superiority over women is protected by the way Islam is interpreted and through their membership in power hierarchies outside the household, such as the religious community and various types of associations. Men maintain their status by public religious observance and by seeking each other out for company. Being Moslems, they do not spend their leisure drinking alcohol as underemployed husbands in many other poor regions of the world do. On the contrary, Bankoni men are perhaps more interested in upholding respectability, both through adhering to elaborate etiquette when consorting with each other, and in insisting on "proper behaviour" on the part of women and children when men are present in compounds. These should speak only when spoken to, and I often saw women scurry for headscarves when fathers or husbands returned home in the afternoon.

But gender constructs are not only received notions of what is male and female proper. They have to be interpreted and enacted, and are consequently modified in everyday practice. If women's increased economic contribution does not result in male authority being overtly challenged, such shifts in the actual division of economic responsibilities may nevertheless have implications for gender relations. Two possible outcomes are (a) new cooperative patterns between spouses, and (b) potentially greater economic and social autonomy for urban women, both single and married.

In earlier sections, it was pointed out that men's and women's productive and reproductive roles in Malian rural society were complementary, and that women in the urban economy never withdrew completely from economic activity. If women could afford it, their economic activity revolved around social obligations of ceremonial gifts and of building up personal funds. Today, their earnings, while still in theory their own and which they are entitled to keep secret, often have to cover everyday household expenses. While it may be in women's interest to keep their earnings secret, when they actually carry a large burden of daily outlays, women may get negotiation power *vis-à-vis* their husbands in the direction of pooling resources and of redefining food and other necessities as joint responsibilities. Particularly in younger monogamous households where both husband and wife earn money, there often can be observed a lot of reciprocity and sharing of expenses, but in combination with at least paying lip service to having separate economies.

As to the possibility of increased economic and social autonomy for women, the urban informal economy not only allows for wider space, entrepreneurship and multiple employment strategies than women have in rural society, but it is also easier to escape the control of kin and neighbours. As Hannerz points out, "when role repertoires and consequently networks are varied, more or less original combinations of experiences and resources offer scope for innovative adaptations and strategies" (1980, p. 173). While identity and worth for a women are still said to depend on marriage and motherhood, urbanization has also led to a larger proportion of women being on their own (Antoine and Nanitelamio, 1989). This is partly because divorce is not as automatically followed by remarriage as before, partly because some women migrants to town choose to live alone, or in looser unions than marriage. Young, adult women may also have a fairly extended period of engagement, because their fiancés cannot afford the expenses connected with wedding ceremonies. When these young women earn money, it is in theory their own, but is often used to help parents and siblings.

However, their having incomes does not necessarily challenge gender hierarchies.

While kin and friendship networks are both a blessing and a curse, both single and married women are in theory allowed to keep their earnings and expenses secret. The freedom to do so becomes rather illusory if the money they earn is barely sufficient to cover the daily needs of their dependants. But there is at least a normative basis for personal enterprise and economic independence for women. Thus, the autonomy of urban women may be more limited by the overall economic situation than by prescriptions of what it is proper for a woman to do. Women do sometimes succeed, and in turn become role models for other women.

Notes

1 The focus of this study was the long- and short-term survival strategies adopted by women who had recently migrated to town. Some of the results have been reported in Vaa, 1987, 1989, 1990; Vaa *et al.* 1989. A more comprehensive report is forthcoming. Drafts of the present chapter have been discussed with colleagues both in the Institute for Social Research, and elsewhere. I want to thank Inger Altern, Grete Brochmann, Anne Lise Ellingsæter, Lise Kjølsrød, Lars Mjøset, Kristen Nordhaug, Arnlaug Leira, Ann-Therese Lotherington and Kristi Anne Stølen for useful comments. Finally, I want to express my gratitude to Natalie Rogoff Ramsøy both for her sustained interest in my Bamako project since its inception, and for her patience in responding to my frequent appeals for help with the English language.
2 See for instance special issues of *World Development*, 1978; *Revue Tiers Monde*, 1980; Bromley and Gerry, 1979, Gilbert and Gugler, 1981; Deblé and Hugon, 1982; Portes *et al.*, 1989; and on women and the informal sector in particular, see *Signs*, 1977; *IDS Bulletin*, 1981; *Revue Tiers Monde*, 1985.
3 Administratively, Mali is divided into "regions", "cercles" and "arrondissements". Until 1978, Bamako was part of the Koulikoro region. It was then renamed District de Bamako, given regional status and its area extended. It is divided into six Communes, and each commune into "Quartiers" and "sous-quartiers".
4 For a general analysis of the situation of children and women in present-day Mali, with a bibliography of published and unpublished material, see UNICEF, 1989.

References

Amis, P. 1989. African Development and Urban Change: What Policy Makers Need to Know. *Development Policy Review*, Vol. 7, pp. 375–391.
Amselle, J. L. 1985. Socialisme, capitalisme et précapitalisme au Mali. In Bernstein and Campbell (1985), pp. 249–266.
Amselle, J.-L. 1987. Fonctionnaires et hommes d'affaires au Mali. *Politique Africaine*, Vol. 26, pp. 63–75.
Antoine, P. and Nanitelamio J. 1989. Statuts féminins et urbanisation en Afrique. *Politique Africaine*, No. 36, pp. 129–133.

Arizpe, L. 1977. Women in the Informal Labour Sector: The Case of Mexico City. *Signs*, Vol. 3, pp. 25–37.
Baker, J. (ed.) 1990. *Small Town Africa: Studies in Urban–Rural Interaction.* Uppsala: Scandinavian Institute of African Studies.
BCR 1987. *Recensement Général de la Population et de l'Habitat (du ler au 14 avril 1987). Résultats Provisoires.* Bureau Central de Recensement, Ministère du Plan, Bamako.
Beneria, L. 1981. Conceptualizing the Labour Force: The Underestimation of Women's Economic Activities. In Nelson (ed.) (1981), pp. 10–28.
Bernstein, H. and Campbell, B.C. 1985. *Contradictions of Accumulation in Africa.* Beverly Hills: Sage.
Boye, A. K. et al. 1987a. *La condition juridique et sociale de la femme dans quatres pays du Sahel.* Etudes et Travaux de l'USED No. 9, Bamako.
Boye, A. K. et al. 1987. La condition juridique et sociale de la femme au Mali. In Boye et al. (1987), section II, pp. 11–32.
Bromley, R. and Gerry, C. (eds.) 1979. *Casual Work and Poverty in Third World Cities.* New York: John Wiley.
Castells, M. and Portes, A. 1989. World Underneath: The Origins, Dynamics and Effects of the Informal Economy. In Portes, Castells and Benton (1989), pp. 11–40.
Chambers, R. 1985. Putting 'Last' Thinking First: A Professional Revolution. *Third World Affairs 1985.* Third World Foundation, London, pp. 78–91.
DNSI *1986: Enquête démographique de 1985* (résultats préliminaires). République du Mali, PNUD/PADEM/29.
Deblé I. and Philippe Hugon, P. (eds) 1982. *Vivre et survivre dans les villes africaines.* IEDES, Collection Tiers Monde, Presses Universitaires de France, Paris.
Diallo, A. 1988. Etre Femme Aujourd'hui au Mali. Unpublished manuscript, Bamako.
Fortes, M. 1978. Parenthood, Marriage and Fertility in West Africa. *Journal of Development Studies*, Vol. 14, No. 4, pp. 121–149. Also in Oppong, C. et al. (eds) 1978. *Marriage, Fertility and Parenthood in West Africa.* Canberra: Australian National University Press.
Gilbert, A. and Gugler, J. 1982. *Cities, Poverty and Development.* Oxford: Oxford University Press.
Grosz-Ngaté, M. 1989. Hidden Meanings: Explorations into a Bamanan Construction of Gender. *Ethnology*, Vol. 28, No. 2, pp. 168–183.
Grown, C. A. and Sepstad, J. 1989. Introduction: Toward a Wider Perspective on Women's Employment. *World Development*, Vol. 17, No. 7, pp. 937–952.
Gugler, J. and Flanagan, W. 1978. *Urbanization and Social Change in West Africa.* London: Cambridge University Press.
Hannerz, U. 1980. *Exploring the City.* New York: Columbia University Press.
Hay, M. J. and Stichter, S. (eds) 1984. *African Women South of the Sahara.* London and New York: Longman.
IDS Bulletin 1981. Women and the Informal Sector. Vol. 12, No. 3, Institute of Development Studies, Sussex.
ILO 1972. *Employment, Incomes and Equality: A Strategy for Increasing Productive Employment in Kenya.* Geneva: International Labour Office.
ISH 1984. *L'exode des femmes au Mali.* Institut des Sciences Humaines, Bamako.
Jamal, V. and Weeks, J. 1988. The vanishing rural–urban gap in Sub-Saharan Africa. *International Labour Review*, Vol. 127, No. 3, pp. 271–291.
Jamana 1985. *Femmes Maliennes*, special issue, May.
Kaufmann, G., Lesthaeghe, R. and Meekers, D. 1988. Les caractéristiques et tendences du mariage. In Tabutin (1988), pp. 217–248.
Keita, Rokiatou N'diaye 1981. *Les indicateurs socio-économiques de l'intégration des femmes au développement; Cas du Mali.* ONU, Commission Economique pour l'Afrique, Addis Ababa.

Lambert de Frondeville, A. 1987. Une alliance tumulteuse, les commercantes maliennes du Dakar-Niger et les agents de l'Etat. *Cahiers de l'ORSTOM, Serie Sciences Humaines*, Vol. 23, No. 2, pp. 89–104.
Le Cour Grandmaison 1979. Contrats économiques entre époux dans l'ouest Africain. *l'Homme*, Vol. XIX, pp. 159–170.
Little, K. 1973. *African Women in Towns*. Cambridge: Cambridge University Press.
Lloyd, P. 1982. *A Third World Proletariat*. London: Allen and Unwin.
Lomnitz, L. A. 1977. *Networks and Marginality: Life in a Mexican Shantytown*. New York: Academic Press.
Meillassoux, C. 1965. The Social Structure of Modern Bamako. *Africa*, Vol. 35, No. 2, pp. 125–141.
Meillassoux, C. 1968. *Urbanization of an African Community*. Seattle and London: University of Washington Press.
Nelson, N. 1979. How Women and Men Get By: The Sexual Division of Labour in the Informal Sector of a Nairobi Squatter Settlement. In Bromley and Gerry (eds.) (1979), pp. 283–304.
Nelson, N. (ed.) 1981. *African Women in the Development Process*. London: Frank Cass.
Oppong, C. (ed.) 1983. *Female and Male in West Africa*. London: Allen and Unwin.
Oppong, C. (ed.) 1987. *Sex Roles, Population and Development in West Africa*. Portsmouth: Heineman–London: James Currey.
Pittin, R. 1987. Documentation of Women's Work in Nigeria: Problems and Solutions. In Oppong (ed.) (1987), pp. 25–44.
Portes, A., Castells, M. and Benton, L. A. (1989). *The Informal Economy*. Baltimore and London: Johns Hopkins University Press.
PUM 1984 *Etude du Développement Urbain de Bamako: Programmation Décennale des Investissements*, Rapport Phase 1, République du Mali, Ministère de l'Interieur, Direction du Project Urbain du Mali (PUM), Bamako.
Revue Tiers Monde 1980. Secteur informel et petite production marchande dans les villes du Tiers Monde, Tome XXI, no. 82, Avril–Juin.
Revue Tiers Monde 1985. La sortie du travail invisible: Les femmes dans l'economie, Tome XXVI, no. 102, Avril–Juin.
Rondeau, C. 1987. Paysannes du Sahel et Stratégies Alimentaires. *Revue Internationale d'Action Communautaire*, No. 1767, pp. 63–80.
Rondeau, C. 1989. Les restauratices de la nuit à Bamako. *Labour Capital and Society*, Vol. 22, No. 2, pp. 262–286.
Sarr, M. 1983. *Bamako et Banconi, son quartier illégal*. Thèse de 3e cycle, géographie, Paris I.
Sidibé H. 1982. Réparation et récuperation à Bamako. In Deblé and Hugon (eds.) (1982), pp. 147–152.
Signs 1977. Women and National Development, Special Issue, Autumn, Vol. 3, No. 1.
Tabutin, D. 1988. *Population et sociétés en Afrique au Sud du Sahara*. Paris: L'Harmattan.
UNDP 1990, *Human Development Report 1990*. New York and Oxford: Oxford University Press.
UNICEF 1989. *Enfants et femmes au Mali*. Paris: Editions l'Harmattan.
Vaa, M. 1987. Urban Growth and Urban Poverty: Women's Strategies for Survival in Bamako, Mali, *Working Paper* 87:5. Oslo: Institute for Social Research.
Vaa, M. 1990a. Self-employed Urban Women: Case Studies from Bamako. *African Population Studies*, No. 3, pp. 72–84.
Vaa, M. 1990b. Paths to the City. In Baker (ed.) (1990), pp. 172–181.
Vaa, M., Findlay, S. and Diallo, A. 1989. The Gift Economy: A Study of Women Migrants' Survival Strategies in a low-income Bamako Neighbourhood. *Labour Capital and Society*, Vol. 22, No. 2, pp. 234–260.

van Westen, A. C. M. and Klute, M. C. 1986. From Bamako with Love: A Case Study of Migrants and their Remittances. *Tijdschrift voor economische en sociale geografie*, Special Issue: Migration, Regional Inequality and Development in the Third World, Vol. 77, No. 1, pp. 42–49.

Wéry, R. 1987. Women in Bamako: Activities and Relations. In Oppong (ed.) (1987), pp. 45–62.

World Development 1978. The Urban Informal Sector: Critical Perspectives, Special Issues, Vol. 6, No. 9/10.

6
What Is She Up To? Changing Identities and Values Among Women Workers in Malaysia

MERETE LIE AND RAGNHILD LUND

"She's wearing pants these days. I don't know what she is up to." This remark stems from the father of a young, female industrial worker in rural Malaysia. It brings us straight to the problems of this chapter – namely, what are the changes brought about by export-oriented industry for female workers and their families?

This context of change poses new demands on the workers, affects their female identity and values, and challenges their traditional position in the local community. "Wearing pants" may be one clue to understanding how they respond in this process.

The industrialization process in Malaysia is part of a restructuring of the international division of labour (Fröbel *et al.*, 1980). This transformation, whereby Third World women have become a new industrial work-force, has gone very quickly. During the 1970s, Malaysia tried to attract foreign industries by establishing Free Trade Zones, where companies were exempted from taxes and customs. This resulted in a geographic concentration of industry, and an extensive migration of young females from the rural areas. Rather poor working and living conditions of the Malay females, especially in the large electronics companies, have been documented in several studies (Ackerman, 1980; Daud, 1985; Heyzer, 1988; Lim, 1978). This has led to a public concern for the welfare and the morals of the female workers.

The district where the quoted father lives has until recently been an agricultural area. Men and women were engaged in small-scale farming or worked as estate labourers. During the last two decades, several factories have been established, mainly employing young women. Among others, a Norwegian factory was set up around 1980.

Mainly young women are recruited to the work-force. According to the traditions of their Malay culture and of Islam, young unmarried women were expected to be shy and reserved and not to participate in public activities on their own. In other words, those who were previously the most protected are now the ones who leave the village on their own and bring new ideas and new values back to the village. As a result, they challenge the cultural and religious tradition which defines men as household heads and major economic providers. Consequently, the young women workers have come in a position whereby they may wish to redefine their status and authority *vis-à-vis* men in the conscious as well as unconscious process of gender negotiations (Rudie, 1984).

On the other hand, a Malay woman always contributed to the family budget. As a youngster she worked as a family helper, and after marriage she had more independent economic functions. In this perspective, taking up industrial work is just another way of performing one's traditional duties. Still, the organization of modern, industrial work in factories run by foreign companies is different from the ways traditional economic activities were organized, thereby influencing who can participate and how. One generation ago, young women worked under family surveillance and did not receive their own wages. Grown-up women were more important providers than young daughters. By entering the modern economic sector young women have considerably increased their economic importance in relation to males as well as older females, thereby acting as promoters, or agents of change.

Like the concept of entrepreneur (Barth, 1963), we would say that being agents of change is only an aspect of a role, relating to certain actions and activities of a person. Therefore, the industrial workers are agents of change when they bring to the local society new thoughts as well as behaviour, while they may at the same time continue to perform many of the traditional virtues and duties of an unmarried daughter.

This brings us to the difficult question of what is to be termed social change. Change in behaviour may be strategies to preserve basic elements of life-style and traditions, only modified to adjust to new circumstances. Or should we reserve the term "change" for events where there is also a change of mind and a change of values? – namely, when people act in new ways to seek for new goals, and not to preserve old traditions. Our data, however, will give evidence of how new and old values may exist simultaneously, thereby creating conflicting expectations and demands.

It is often held that economic change happens faster than conceptual change, meaning that people's minds cannot really follow rapid modernization processes. To us it seems that when people are exposed to rapid economic and social restructuring, they try to come to grips with their new circumstances by making use of new concepts, or alternatively modifying traditional ones, to explain their new situation. Hence, conceptual modifications may also take place quite quickly, and new values and different ambitions of life may be the outcome. However, this process is not always easy, and may go more quickly for some than for others, resulting in a disparity of values within a community and between family members.

In our case, parents and working daughters have grown up under very different socio-economic realities. They have different ways of understanding and interpreting processes of change. Change in behaviour seems to be followed by new goals and values, thereby leading to conflicts or lack of understanding between the young workers and people to whom they relate in their local community. To the young, as well as to the old, this may be very challenging as traditional hierarchies are questioned. To study these processes of change, we shall follow the young women in different social settings.

Our basic understanding is that gendering processes cannot be singled out to one single sphere from which its consequences spread to other spheres. This means, for instance, that we do not see women's inferior position in the labour market as a mere reflection of the sexual division of responsibilities in the home. In our view, gender negotiations are taking place in all different spheres of life. Therefore, we find it important to study women's situation in different social settings, such as the family, the local community and the place of work. In a period of rapid economic change such as here, we expect that the processes going on in these different social settings may follow different directions and that change may be more prominent and occur more quickly in some spheres than in others. The individual woman, therefore, may experience both conflicting expectations and ambivalence.

I. Problems and Data

The chapter is based on the findings of an in-depth study of one Norwegian-owned company and one village from where female workers are recruited.[1] In our work we have combined various methods of data collection. Here, we rely mostly on qualitative data collected through question guides, supplemented by observations and conversations at the factory and in the village. Interviews were conducted with all the workers from one village (37), their mothers, other female household heads such as married elder sisters, organizational leaders in the village and the management of the factory.

To provide an understanding of women's role in the processes of change initiated by industrialization, we need insight into both gender-specific and gender-relational aspects. Therefore, we have aimed in two directions: one to study the female workers as agents of change, their behaviour as well as their plans and dreams; the other to look at changing social relations, more specifically women's possibilities of negotiating their position within the family, towards the other sex and other age groups.

Regarding the gender-specific aspects, we shall discuss the following issues: What does the work and the social life at the factory mean to the female workers' self-image? How do they perceive themselves as women and as workers? What do they think about their future as wives, mothers and perhaps also wage earners? How do they adjust to old and new value systems – in other words, do they know more clearly what they are up to?

Regarding changing gender relations, the questions are: How are women workers regarded by other people in their village? What do young women's cash contributions mean for their status, autonomy and decision-making power inside the family? Has the new work role altered their relations within their families? Has it altered the relationship between young males and females in the village, perhaps affecting prospective marriage relations?

To sum up, our main object of study is new patterns of behaviour among young women as compared to the previous generation, and how the changes are perceived by themselves as well the people they are relating to in their daily activities.

II. The Factory – a Place to be Together

The factory is located in rural Johor, in a previous estate area. The workers are recruited from the surroundings, commuting every day by company bus. More than half of the workers originate from nearby settlement schemes such as the Federal Land Development Agency (FELDA), and we chose one of these for our in-depth study.

Malaysia is a multi-ethnic society, the largest groups being Malays, Chinese, Indians and different aboriginal groups. However, in the rural villages, and especially in the governmental settlement schemes, the overwhelming majority of the population is

Malay. The Malays adhere to the Muslim religion, and the influence of Islamic revivalism has been strong during the 1980s (Anwar, 1987; Muzaffar, 1987). The workers recruited to the factory of the study are nearly all Malay, females and young (86 per cent are 25 years old or less).

The factory produces fishing tackle and has about 190 employees (varying according to season). The work tasks are simple and mostly done manually. The workers are seated around tables, 6–10 together, still working individually. The division of labour is organized in such a way that male workers tend the bigger machines, which are very few, while women do the manual tasks.

However, the factory has an all-female leadership, consisting of three women, in charge of personnel as well as technical matters. Also, most of the female workers are under female supervision, and the factory has a reputation of offering a female environment. This fact is very important to the workers, and especially to their parents. Parents have a great concern for their daughters' safety and moral reputation, and a personnel policy with concern for these matters apparently has a great recruitment potential.

Traditionally, an unmarried woman would be expected to work only inside the house or under supervision of an elderly relative. In this factory, the workers live within daily commuting distance. This means that they can be living with their parents, as protected daughters while at the same time having a job and earning an income. The moral problem of leaving the parents' supervision is reduced by the companionship of girls from the neighbourhood and by sisters working together. Also, some of the supervisors are recruited from the same villages as the workers and are known to the parents.

In many ways the personnel policy resembles the treatment of dependent daughters more than grown-up employees. The workers are kept under close supervision from the moment they leave the home. They are picked up by the company bus outside their houses and brought directly home after work. Only during lunch hours are workers allowed to leave the factory premises, but as the factory is located in a rural area, there are hardly any houses around and no shops or coffee houses. Management is concerned with other aspects of the worker's behaviour than what strictly matters for their productivity. Discipline and politeness, for instance, are among the criteria used for promotion. The young age of the workers is considered a reason for the need of close supervision, and they are consequently referred to by management as "girls".

To the workers, the factory serves as an important meeting place. The social relationships with girls of the same age are, besides the wages, what is appreciated most. They meet different girls and observe their behaviour. Besides, village gossip overheard from the elders may be shared and talked over. When they are not at work, their time is mainly spent at home and much of it on housework. Occasionally they do go out, however, and to go for instance to the weekend market or shopping in the nearest town one needs girl-friends to go with and money to spend. Thus, the job increases the girls' independent activities in more than one way.

Consequently, the factory is a place where girls meet while they earn some money. They are not there to do something together, it is rather a place to be together. The importance of the social aspect at the expense of more work-related aspects, such as learning, personal development and economic self-support, makes it a less attractive place when they get older. The majority of the workers consider their job as temporary. Most of them plan to leave when getting married, if not earlier. During the period at the factory they observe that very few continue working after getting married, and that nobody works there after having children.

However, a small minority have continued working in the factory even if they have passed the age considered appropriate for marriage (22–23 years old). Some girls may want to extend a period of relative freedom while having their own income. As we shall see, also, the parents may be reluctant to lose their daughters' income. Moreover, some have achieved senior positions as supervisors or quality checkers, while others again have raised their wages considerably above the average by being efficient and quick workers. This tendency to stay on may also be a result of the social relationships among the workers, increasing their commitment to the place of work.

The workers hold that it is important, and also common, for a girl to have industrial work today. Most think of this as a temporary phase in their lives, however. But although most aim at getting married and devoting themselves to the family, we still see the tendency that some stay on. These girls have not married. Does this mean that the girls do not consider it possible to combine their new role as "modern working women" with the traditional role as wife and mother? Do they feel they have to choose the one or the other? We shall come back to these questions after looking into the workers' relationships to their families and in the local community.

III. The Integration of Workers in the Local Economy

As mentioned, the majority of the workers at our factory come from various resettlement schemes in the vicinity. The idea behind these schemes has been to allocate land to landless, poor, but enterprising farmers, and to raise the level of living among the Malay population.

The Federal Land Development Agency (FELDA) was established at the eve of independence from the British colonial regime during the 1950s. FELDA schemes are so-called integrated land settlement projects. This means that each scheme is packaged as a new community, complete with roads, dwellings, schools, community hall, clinic and mosque. Each farmer has been allocated about ten acres of land, either for rubber or oil palm cultivation.

Our FELDA settlement is a big palm oil producing one, inhabited by 666 households and has about 6,000 inhabitants. The settlers arrived in the period between 1968 to 1975, most of them during the early years. This means that most of the workers have grown up in the FELDA, even if they were not always born there.

The settler families who came to this community consisted of mother, father and children; a two-generational pattern prevailed. Today, this is still so in the majority of cases, even if the parents are becoming old and the children have grown up. There are few grandparents residing in the settlement. The ordinary family consists of parents with six to nine children. The average age of the male settlers is 55 years, and the mothers we interviewed were generally in their forties. Most of their children were grown up, but, having given birth to many children, several mothers also had children of school and preschool age.

Consequently, we find here a settlement with a population fairly homogeneous in terms of age and family structure. In addition, we face a population which is rapidly becoming old and dependent on younger forces to support them and take over the family farm. But becoming a farmer is not so attractive these days because of a deteriorating economic situation for palm oil producers. The latter has led to the development of a more heterogeneous society with respect to occupational structure. Many settlers have taken up wage work in addition to farming, and many of the adult children work in industry or in the service sector outside the FELDA.

The economic situation of these families has fluctuated. Originating from a poor stratum of the rural population, they went through much hardship during the first years in the FELDA. Only after 6–8 years after planting and tending did the trees start yielding fruits. Since then, their incomes have been dependent upon fluctuating prices on the world market. While many farmers were quite successful during the 1970s and early 1980s, during the later years, the prices of their products have been declining steadily. At the same time, the trees are getting older, and so is the farming population. At this time of the families' cycle, however, their children are growing up and start contributing to the family economy.

Today, the FELDA represents a rural society in stagnation, with a weak economy due to recession on the world market and a high rate of unemployment. Many a family is faced with severe economic problems. Besides, their number of dependants is high. The adult daughters' contributions are therefore important, not only to themselves but to their families and to the local community from where they come. Hence, the economic role of the young worker is intrinsically linked to the processes of change taking place at the national and international levels.

The farm produce was originally supposed to cater for the needs of one nucleated family. However, during the present recession this has not been possible. We found that the average monthly income from the settlers' farms amounted to less than MS 300 (NOK 780) per household. Given that the average household has about 6–8 children, this is too small an amount on which to live. Hence, the settlers and their grown-up children have had to find their means of living in alternative ways and rely on a pooling of resources of different household members.

Various means of survival were identified in the FELDA depending on people's social and economic status, the age structure of the household, previous occupational and educational background. In the agricultural sector, subsidiary work such as rubber tapping was undertaken. Others were engaged in manufacturing which could be both factory work and private petty production. Within the service sector there was a wider choice; teacher, nurse, driver, technician, policeman and private business/trade. In the case of young women, work in industry was the major activity.

Other studies have also shown that a pooling of several household resources is a strategy of household members for pulling together in crisis (*World Development*, 1989). However, it has been shown that women and men do not always pull together towards a common benefit of household and family members as they display different needs and loyalties to dependants. Often, women serve as better care-takers than men during crisis (Roldan, 1988). Here, we have not compared the coping strategies of women with those of men. We have found, however, that women feel a strong obligation to contributing in various ways to the benefit of the family unit.

Furthermore, the economic participation of women relates to class. In societies where women have restricted freedom of mobility, it is often a weak economic position which initiates participation of women in the formal labour market. In our study area, the majority of the industrial workers (approximately 80 per cent) come from the less wealthy households.

However, although women earn their own income, they are not free to allocate it as they may wish. A major share (around two-thirds) is given to the workers' parents, and especially to their mothers, in the form of cash, for paying bills, for provision of food and other consumer goods, and for gifts and schooling for younger brothers and sisters. Such contributions prove important to sustain the livelihood of the parents' household. Contributions are even made in cases where the daughter has left the home, expressing life-long obligations towards her parents.

Only a lesser share (around a third) is used by the female workers to cover the needs defined as strictly personal, such as sanitary articles and cosmetics, occasionally some sewing material or a visit to a cafeteria. The fact that women cater more for the needs of their families than their own personal needs has also been documented in other studies (Firth, 1966; Lund, 1978; Vandsemb, 1987; Papanek and Schwede, 1988). Generally, it has been shown that women's control over their income is limited as compared to that of men or houschold elders. A study of industrial workers in Taiwan, for instance, has shown that women are bound to life-long obligations towards parents to repay for support during childhood (Greenalgh, 1988). Greenalgh further argues that the income provided by women is directly invested into the education of brothers, thus indirectly favouring men. In our study area, no differential treatment of boys and girls could be observed in this respect. Still, women's earning opportunities seem to have given them little economic control. Although the workers have a keen awareness of economics, their economic freedom and independence is limited.

In the FELDA households, a division of labour pertaining to work tasks, consumption and income prevails between men and women, the old and the young. Men and women have different spheres of responsibility relating to their respective work tasks. The senior man of the household generally has the final word in handling money. However, neither the old nor the young manage to fulfil household needs. The young also perceive new needs. Thus, a relationship of mutual economic dependency prevails. However, the traditional authority structure is changing. The influence of the parent generation is decreasing, whereas that of the younger generation is increasing.

IV. The Young Generation and Perceptions of Factory Work

Today, the FELDA faces a severe problem with its second generation. As only one child can take over the farm (usually the eldest son), the big size of the families means a heavy demand for alternative employment. Within the scheme itself there are few job opportunities, and there is no more land to allocate. Moreover, among the young, there is a reluctance to take over the farms, due to the present situation of economic decline. Taking over the farm means an unreliable source of income combined with hard work. One can earn much higher wages in a job in the service sector.

Also, many children do not identify themselves with the occupation of a farmer. As young children they have gone to school instead of helping their parents in the field. Through schooling they may have got alternative views on their scopes and abilities. Through improved means of transport and increasing mobility around the area, many young have got perceptions of urban lifestyles and material welfare. So even if better paid and higher status jobs are difficult to find, the children are still unwilling to take over the farm and are in search of an alternative future.

In the type of industry that has become the major job alternative outside the FELDA, it is easier for the young females to get a job than for the males. The factories established in the area are labour intensive, light industries demanding female labour. Besides, according to the mothers, the young boys are more choosy about jobs than the girls. Thus, the unemployment among young boys is high in the settlement. There is also underemployment, as often several brothers are helping on the farm, due to lack of other employment. The fact that girls generally have stable jobs and incomes, whereas many boys are unemployed and idle, leads to an increasing social esteem of the girls. Boys get to know the girls' work efforts and economic contributions through the work of their sisters (Ong, 1987).

Furthermore, the mothers judge their daughters as more trustworthy than their sons in contributing regularly to the family. Whereas daughters are not expected to spend much on themselves, the boys are expected to save for a future marriage. Apparently they also have more personal expenses as they are allowed much more freedom of action.

Looking into how local people view women and industrial work, the attitudes expressed are on the whole positive. Generally, people claim that industrial work has increased the welfare of the worker as well as her family. They also emphasize the importance of economic independence for the young: "she can afford to buy more clothes. When she gets her salary, she first gives us (read: the parents) what we need. Then she decides what she will do with the rest. . . ."; or "Now the young people can become more independent than before. They can have their own money and buy things for themselves."

Many parents also emphasized that industrial work was positive as their daughters have got new friends and are happier than before. However, it seemed very important to the respondents to emphasize that although the young worker has got industrial work, her behaviour has not changed. In fact, this argument was stated more often than those related to the importance of economic freedom and social happiness. About two-thirds of the mothers claimed that their daughters were the same in spite of the changes to which they were exposed: "My daughter has not changed or become more modern. She still goes out very little, only occasionally she goes on trips with the factory people." Or "Factory work has affected her way of dressing as she can afford to spend on herself. Her behaviour has not changed." Evidently, it is considered most important to cherish the reputation of their working daughters. Even if increasing economic freedom is appreciated, still the traditional virtues of young women are appreciated most.

V. Mothers and Daughters: Work and Marriage

Returning once again to the quoted father, we would illuminate his lack of understanding of his daughter's behaviour by comparing the lives of the older and younger generation in the village. Much has changed in Malaysian women's lives during recent decades. The parents grew up during times of political unrest and rural poverty. Their children, however, grew up during a period of stability and increasing economic growth. The contrast is even more marked because the last generation was brought up in a new settlement. The old Malay villages were characterized as a chain of family circles with little formalized structure (Maeda, 1975; Kushiba et al., 1979).

A major characteristic of the FELDA is the "one generation society". Another is the formalized social organization. The FELDA settlers' economic and social activities are organized in block units and with block leaders. All the settlers' wives are members of the Womens' Organization, also by blocks. It arranges classes in cooking and handicrafts, religious groups and social events. The children join the Youth Organization. Such organizational life is unknown in traditional villages.

Apart from FELDA-organized activities, and ceremonies such as weddings and funerals, we got an impression that the settlers do not mix very much with each other socially. Although the women we talked to were quite familiar with their neighbours and people from the same block, they seldom got together informally or visited non-relatives. This corresponds to the Malay tradition of intra-family networks. The settler families usually visit relatives in their village of origin on special occasions. It does not seem, however, that neighbours in the FELDA have taken the place of relatives in forming close social networks.

The mothers, growing up in a village milieu with many female relatives in the neighbourhood, would have a broad spectre of female role models, as regards different age groups as well as personalities. In the FELDA, the nucleated family is not surrounded by such a network, but by neighbours of the same age groups. Here, women meet at formal meetings, and less often by informally dropping in to see each other. Thereby, the socialization of girls becomes more strictly a matter of the mother–daughter relationship. In addition, the importance of age mates in the socialization process has increased because girls go together at school and later to work.

According to Rudie (1987), one of the most basic characteristics in Malay households was the very intimate relationship between mother and daughter. However, we often found tendencies towards the contrary between mothers and their working daughters. Many mothers complained that they knew very little about their daughters' lives, both at work and in the village. Mothers often commented that their daughters were away at work during most of the daytime. The new arena the daughters had entered was unknown to them. They did not know what type of job their daughters did, nor how much they earned, and some girls also had a social life in their free time which they did not know much about. As the mothers had their marriages arranged at an early age, they had no experiences of their own to relate to.

Apparently, there is a lack of understanding between the former and the new generation concerning what is a secure or a promising future. The parents' generation has been raised during times of hardship. The mothers have always worked hard, as family helpers while they were young, as rubber tappers or farmers after they got married. The children, however, have grown up in a community where security, at least in part, has been secured by the Government. Whereas land always has been, and still is, regarded as the source of economic security by the older generation, education has taken over this place for young people today. Education is regarded as the source of money as well as social esteem by the young, for girls as well as for boys. However, even when secondary education is completed, if not with the best results, industrial work is the only job opportunity locally.[2] What the girls see as the alternative is staying at home and helping their mothers.

The girls say that the decision to take up work was their own. Permission had to be given by the parents, but there was rarely any resistance. The question seems to have been settled in the way that factory work for young females has gained general acceptance, at least as an economic necessity. And although parents complain that they know little about their daughters' lives, they apparently feel there is little to do about this. They have, some tacitly and others complainingly, accepted the daughters' increased freedom of action.

Girls nowadays have much more say regarding whom they are going to marry and at what age. Different from the mothers' time is that girls have the opportunity to meet boys, at least to see them, and also get to know them. Even going out with a boy may be allowed if he is recognized as her boy-friend and she is trusted to behave properly. While the mothers were married in their teens, the girls find the early twenties a suitable age for marriage. The marriage negotiations as well as the marriage rituals follow the old traditions, but the negotiations between the parents will now usually start after the young couple have agreed.

The majority of the workers plan to leave the factory upon marriage, as their colleagues have done, as well as their elder sisters. The decision is left to the prospective husband, however, but still the girls voice their own opinion. The reason they give is that they want to give full attention to their family. But many add that it depends on circumstances, more specifically the husband's income, indicating by this a concern for the family economy making the decision less than easy.

The new housewife ideology is most clearly voiced by the agents of Islamic resurgence. This movement has singled out women as the bearers of traditional values and morality (Heyzer *et al.*, 1989). The way to recreate moral order goes mainly through the control over women by stressing male–female segregation, Islamic dressing and women's role as wives and mothers with increasing emphasis on the importance of motherhood. Disregarding the strength of this movement and its roots far from ordinary village people, these ideologies have become widespread and influential.

Thus, it seems as long as the participation in industrial work is confined to a period between school and marriage, it does not profoundly challenge local values as to what is becoming for a woman. The young women have broadly extended their freedom of action. However, for their future, the workers seem to be trapped between conflicting ideologies, concerning the role of a Malay woman as an important economic provider versus a new role as a housewife.

VI. Women as Carriers of Alternative Values and Ideas

Here, we are exposed to a society in economic stagnation where young women have come in a situation where they are substituting, or complementing, the previously important economic role of their fathers. However, the role as agents of change challenges the image of the woman. On the one hand, women meet with the demand to be pious and obliging daughters, and later housewives and mothers taking care of children and the home. On the other hand, they have taken on the important function of providing for their families' level of living. This position between new and traditional roles has posed new dilemmas, and the women tackle them differently. Also, the response in the local community varies in different types of relationships.

The daughters voice a positive attitude towards more freedom, but it takes a longer time to change the mind of the elders. Several of the mothers complained that they preferred the old days, precisely because then young people obeyed their parents. The new freedom for the girls therefore has certainly not always been gained easily and still involves the cost of affecting their reputation.

Going back to the quotation above, we find that the father does not sanction his daughter wearing pants, which is an indication that the framework of behaviour between fathers and daughters has changed. How does he perceive her? Most important is that he apparently does not know what her message is, as she has changed the rules of behaviour and introduced new signals. Is the reason why he does not sanction her that she, i.e. the young woman, has taken the offensive in defining the new signs of femaleness and the framework of interaction? Is he on the defensive and powerless just because he does not know what the new pants mean? He understands that she is trying to change something and that she wants to live her life differently, but he does not understand how. He cannot relate to her new ideas as he does not know them.

Studying social change in a Spanish community during the same period, Collier found, to her surprise, two generations with differing ideas and values living together without really understanding each other. The lack of understanding is not so apparent because members of both generations act in ways they think will please the other (Collier, 1986). In our area of study, we find that most workers adhere to traditional ways of dressing and behaviour, thus conforming to the ideas of the older generation.

Telling that important decisions will later be left to the husband, the girls do not openly challenge the traditional authority structure. However, they still expect to voice their meaning. Moreover, the mothers reacted to questions of making plans for their daughters' own future as something nearly improper for a young girl, and at least as futile, as decisions were always made by others. Their daughters have clearly articulated meanings on topics such as marriage, children and work, thus indicating a new interest in planning and deciding over their own future.

The girls are the agents, the carriers, of change in connection with industrialization. Their families are more indirectly involved, positively by the economic contribution, more negatively by having daughters who break barriers by their behaviour. The families have, only reluctantly it seems, had to accept their daughters' extended freedom. Moreover, they defend a daughter's reputation by telling us that the daughter is trustworthy and therefore may go out with friends, and may choose her own spouse. A new attitude of responsibility has taken over from the previous guarding of a young daughter. A daughter may now influence important decisions concerning her own life and taking the risks involved. She has thereby become more responsible for the esteem of her family than the mother was in her generation.

What apparently has changed is what young girls can do. Compared to their mothers, they are allowed to do a lot of things that girls could not even think of before. What has not changed, however, is the image of, and the importance of, being a respectable girl. Being a Malay girl implies being a Muslim and adhering to Muslim rules of behaviour. The new freedom of movement, therefore, should not threaten male supremacy, nor the image of the pious, Malay young woman. Now, people say that she can do this and that "as long as she does not do something wrong". Before, a girl was protected from anything that could be associated with sexuality and improper behaviour by never being left on her own, whereas now, it is up to the girl to decide what is on the right and wrong side of the scale.

Responsibility for their own decisions and actions has come into the young women's lives. She is responsible for getting to work in time, for her performance at work, for her behaviour and for handling her money. All of these acts demand alertness, as proper behaviour not only concerns guarding her sexuality but also performing her duties properly and in a nice and graceful way. Handling her own money demands care, as it is associated with – by village people as well as the girls themselves – improper behaviour such as buying cosmetics and modern clothes, going out on her own, even visiting restaurants. As people see it, when she is no longer confined to the home she is constantly exposed to temptations, and consequently, has to prove her good morals.

Adding to the cost for the girls is that they have to defend their reputation. As the work in industry does raise their status in the local community in an alternative way, they still have to adhere to the traditional ideals. First, they go out to work to earn their wages. Next, they go home to fulfil their obligations as dutiful daughters, obligations which, it seems, must be fulfilled even more thoroughly than for a homebound daughter. A daughter who stays in the house is by definition a pious daughter, while the daughter who works in industry must confirm her duties by adhering to housekeeping and religious duties when she is not at work.

Integration in the formal labour market has led to new positions for these women *vis-à-vis* men. However, although industrial work for young women is largely accepted in the local community, it is generally regarded as temporary. A proper profession for a woman is, for example, teaching or nursing. Hence, even if the job does not threaten their identity as women, it does not confirm it either. Their identity and value as women has to be gained in other ways. One way is to adhere to traditional ideals, another is to expose oneself as a modern woman.

The majority of women workers have chosen to conform to traditional values. This is how they win the acceptance of the local community. Still, that most do not openly signal modern ideas does not mean that they are going to live the life of their mothers, but it means that it is more difficult to figure "what they are up to". Even if factory work does not provide economic independence and an alternative future, it is an important arena of interaction and socialization in a special phase of young women's lives. The young women have got a period in life when they are neither under surveillance of parents nor husbands. In this community of young girls, new ideas are expressed and discussed.

Notes

1 The chapter is based on data from the project "Women in Norwegian Industry in Malaysia: integration or marginalization?" Data were collected during 1987–89, altogether a field study period of five months. The project involved several part studies, and various methods of data collection were used to provide information on different aspects of Norwegian industrialization (Lie and Lund, 1990). One perspective was to study the economic impact of industrial work for the workers, their families and the local community. Thereby, focus has been on relationships within the family, the village and the wider community. Another perspective was related to changes in life course from the mothers' to the daughters' generation, thereby seeking for the women's own view on processes of change, their perceptions of themselves and their environment.
2 53 per cent of the female workers have completed secondary education (the SRP or SPM exam).

References

Ackerman, S. 1980. *Cultural Process in Malay Industrialization*. PhD dissertation. Ann Arbor University., Michigan.
Anwar, Z. 1987. *Islamic Revivalism in Malaysia. Dakwah among the Students*. Malaysia: Pelanduk Publications.
Barth, F. 1963. *The Role of the Entrepreneur in Social Change in Northern Norway*. Bergen/Oslo: Universitetsforlaget.
Collier, J. F. 1986. From Mary to Modern Woman: The Material Basis of Marianismo and its Transformation in a Spanish Village. *American Ethnologist*, Vol. 13, No. 1.
Daud, F. 1985. *Minah Karan. The Truth about Malaysian Factory Girls*. Kuala Lumpur.
Dwyer, D. and Bruce, J. (eds) 1988. *A Home Divided – Women and Income in the Third World*. Stanford: Stanford University Press.

Firth, R. 1966. *Housekeeping among Malay peasants*. New York: Humanities Press.
Fröbel, F., Heinrichs, O. and Kreye, O. 1980. *The International Division of Labour*. Cambridge: Cambridge University Press.
Greenhalgh, S. 1988. Intergenerational Contracts: Familial Roots of Sexual Stratification in Taiwan. In D. Dwyer, and J. Bruce (eds).
Heyzer, N. (ed.) 1988. *Daughters in Industry*. Kuala Lumpur: APDC.
Heyzer, N., Anwar, Z. and Zain, K. 1989. *Islamic Revivalism and Women in Malaysia: A Case Study*. Kuala Lumpur: Asian Pacific Development Centre.
Kuchiba, M. *et al.* 1979. *Three Malay villages: A Sociology of Paddy Growers in West Malaysia*. Honolulu: University Press of Hawaii.
Lim, L. Y. C. 1978. *Women Workers in Multinational Corporations: The Case of the Electronics Industry in Malaysia and Singapore*. Michigan Occasional Papers no. 9, University of Michigan.
Lund, R. 1978. *Prosperity to Mahaweli. A Survey on Women's Working and Living Conditions in a Settlement Area*. Peoples' Bank Research Department, Colombo.
Lund, R. and Lie, M. 1989. The Role of Women in the New International Division of Labour – the Case of Malaysian Women in Norwegian Industry. *Norsk Geografisk Tidsskrift*, Vol. 43, pp. 95–104.
Maeda, N. 1975. Family Circle, Community, and Nation in Malaysia. *Current Anthropology*, Vol. 16, No. 1.
Muzaffar, C. 1987. *Islamic Resurgence in Malaysia*. Malaysia.
Ong, A. 1987. *Spirits of Resistance and Capitalist Discipline – Factory Women in Malaysia*. Albany: State University of New York Press.
Papanek, H. and Schwede, L. 1988. Women Are Good with Money: Earning and Managing in an Indonesian City. In D. Dwyer, and J. Bruce, (eds).
Roldan, M. 1988. The Black Four of Hearts: Toward a New Paradigm of Household Economics. In D. Dwyer and J. Bruce, (eds).
Rudie, I. (ed.) 1984. *Myk start, hard landing*. Oslo: Universitetsforlaget.
Rudie, I. 1987. Development Ideologies, Family Systems, and the Changing Roles of Malay Village Women. Department of Social Anthropology, University of Oslo.
Vandsemb, B. H. 1987. Arealbruk, velferd og kvinners arbeid – en studie fra Moneragala, Sri Lanka. Master's Thesis, Department of Geography, University of Trondheim.
World Development, Vol. 17, No. 7: Beyond Survival: Expanding Income-Earning Opportunities for Women in Developing Countries. Special Issue. Oxford: Pergamon Press.

7
Housewifization of Peasant Women in Costa Rica?

HALLDIS VALESTRAND

The past 20 years have witnessed a debate over the possible impacts of agricultural change on rural women in Third World countries, a discussion launched with the publication of Ester Boserup's *Women's Role in Economic Development* (1970). The basic notion is that changes in agriculture affect rural women negatively, either because no one takes them into account, or because they are in the most vulnerable position in the first place. Following the appearance of Boserup's book, several concepts have been employed in order to grasp the processes involved in the perceived worsening of the situation of rural women. The most frequently used terms are "marginalization", "proletarianization", "feminization" and "housewifization". In this chapter I will discuss the "housewifization thesis" in relation to the changes peasant women in the agricultural settlement of Coto Sur in Costa Rica have experienced after the introduction of a new crop.[1]

When I returned to Coto Sur in 1990 where I had conducted fieldwork four years previously, I noticed that housework and the ways in which women organized their daily lives had changed substantially in the interim.[2] Many of my informants live on farms currently in the process of substituting semi-subsistence farming with African Palm. As dark green "forests" replace yellow maize fields, there are also repercussions inside the homes, on the division of labour and interpersonal relations. My first thought was that these farm women were now becoming housewives, as I recognized many traits of "housewifery" in the women's recent adaptations. Could these changes be analysed as part of a worldwide "housewifization process" (Mies, 1986), and how useful is this concept for understanding the processes of change in a place like Coto Sur? I will discuss this by comparing how the farm women spent their time and what their work involved before and after starting with African Palm production, as well as linkages to their life courses and their perception of the new situation.

I. "Housewifization": An Effect of Economic Processes Alone?

María Mies in her book *Patriarchy and Accumulation on a World Scale* (1986) introduces the concept of "housewifization". Her theme is the situation of women in the present state of the world economy; late capitalism, neocolonialism and the reign of the New International Division of Labour. Mies asserts that "housewifization" is an international and ubiquitous phenomenon. On the basis of my own field-work among peasant women in Costa Rica I will voice a certain scepticism to applying such a concept uncritically whenever women are observed in the role of "housewives". Especially when working with empirical material from cultures other than our own, we should be careful when applying the term "housewife", which is a concept loaded with European connotations. Harris has pointed to such a danger concerning the concept of "household", noting how many authors assume that "the domestic" is a universal category, without taking all the empirical variations into consideration (Harris, 1981).

Let us briefly return to the source, to María Mies's own use of the concept "housewification". Her thesis is that this is a process taking place on a global scale, with women increasingly being pushed back to a position as dependent home-makers, under the aegis of an ideology favouring women who work in the home. Mies takes as her point of departure the structural changes currently taking place in the world economy, the seemingly never ending exploitation of the earth and its peoples. With the industrialization of Europe as her point of departure, she notes how first middle-class and later working-class women were confined to the home, as work-place and household became physically separated. The most important effect for women was economic dependence on a male "bread-winner". Mies claims that this process was made possible not only because of industrialization, but also because of changes in the world economy in the colonial era from the sixteenth century and onwards. Her specific contribution has been to relate "housewifization" to the emerging New International Division of Labour. Mies focuses on how women, because they are universally being defined as "housewives" and not as "free" workers, can be over-exploited in the export-oriented industries in developing countries, by transnational companies that shift their production sites around in the Third World, by the small-scale putting-out production found in many of those societies and by the way in which international agribusiness utilizes this situation.

Mies also claims that this ideology of viewing women primarily as housewives is actively being put to use in the development strategies in many countries by the national states as well as by foreign-aid agencies. What women actually do is defined not as "work", but as an "activity" (Mies, 1986). This is a point also noted by others (Rogers, 1980; Moore, 1988). Several authors have used the concept of "housewifization" in analysing empirical material from different parts of the world, be it Third World agricultural societies, newly industrializing countries or the consolidation process now taking place within the European Community (Bennholdt-Thomsen, 1988; Townsend, 1989; Skjønsberg, 1990).

Veronika Bennholdt-Thomsen shares Mies's view of "housewifization": "The housewife is not characterized by what she does but by the conditions and the relations under which she does it" (Bennholdt-Thomsen, 1988, p. 160). Both Mies and Bennholdt-Thomsen see "housewifization" as a parallel to a concept like "proletarianization", arguing that one is dealing with a seemingly endless process where the economy is decisive, but where the Church, the state and capital all act to reinforce one another.

> The contrasting conditions of work between the free wage labour and the housewife constitute the two poles of a continuum of capitalist conditions of work and relations of production (Bennholdt-Thomsen, 1988, p. 176).

We can certainly agree with Mies and others who stress the importance of looking at "housewifization" on a world scale in order to understand the nearly universal subordinate position of women. But when Bennholdt-Thomsen claims that "The relation between husband and wife is repeated in the relation between the first and the third world" (p. 177), this would seem more problematic although both she and Mies point out that they are not referring to concrete housewives, but are concerned with what they call "generalized housewives". Even more problematic is that the concept "housewifization" seems to be a tempting one to apply precisely in specific cases. However, as such, it is a comprehensive concept which needs to be further supplemented and discussed through specific empirical research in different settings and from a variety of theoretical considerations.

1. *Some Aspects of "Housewifization": Housewife, Housework and Strategy*

Let us start by scrutinizing two basic concepts: "housework" and "housewife". Mies and others do not consider the actual tasks performed by a housewife to be important in an analysis. I will claim that in order to say anything at all about the changes observed in Coto Sur, we will have to look at what housework implies. And finally, we need to examine Mies's and Bennholdt-Thomsen's position concerning "housewifization" as an effect of economic changes.

We also need a more precise basis for discussing what a housewife is. Anne Oakley (1974) takes up this question. Like Mies and Bennholdt-Thomsen, she uses observations from industrialized countries to explain the rise of the housewife in Great Britain. However, she also discusses at some length the definition or concept of a housewife:

> The synthesis of "house" and "wife" in the single term establishes the connections between womanhood, marriage and the dwelling place of family groups.

And from the Oxford Dictionary:

> A housewife is a woman who manages or directs the affairs of her household; the mistress of a family, the wife of a householder... [and] through the location of the housewife role in marriage, housewifery is an economically dependent occupation (Oakley, 1974, p. 2).

Ann Oakley's main points are as follows (1) The housewife's primary economic function is vicarious; by providing services to others she enables them to engage in productive economic activity. (2) Instead of playing a productive role, the housewife acts as the main consumer within the family. (3) The housewife's work is not regarded as work because she receives no salary for it; and in most industrialized countries the housewife as a houseworker has no legal rights to benefits such as sick pay and so on (Oakley, 1974).

Oakley draws attention to the contradiction that housework is work and housework is not work, which is a constant theme in any analysis of the housewife's situation. In our Western societies the housewife has been told that she has an honourable position but at the same time she lives in a situation of economic dependence and holds hardly any of the rights entailed in people's status as wage earners. Oakley also discusses the concept of housework at some length. Here she focuses on the private nature of the work, and the fact that it is self-defined and integrated into a whole complex of domestic family-based roles which define the situation of women as well as that of housewives. The roles of wife and mother are not distinct from the role of a housewife, and a woman can strive for perfection in all three roles; mother, housewife and wife. In her historical assessment Oakley examines the ideological construction of a housewife from ideas of the home as a refuge, as a private place, and then turns to the domesticity of women that prevailed towards the end of the nineteenth century, and how "housewifery" gradually became a full-time occupation for women. Not until the twentieth century did women's economic dependence on men become an accepted fact in England. By then, the family had increasingly become the locus of all meaningful personal life. Society had become more and more "family-oriented", and the family itself was identified with its physical location, the home (Oakley, 1974).

Oakley's analysis concentrates on the role of the housewife, less on the structural aspects of a housewife's situation, although these always underlie her argumentation. Oakley refers to the role of the housewife in industrialized countries, and Mies to the global process. In many ways the two authors supplement each other. Both emphasize women's increasing economic dependence on men. One important point to clarify concerns this economic factor: what access has the housewife to money earned by other members of the household? To explore this further we will have to find out how money and resources are distributed within the household or family (Harris, 1981; Whitehead, 1981; Roldán, 1987).

However, there is obviously more to "housewifery" than this. Melhuus and Borchgrevink (1984) argue that if we are to say anything meaningful about housework and the person who carries it out, we will have to be explicit about the historical and social setting. Many fail to do this, thereby giving housework the character of being ahistorical, unilateral and unchanging.

The two authors point to the fact that housework performed by women has a dual character. Housework is both economically and culturally contingent, and so is the result of housework. Any analysis that does not take both dimensions into consideration must necessarily be biased. This means that the same empirical phenomena must be studied both as concrete tasks that can be registered and quantified, and as reproduction of the cultural order. Housework is therefore more than the sum of all its various parts. The result is not merely the products and services, but the "home". It is a question not only of survival, but also of well-being. Housework produces not only workers, but also social persons, and studying housework can enable us to understand how social identities are created and sustained for both women and men. Concerning cultural differences we can observe that the combinations of productive and reproductive activities are quite distinct in different societies, also varying with the stages of the households' cycles.

Melhuus and Borchgrevink suggest that in our society, housework is the price women have to pay for the love of their husband and children. They exemplify this by showing how housewives in a rural community in Norway discuss and negotiate standards of housework by referring to their time use and by gossip intended to make their housework more visible (Melhuus and Borchgrevink, 1984).

Much in the same vein is Rudie (1984), who splits modern housework in industrialized societies up into three; what she calls an economic, a care-giving and a ceremonial component. In this way she is able to show how in our society there has been a movement away from what used to be most time consuming and important for survival in "traditional" society, namely the economic or productive component, towards more emphasis on ceremonial (symbolic) activities. Her point is that these components can be negotiated between women and men and among women; further that some areas are more difficult to negotiate than others, but that those probably differ culturally. In Scandinavian societies the care-giving component appears the most difficult aspect to negotiate (Rudie, 1984).

Returning to Mies's concept of "housewifization" and contrasting it with the other views mentioned, we find that she uses the concept as a structural term. Becoming a housewife is a situation that is forced on women by capital, state and religion reinforcing each other. When referring to "housewifization" Mies (and others) see women as victims and objects, not as strategic actors. And yet, do not the women themselves have any say in the changing circumstances in which they live? Might it not be that "housewifization" could also be something that people desire? That many women, in striving for a better quality of life, will consider becoming a full-time, financially supported housewife as a good strategy for them?

If we are to choose whether or not to apply the concept of "housewifization", we will have to be more accurate about the content of the concept itself, by also including women as subjects in any "housewifization" process. We will have to take both women's and men's strategies as well as gender relations into consideration when discussing "housewifization". For instance, we should examine gender relations both at the household level and in society at large, since they are likely to determine the degree to which a housewife can maintain some independence and thereby be in a stronger position to negotiate the terms under which her services will be available to the others in the household.

The importance of women's bargaining capacity is decisive here and this is a situation in which age and generation are obviously central factors. For example, in most societies a young wife will have fewer opportunities than an elderly woman. Moreover, the history of the spouses as social persons must be considered: how they have acted as strategic actors both individually and together, in different life situations. It is necessary to emphasize that even though in most societies women have a secondary position compared to men, we cannot take it for granted that we will find the same "secondness" cross-culturally; that is an empirical question.

On the basis of the foregoing discussion, let us now turn to the processes of change observed in Coto Sur, Costa Rica. Fiona Wilson (1985) asks to what extent economic development has sufficient explanatory power to interpret the particular experiences of women, arguing that it is the socially constructed relationships between men and women that will be decisive for the situation at any given time, not any "impact" alone. This should be borne in mind when considering an agricultural area like Coto Sur which is being so fundamentally transformed.

II. "Life Hasn't Been Easy..." – Peasants in Migration

Coto Sur is a rural settlement inhabited by peasants who live on farms ranging from 7 to 25 hectares in size. The approximately 1,500 farm households were established 10–15 years ago, as part of a settlement scheme.[3] The area, which comprises large tracts of former banana plantations (United Brands (Fruit) Company), was initially invaded by former banana workers when the Company started to withdraw from the Golfito Division in the Southern Pacific Zone in the early 1970s. The banana workers were followed by a great number of landless peasants, largely originating from Guanacaste, a province bordering Nicaragua, with a farming structure based on big haciendas. The population living in the settlement today, which numbers around 12,000, is therefore a mixture of former banana workers and landless people from other parts of the country as well as a substantial number from the neighbouring countries of Panamá and Nicaragua. Most of them live on individual farms, or "parcels" and are usually called "parceleros".

The life stories of the adult peasant women have some essential features in common. Almost all of these women have been born and raised on a farm, have had to work hard all their lives, and have either no schooling or perhaps just a few years. They have had their first child at the age of 15–16, and a majority of them have also been abandoned one or several times by the father(s) of their child(ren). The women were between 17 and 35 years old when they first came to the settlement.

One group of peasants came to Coto Sur directly from other rural areas, most of the women arriving together with their families. They had been born and raised in Guanacaste on small farms, or on haciendas as daughters of landworkers, and they "heard that they were giving away land in the South", as so many put it. In their home region there were few possibilities to earn a living from agriculture in the 1960s and 1970s. Pressure on land and technological changes meant that a great many landless persons were forced to move out.

A second group in Coto Sur is composed of those who have spent some time on one of the many banana plantations in the Golfito area. They also originally come from Guanacaste or other agricultural regions. Quite a number of the women in this group came to Coto Sur on their own to seek a living for themselves. This zone functioned like a magnet for landless people for several decades. Approximately three-quarters of the "parcelera" women in the central part of the settlement are daughters, mothers or wives of "bananeros".[4]

The banana plantation was basically a male world, since very few women were employed by the Company. It was only men who worked in the fields and in the packing stations. Some women were typists, cooks, maids for the "gringos", or were petty traders of food. In this system a woman's best strategy for survival was to establish a relationship with a "bananero", preferably someone who had a permanent contract with the Company, with rights to his own (half) house. Bossen (1984) reports on similar strategies on a sugar plantation on the coast of Guatemala. Some of the women in Coto Sur lived for 20–30 years in different "cuadrantes" (worker compounds), before getting their own parcel of land.

On the banana plantations women were normally financially dependent on a man, usually the husband, who was expected to give them money to feed their children and themselves. This seems to have been difficult at times. The main threat experienced by women in Coto Sur was that other women might claim that their husband should pay for children he had fathered. Giving birth to his child was considered a strategy to obtain support from a man. If one succeeded, the next step was to uphold the relationship. Some of the peasant women mentioned they had been very happy as "bananero's" wives, that their husbands always gave them money for food first, before going off on their own to drink and play. Such men were considered "responsible", a word the women often repeated when talking about how a man ought to be. Apparently, responsible men were hard to find. To maintain a stable relationship with a banana worker meant cooking for him, washing his clothes, serving him and taking care of the children. He would leave the house early to go to work, come home for lunch and a nap, then go back to work, come home for supper and normally would go to the "Club" to drink with his companions at night.

Seen from outside, this group of women could in many ways be said to "have been made into housewives" on the plantations, either after they had come, alone in search of a living and had found a companion; or when they moved in with an already established family. The life on the plantations provided for by the Company infrastructure was far more comfortable for the women than a smallholder life in Guanacaste, or working as maids in private homes. Life with a "bananero" could be pleasant, but it was completely dependent on the kind of relationship and negotiating power a woman established *vis-à-vis* her bread-winner, and on relations to other women in the compound. Thus, being a bananero's wife was not always easy; many of the women report hard times in making ends meet, because their provider did not turn enough money over to them, because there could be many persons to be supported by one man, or because he spent it on drinks and other women. In such cases the women tried to supplement their household economy by preparing and selling food, by sewing and other income-generating activities. There was always the lurking threat of being thrown out if their "compañero" found another woman. Doña Luisa, who had lived on various banana plantations since she arrived in the Southern Zone as a 15 years old newly wed, had to maintain nine children more or less by herself, as her husband was not much worth:

I had to get up at 1 in the morning to start grinding maize, in order to make tortillas, they were sold for 10 colones (a stack), they had to be ready for breakfast for the bananeros and were brought out at 5 a.m. by my children. I was buying and selling all the time, making biscuits, atól [a drink], bread, and was constantly searching for firewood. I had a small pushcart wherever I went, and everybody knew me.

Against this background it is perhaps not so strange that it was often the woman in a banana worker household who had pressed to leave when possibilities for land opened up in Coto Sur. Men tended to be more reluctant, wanting to remain in what they saw as the security of the banana plantations, if they still could.

III. "Parcelero" Life: Settlers in Coto Sur

For those who settled in Coto Sur, the first period was tough. They had to clear the land, often dense tropical rainforest: then get hold of seeds, and try to survive until the first harvest. There are numerous stories of living from hand to mouth in a "rancho" (hut) made of bamboo or corrugated tin plates that they carried with them on the local train. The climatic conditions are difficult: tropical heat, high humidity and lots of insects, which added to the settlers' problems. According to the land reform law, priority to land was given to "heads of households". A pattern of property rights was established, in which 98 per cent of the owners were male. To many of the pioneering peasants, running their own "enterprise" was a new experience, to be learnt by trial and error. Many did not succeed and left; others barely survived; and a few have done relatively well.

A smallholder agriculture developed in the settlement, based on maize, rice and cattle, mixed with beans and a few other crops. Crops varied according to the location of the farm and its size. This pattern emerged as a result of the know-how the peasants already had, and the establishment of a CNP (Consejo Nacional de Produccione) state receiving station (maize, beans) in the settlement. Most of the farms in Coto Sur are poorly provided with tools; some did have a horse or a mule.

Maize cultivators were in the majority. Their lives revolved around the two annual harvests. Although many based their survival on maize, they would often grow some beans, green bananas and other crops. They would sell off what they could to middlemen who passed by, buying local produce and then taking it the long way to the larger markets in the Valle Central.

The sexual division of labour on the farms varied considerably. On some farms, the woman would participate and even direct all agricultural activities, whereas at others she might never set foot in the fields at all. The overall pattern was that after the initial clearing of the land, where all hands were needed, the woman was an active participant in the harvest seasons, depending on how many small children and other women there were in the household. In most farm households her task was co-ordinating the work of others and providing food. At times she would also have to send children off to work elsewhere, or find some ways of making and selling things. The pivotal role of women in the peasant households in Coto Sur in the 1970s and 1980s was extremely central for the households' viability. It was apparent from the women's knowledge of prices and acreage and what they were growing and how, even among those who never set foot in "el monte" (the field). With a very few exceptions all the "parceleras" in one way or the other took part in agricultural activities. This position gave them the autonomy which they had felt they lacked as "bananero" wives.

IV. Women's Daily Life on the Farms in the 1980s

Women's work and daily life have changed along several dimensions. We will start by looking at how peasant women organized their working day in the 1980s. The setting is a "finca" (farm) of 7–20 hectares, producing staple crops (maize), which was delivered to the state receiving station (CNP) twice a year, in addition to growing some beans and cocoa or green bananas. The household economy was based on the results of the two annual harvests. In order to sow, the majority needed credit from the bank. First to be paid off after the money came in from the CNP would be the bank, as the farmers feared getting into debt. From around 1980 each year yielded a smaller and smaller surplus, and the smallholder economy never seemed to improve. If there was any surplus, the most thrifty households secured provisions (such as coffee, salt, rice and so on), followed by clothes for the children and necessary repairs. Otherwise it was just to try to get along on what could be made and sold, trying to save on anything that required cash. Often this meant taking the children out of school for a while.

The diverse activities which constituted a typical working day for a smallholder's wife are summarized in Figure 1. The different tasks have been classified according to average amount of time spent and where the activity is performed. Altogether the "parceleras" spent approximately 15–16 hours working each day. The woman got up first, between 3.30 and 5 in the morning, to make coffee and tortillas for the other family members. Cooking was over open fire or by gas cooker. Most households alternated depending on cost. These activities the women themselves would classify as "oficios domesticos" (domestic work), together with a great number of other chores.

The domestic chores took on average five hours a day. Variation in time use depended on how many daughters or daughters-in-law could be put to work. Cooking, laundering and ironing were the most time-consuming tasks. Laundering took place either outside in wash basins, or in a nearby stream or canal. Most farms now have their own well, but still water generally has to be hauled for cooking, laundry and personal hygiene.

Women in Coto Sur can seldom tell the exact size of their household, because there is constant change with people coming and going. A daughter might return with a child or two, after several years away from home, stay for some months, then leave to find another job, and leave her child(ren) behind. The women kept track of their households by the number of mouths to feed, a number which would not necessarily correspond to the number of people sleeping in the house. Women could for example feed "peones" (day workers), or send food to older relatives who lived elsewhere.

Looking after children and the elderly (2) occupied some 2–3 hours of a farm woman's day. This included direct surveillance, in addition to constant awareness. Many farmers were quite young when they came to Coto Sur, so the number of children is high, the average being 6–7 in each household. In recent years, older relatives have moved in to be taken care of in their old age. This can represent a heavy burden for many women. On the other hand, grandchildren are often taken care of by their grandmothers when their mothers leave to find work as maids or in factories in the Valle Central and the capital.

The peasant women in Coto Sur have a difficult life, and have learnt to survive by hard work. They have worked in agriculture or have found other ways of getting along – making food for sale in the streets, tortillas, bread, tacos and so on. If they had hens, they could sell eggs and poultry meat; they knitted, sewed, had some vegetables and a few cocoa trees, brought up a pig, and generally had

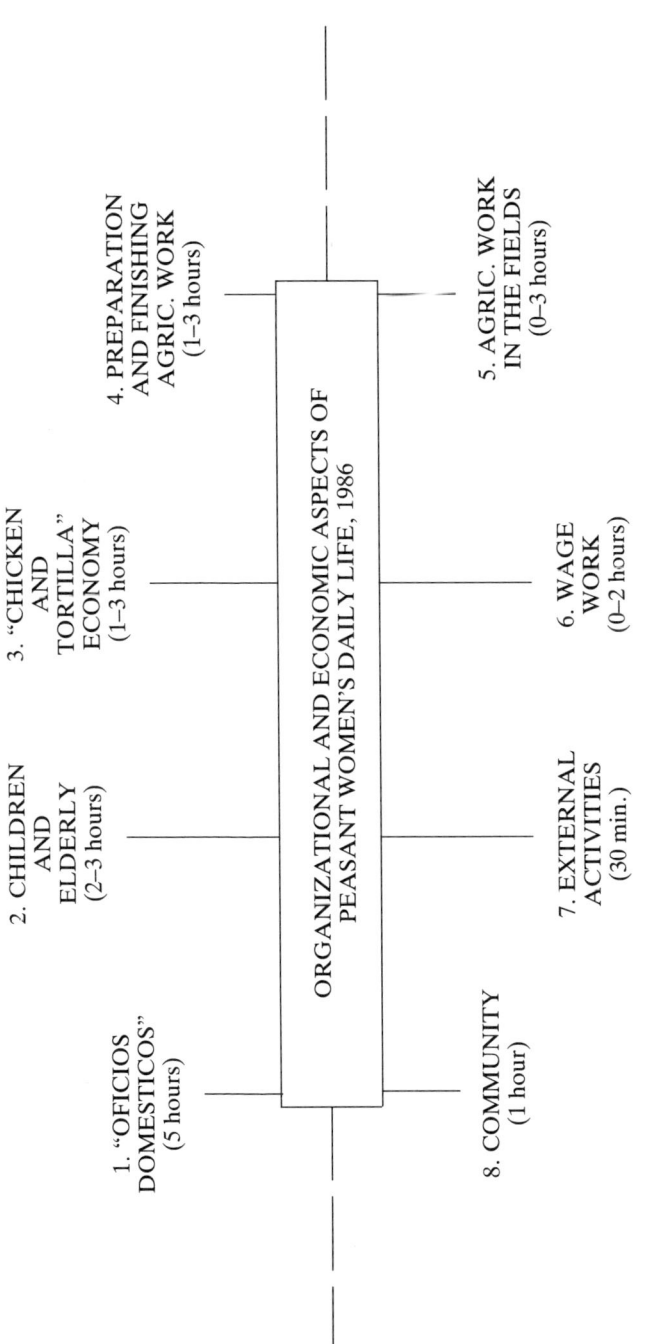

Figure 1. Peasant women's daily activities and time use in Coto Sur, 1986. (The activities above the dotted line are performed on the farm and in or around the house. Selling of produce (3) usually also took place there, but might occasionally involve leaving the house.)

great flexibility. In Coto Sur the market has been limited for their products, so the women always brought along something to sell when travelling to other places. Because of the seasonal variations in the economy of most farm households, what we can call the "Chicken and tortilla" economy (3) – run and organized by the women – was important for day-to-day survival. The household was thus heavily dependent on the woman to keep things going, to buy the little "extras" that demanded cash (i.e. a pencil or a notebook for the children, a bus fare, medicines). Food could be obtained from the farm, tortillas (maize), eggs and beans and even rice. Farmers living in the outskirts of the settlement were most self-sufficient, with larger farms and less contact with the market. For "parcelera" women it would take 1–3 hours of their time to keep this "system" going. Their main occupation then was to organize, to keep an open eye on everything.

The fourth work area I have called "Preparation and finishing of agricultural work" (4). This was work connected with the agricultural production of the farm, but performed in or near the house. As it was all women's work it meant that they hardly left the farm. Preparation and processing of agricultural products could mean things like filling sacks with corncobs, opening the cocoa pods, removing the cocoa seeds to dry, cleaning and milking the cow(s), and so on, depending on the season and what the farm produced.

The most time-consuming "external" activity was the actual work in the fields (5). In the busy seasons this would mean many hours in the sun, weeding or harvesting maize or other crops. If the woman had somebody at home to cook and take care of the house, she might well spend most of the day in the fields. A normal work day in Coto Sur occupies the morning hours from 6 to 10–11 a.m. Fieldwork sometimes continues in the afternoon, but heavy rains usually make this impractical. To say that farm women in Coto Sur were "unpaid family labour" (Deere and León, 1987; Long, 1984) is both true and untrue. In some cases women were paid day labourers' wages by their husbands/sons for the days they actually were in the fields, like the other workers.[5] This would depend on the size of the pay cheque from the CNP. But women were not paid for what they did inside the house.

In Coto Sur we also found examples of a triple day for farming women. By this is meant when women, in addition to working at home and in the fields, also went out to work for others, or took in paid work to do at home, like washing and ironing. Those living near the "cuadrantes" of the ex-plantations might do cleaning, laundry and ironing in other peoples' houses. There were also a few cases of women working as day labourers on other people's farms, but I was told that this had been more common before.

The final two areas in Figure 1 cover activities that do not account for much time on a normal day. "External activities" (7) might be visits to the bank or the doctors; "community" (8) could be visiting others, going to church or to a local meeting, and so on. In Coto Sur there are few external organized activities for women, and the parcelera women in Coto Sur did not leave their homes very often.

This then was basically what an "organizational budget" would look like for parcelera women in the 1980s. Life yielded little but the bare necessities; worries about how to meet the next day, and how to face debts with the bank and the local grocer's were considered the main problems (Valestrand 1990). With so little extra income in most households, any discussion on how to spend the money was rare. In many households, women had quite a say in budgetary matters, being the ones in contact with the bank or other credit institutions. But in others there was a different pattern. There were households where women never left home, and others where they did so relatively frequently.

One thing was clear, however: most farm women had extensive control over important farm resources. They were largely the ones who could manage to make things run economically if storm should ruin the harvest, or prices on their produce should fall substantially. Still they did not always consider themselves farm wives, very often calling themselves "amas de casa" (housewives). Into this housewifery they put both productive and reproductive activities with an extensive degree of flexibility. To these women being a housewife in the 1980s in Coto Sur included being available to "help out" in the fields whenever necessary, being well-informed on the prices of inputs and grains, in addition to providing services to everybody in the household.

1. *From Maize to Oil Palms: "Agricultura de Cambio"*

The first planting of African Palm in the Southern region was initiated by the Banana Company, when it started to withdraw from the Coto Valley in the mid-1970s, on the plantations bordering Coto Sur to the north. Unlike the system on the plantations, the Palm Project in Coto Sur is based on individual ownership and farm management. This major agro-industrial project was planned as an alternative for the peasants, as climatic and soil conditions are far from optimal for growing maize, and the consumer markets are far away. While the domestic market was dependent on importing edible oils (for frying fat, margarine and cooking oils), the Government was also concerned to expand export production. This was part of the conditions set by the International Monetary Fund and the World Bank for renegotiating the foreign debt – the well-known "structural adjustments". In Costa Rica this policy is termed "Agricultura de Cambio" (agriculture of change). The Palm Project is part of these new policies, and is referred to as "agricultura de cambio" in daily speech by the officials now working in the settlement.

The oil palm takes from between two and four years before it starts to yield. During this period, people have a difficult time as participants in two different worlds – the future "palmero" world, and the old "maizero" world. Not all peasants are enthusiastic about the new crops, and experts spend a lot of time and energy motivating and convincing them to join the programme. Some peasants have rejected the idea of planting palms. Arguments vary, ranging from "palms we cannot eat", via ecological considerations and the danger of relying on monoculture alone, to worries about incurring heavy debts.[6]

A weekly transport system has been established to collect the produce. On a particular weekday the palm berries are to be harvested and stacked up at the entrance of each homestead to be collected by truck the next day. This makes one day every week a labour intensive harvest day while the other six days are used for maintenance and clearing around the palms, requiring fewer people. Once in the soil, the plants really demand little attention, except for some weeding.

As for the sexual division of labour the following pattern emerges. Men do the work that requires physical strength – cutting down the heavy clusters of berries, and loading the mule and carriage. Women and children pick dropped single berries and otherwise assist the men. Men work with and have the main responsibility for the palms. Women help or assist them, or they stay at home. Their participation depends on the number of male hands in the household. Information on technical matters is disseminated by experts connected with the project. They travel around in jeeps or on motor bikes to talk to the farmers, to invite them to field demonstrations and other events. The experts are all young, professional and male. In order to get this project started, it was necessary to organize a producers' co-operative, but the project staff as well as the paid secretariat of the palm co-operative are professional people from outside. Some women belong to the co-operative, but they are owners of land. Very few are active farmers themselves, which some of them used to be as long as the main crop was maize. Because of its economic possibilities, the palm co-operative is set to be an important actor in the agrarian/co-operative sector in Costa Rica. It now appears that its establishment is also giving men an important foothold and an economic/political channel to society at large. These possibilities are not open to women in general.

V. Daily "Palmera" Life, 1990

One of the women, Doña Lígia, is very satisfied with the recent changes in Coto Sur. She thinks that her life has improved after starting with oil palms: "Look, I can dedicate more of my time to the house, make it look more orderly, buy more things for it." The past two years, after she and her family started to deliver oil berries, she has been able to buy a new colour television, a new fridge, an electric fan and a cupboard. Nor is she the only one: most women are happy with the changes, because they can now spend more time on housework and afford to buy things they could only dream about before. When we look more closely at the daily routines on the palm farms, the first thing we notice is the stability of incomes. Previously, incomes used to be limited to the harvests twice a year. Now income, although variable, comes in steadily on the first Friday of every month, just as in any other wage-earning family.

Palm farmers in Coto Sur now have an income (after deductions) at least 3–4 times higher than what they used to have. Although it is still not much in absolute terms, to them it is a lot. Their debts are scheduled to be repaid in 12 years, and as the plants are expected to have a 25-year life-cycle, farmers are also promised good incomes in the future. Before, they could not afford anything. They still cannot afford so much, but now they have cash to pay for the goods they need.

Second, there have already been some changes in the housework of farm women: it has become more concentrated. There are not so many different tasks to attend to. The daily routines of women on palm farms are still time consuming as their houses are impractical and considerable effort is needed just to keep them clean. Especially in the kitchen area, much is old-fashioned. What we do notice, however, and the women themselves emphasize this, is that life has become easier. There are fewer worries: worries about money to pay for medicines, pesticides or bills, about a storm that may ruin the maize fields and plunge them into debt. "We sleep better at night", they say. Until recently life for them has largely been a matter of wondering how to get to the end of the day, the week or the month, and always work, work and work to keep things going.

With the situation from 1986 (Figure 1) in mind, we can draw a new figure (Figure 2) of the situation today. Several areas of activity have vanished from the farm women's daily schedule: the "chicken and tortilla economy" (3) and "wage work" (6), the two income-generating activities to which the farm women resorted when necessary. Moreover, most women have now left the fields (5). A farm woman's participation in agriculture now seems to become more a question of whether she enjoys working in the fields or not. According to the women themselves, they have "saved" 2–3 hours a day after they started growing palms.

Most of the palm farms have dropped or are in the process of dropping their "milpa" (maize field). Some still plant a hectare or so of maize, for their own consumption, but the general trend now is to plant palms on all the acreage. For the women, the disappearance of maize has led not only to their retirement from agricultural work, but has also led to some changes in their other activities. Previously women used to keep a few hens as a little "reserve" which they could use to pay a debt at the general store, a notebook, or other expenses that could not be covered elsewhere, or for feeding themselves. Nowadays, a big firm, "Pollo Pipasa", is expanding; in the new supermarket they can buy ready-cut, cleaned and frozen chicken. Chickens and hens are disappearing from the small farms since it does not pay to buy maize to feed them. The same is the case with tortillas. On the palm farms, few of the women grind their own maize any more. They buy "Masarica", maize flour, at the store instead. Only for special occasions do they still buy and grind maize, for instance for making the traditional dish of "tamales". In fact this all means that an important part of their culture is about to disappear: for thousands of years it was the "milpa" that saved people in these regions.

"Preparation and finishing of agricultural work" (4) has also become of less economic importance. In the future it may be that other activities connected with farm production, like bookkeeping and contact with the administration of the Palm Project, will have more female participation. This, however, will require skills in

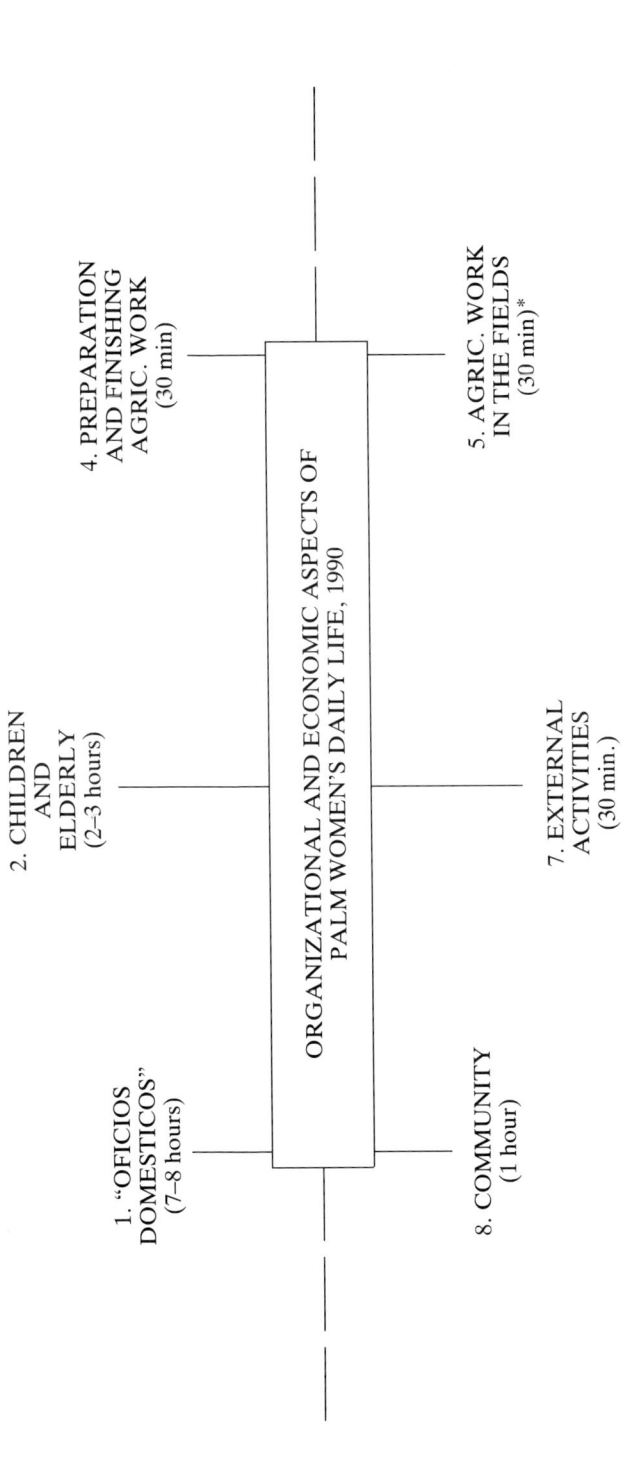

Figure 2. Palm women's daily activities and time use, Coto Sur, 1990. * = Changes in content compared to 1986.

- 1. "OFICIOS DOMESTICOS" (7–8 hours)
- 2. CHILDREN AND ELDERLY (2–3 hours)
- 4. PREPARATION AND FINISHING AGRIC. WORK (30 min)
- 5. AGRIC. WORK IN THE FIELDS (30 min)*
- 7. EXTERNAL ACTIVITIES (30 min.)
- 8. COMMUNITY (1 hour)

ORGANIZATIONAL AND ECONOMIC ASPECTS OF PALM WOMEN'S DAILY LIFE, 1990 writing and accounting that few of the women as yet possess. The agricultural activities have not disappeared completely, but have changed their content.

The five hours that peasant women used to spend on "household chores" ("oficios domesticos") have now been increased to 7–8 hours a day. They carry out much the same tasks as before, as household technology is still rather rudimentary. But they also engage in new activities; moreover, they themselves report that they try to improve their standards of housekeeping. For instance, they try to cook better food, or food they never made before, polish their many pots, or learn to sew. They buy detergent instead of the cheap blue soap, thinking that it will make the clothes of their family look better. They may learn to crochet to make more "adornos" (decorative items) for the house, and so on. And not to forget: they now watch more "telenovelas" on television than before.

So far the palmera women do not spend more time on external activities (7, 8), perhaps less. The exception is the women who run their own farms and who need to go to town for paperwork and to attend co-operative or project meetings. One notable difference is that the women now generally have less information concerning household income and budgets than before. They are perhaps also less interested. The pay cheque comes regularly on the first Friday of the month, and people can calculate how much they will receive. For most of them, there will be enough money to buy the necessary food. What they owe the Project has been deducted before they even see the cheque. Discussions within the household are not on how to survive, but how to spend a possible surplus. Will it be a down-payment on a television set, or new clothes for the children?

Summing up, we can say that a "palmera" woman now has fewer different tasks to organize, but that she spends more time on them (Figure 2). Although we find variations from household to household, most women say that they can now spend more time on housework and still allow themselves a 15–30 minute rest during the day. They themselves feel that the quality of their services to other household members has improved.

VI. Can We Talk About "Housewifization" in Coto Sur?

Now we return to our initial problem: whether "housewifization" is a concept appropriate to describe and analyse the changes we can distinguish among "palmera" women in Coto Sur when comparing 1986 with 1990. The changes in women's housework (Figures 1 and

2) go in the direction described by Rudie (1984): so far the women's work burden is diminishing in its productive or economic component, and increasing in the services to their family members. However, the third aspect – the ceremonial component – is not very important in this culture, where people rarely visit each other in their homes. So far the ceremonial side of their lives finds expression elsewhere. However, some changes can be detected – for instance, the interest in learning to crochet, to make decorations for the home, and so on. Here we will undoubtedly see more activity in the future.

A structural view of these changes, using the agricultural sector as our point of departure, could certainly give the impression that farm women are being pushed away from the fields and back to their homes. Palm growing has become an almost exclusive male arena. The big agro-industrial Palm Project is considered to be a "gender-neutral" project – at least that is how it is presented by project employees. They assume that they are dealing with "family farms", with unitary households. Women who are successful as palm growers are well treated and even cited as good examples at meetings and so on. But no study was carried out concerning how daily life was organized on the farms before the implementation of the project, nor the possible social consequences of it.[7] The administration considers it to be a very successful project, despite some technical and bureaucratic problems. Their view is based on yields and participation, and to a certain extent on mentality change among "maizeros" to make them become efficient farmers and contributors to "agricultura de cambio". Whether women become "housewives" or not, or to a greater extent than before, is of little interest. Or perhaps this is in accordance with the experts' ideas about "the order of things"?

Among the "palmeros" in Coto Sur, we can see a pattern where women are becoming more financially dependent on men than before, but this is not necessarily based on a traditional "breadwinner ideology". My impression is that they are well aware of the qualitative difference between being a "bananero" housewife on a plantation and their present situation. Of course this also has a lot to do with age: older women have more bargaining power than younger ones, and the women in our group are all above 30 by now. But this is also connected with the labour the women still provide on the farms, and the skills they possess. Although the burdens seem to become somewhat lighter for most of the women, as they now spend less time in productive functions on the farm, they still do the cooking and serve the people of the farm. Since it is only a few years ago that they supported their families when necessary, this is a capacity that may still be mobilized in emergencies. Having actively participated in the decisions to switch from basic grains to oil palms, the Coto Sur women have moved into this situation with their eyes open. Many of them have been quite enthusiastic. They are well aware of the reasons for changing the crops, and they discuss it with anyone willing to listen. As their main argument they mention security; it was they who earlier had to think of how to survive the next day, next week or month, and of how to feed their children. If the harvest failed, the women would have to step up their efforts, sending the children out to work, trying to find work themselves, trying to think up new survival strategies. Some of the women, especially the youngest ones, also see themselves as "partners in enterprise" together with their spouse. Only time will show if this becomes a general pattern.

An important factor in the women's arguments is the future for their children: that their investments now are for the good of their offspring, not for themselves. They feel strongly that they have to give them something – money, or valuable land or education, for their future. This has been far more important to the women than getting more time for themselves, which to some has come more as a pleasant surprise.

Another perhaps unexpected effect is that this kind of farming has served to induce discipline in the members of the family. It unites them in a way that the old system seldom did. The fact that the farm has to have its produce ready when the truck arrives each week is a new experience for many, in a culture that has never emphasized keeping to the clock. Many of the farm women say that having the new crop has disciplined their family, although they also admit this has been difficult at times. They all say that their family will have to become more responsible, a value they place in high esteem.

1. *Gender Relations*

Changes in the structure of family members' responsibility are in line with Coto Sur women's long-standing wishes to improve the moral qualities of their families. This has led us to the question of other aspects of housework than the concrete tasks – to what several authors have called its symbolic and identity side (Melhuus and Borchgrevink, 1984; Rudie, 1984; Oakley, 1974).

Women's housewifery has to be considered in the light of gender relations in general and the conjugal contract in particular. Many of the farm women in Coto Sur feel that they as women gained a stronger position in the household after establishing themselves as "parceleras" in the settlement some 10–15 years ago. A pioneer household could hardly survive without a clever woman to organize the productive and reproductive tasks on the farm. In earlier stages of their lives, these women had been highly dependent on men, at least if they were to lead a relatively decent life in their own and others' eyes. Single women without education had few possibilities to survive on their own with the children most of them have from an early age. In fact, the central point here concerns expectations held by men and women: what to expect of a spouse, in the formal or informal conjugal contract.

Women think that men should behave responsibly and take care of a woman and his children. But getting men to take responsibility for their children has often been a problem, and it still is. The laws may be stricter than before, but it is not easy to resort to legal action in this part of the country where lawyers and law-enforcement agents are few and far between.[8] The conjugal contract can have various forms, and it can also be renegotiated (Roldán, 1987). Among 40 farm couples interviewed in a small survey, about half had been married in church once, but not necessarily to the one they were now living with. It often turned out that they had first been married at a young age, but never bothered to get a divorce. For one thing the Catholic Church does not allow it; and although Costa Rica has liberal divorce laws, they have been living far from any lawyers, and people have no money to pay for a divorce anyway. Common-law marriages are therefore frequent. Women often say that they are married and speak of their companion as "mi marido" (my husband). Whether this is formally correct or not really makes no difference. Some women also said that they feel less dependent on a man when they are not legally married to him. They were then able to negotiate with their compañero, since they could threaten to withdraw from a relationship if he did not give them money for cooking and other services. Being married would not give them the same liberty. Others wanted to get married to "safeguard" having a provider, and considered that gave better security. In my material there is no evidence for claiming that one or the other solution was preferred, although church marriage did enjoy higher status.

What seems clear is that if expectations held by men and by women are not fulfilled, this has different consequences for them.

Women's expectations of becoming provided for by a man have also been embedded in all their survival strategies. In a relationship, women were therefore ready to endure much as long as they were provided for. When they were not, they would have to provide for themselves and their children, but they very seldom broke out of a relationship for that reason. That would not have been acceptable, nor would they have had many chances as single mothers.

When men did not fulfil their own expectations of providing for a family, or things became complicated otherwise – they had been "tempted" by another woman, for instance – a relatively normal procedure would be to abandon the "wife". "He left" ("se fué") is such a common saying among women in this region that one may easily think it is the order of the day.

All cultures have ideas of maleness and femaleness. In Mesoamerican rural society there are also quite explicit prescriptions for gender behaviour. To be a good woman means to accept not to leave the house without asking for permission, never to question the work burdens inside the house, and always to behave in a subordinate way (Biesanz et al., 1982; Ferro and Quirós, 1988). It also means that any activities outside "their sphere" are performed for the common good of the family. Agricultural work is, for instance, always referred to by the women in Coto Sur as "ayuda" (help). In this culture, to be a farmer does not form part of the "natural" role for women. On the other hand, the few women farmers living in Coto Sur are admired by others if they farm in order to be able to take proper care of their children. But a woman who is a farmer because she wants to be one, or is interested in such work, is considered "hacerse muy macho" (to make herself much of a man), which is a negative label used by men and women alike.

To be a woman means first of all to be a mother; the idea of men as providers for women and children is very strong among both women and men. Motherhood underlies everything else. Being a mother is the most important part of any woman's identity, and to be esteemed by others as a good mother means that your children behave well. That they do not go "vagabonding", running off or making trouble in society, and so on. Women dedicate quite a lot of time and energy to organizing the lives of their children long after they have left their mother's house.

To women, housewifery and motherhood is one and the same thing, and cannot be separated. Both women and men have very strong ideas about women's position as the centre in the home. To be able to establish a home of their own is therefore vital to women, to try to fulfil their own and others' expectations. Most of the farm women in Coto Sur have devoted all their efforts to trying to establish and to keep up some kind of a home. At times it has been very difficult, both on the plantations and later as pioneering poor peasants.

Nor did becoming "parceleros" in the 1970s prove to be the realization of the men's dreams either: with a few exceptions the farms did not yield much. Many peasants were not used to individual farming and they remained poor, without possibilities of providing adequately for their families. What we are now beginning to see, with the introduction of oil palms, is an increasing differentiation between men in the area, depending on how professional they can become as palm farmers.

It remains to be seen what will happen within the palm households concerning internal negotiations – if and how gender relations will decide the directions they are to take. For one thing, the financial obligations of the palm farming households will necessarily be decisive for all negotiations. Households run up huge debts, and are embedded in a system where banks and projects have legal demands on them as never before.

Nor is it given to know how financially dependent women will be on their bread-winner. This will depend on how money is distributed among members of the household now that women do not have the option of making their little "pin" money. The women are well acquainted with a cash economy, especially those who have lived on the banana plantations. It seems that the men now have more control over the money, as they as landowners have to go to pick up the cheque from the Palm Co-operative every month. Struggles within the households have started, but it is difficult to predict any specific outcomes.

VII. "Housewifization" Rejected?

Our initial question concerned whether the changes observed in Coto Sur can be seen as part of a "worldwide housewifization process". With the incorporation of this area in the world economy through the "Agricultura de Cambio", the Palm Project, have come major changes in the daily work of women, changes that may well look like "housewifization". Indeed, they may seem to be part of a process where household and enterprise in Coto Sur may eventually become completely separated. This process is well known from industrialized countries, the so-called "decoupling of farm and house" (Adams, 1988). It has led to a new division of labour, sometimes said to masculinize agriculture, at other times to increase women's participation through work in the fields. Frequently it has led to increased wage employment for women; time will show if Coto Sur also will experience such a development. Of main interest to politicians and others are such quantifiable changes. Using a concept like "housewifization" to describe these can be highly inaccurate, because, as we have argued, the term would need to be expanded.

We should note, however, that all this presupposes the existence of a wage labour market, lacking in this region. It also raises another question that needs to be investigated: women are losing their control of the farm's resources; while men seem to be reinforcing their position through modern agro-politics.

Many of the findings in this study indicate that the peasant women in Coto Sur are in a process of becoming more "full-time" housewives than before: becoming more economically dependent on a male bread-winner, they spend more time inside the house, dedicate more time and energy to service for others, as well as stepping up their consumption, and so on. Seen in isolation, these findings seem to support the "housewifization thesis" as they meet Oakley's definition of a housewife.

However, in our study we have noted that the changes now taking place in Coto Sur also make it easier for men and women alike to fulfil cultural expectations, both to themselves and to each other. Both women and men of this generation in Coto Sur agree on what is happening, that women can now dedicate more time and energy to being mothers and wives, and men can live up to the ideal of being providers. Many farmers in Coto Sur can for the first time realize their visions about the good life. On the other hand, they will also have to renegotiate their conjugal contracts in the light of these new conditions. Most "parceleros" in Coto Sur do not have a "straight" family record: we find very few life-long monogamous relationships. Yet, in discussing "housewifization", such a situation has not been taken into account by most writers.

VIII. Concluding Remarks

This leads me to conclude that the changes observed in Coto Sur cannot be analysed merely as part of a new trend whereby all women are becoming "housewives worldwide", as Maria Mies would seem to suggest. I find difficulties in applying "housewifization" as a concept to cover the changes currently taking place in Coto Sur. It might even blur the outlines and make them less visible. The change processes experienced by these peasant households are far more complex than the situation captured by Maria Mies's concept of "housewifization".

Concrete case-studies focusing on change over time can draw attention to the complex interplay of gender, capitalism, agropolitics and individual strategies, to mention a few points. This is the kind of perspective we need in connection with "housewifization". It is a difficult term because it indicates an overall process, a movement, rather than describing a given situation. And when many different processes are taking place simultaneously, one concept alone cannot incorporate them all. There are, for instance, differentiating mechanisms between the households; we see proletarianization and marginalization of groups of peasants, the impact of state actions, and so on.[9]

This, however, does not lead me to conclude that we should abandon the concept completely, only that we should be very careful in applying it in research as an analytical tool. The term has so far been applied rather too leniently, I think. It needs to be scrutinized and perhaps further developed, as it undoubtedly does possess a political value in feminist scholarship. The possible analytical value of the concept lies in its pointing to theorizing structure, but we need to understand if and how it is related to human agency and contextuality.

The women in Coto Sur demonstrated the significance of contextuality, both by the strategies they chose in order to be provided for, and in how the term "housewife" to them can have different meanings at different stages in life. It certainly puzzled me the first time I conducted my field-work and many women introduced themselves as "ama-de-casa" (housewife) when they, to my European eyes, were obviously bearing quite a heavy burden of the productive work on the farm. This should remind us as researchers to analyse concepts within their relevant cultural settings. The way Mies *et al.* address the problem, it tends to oversimplify such issues as social change, gender, dependency, and so on, which convinces me that it is a concept embedded in Western thinking.

Finally, we must ask: why has this concept become so popular? Is it because Western feminist scholarship has been struggling so much with the paradoxical situation of the housewife in industrialized societies? Or is it because we have so far lacked analytical tools to handle macro relations in women's studies? Or because we assume that women are subject to the same oppression the world over? Will it help us and other women to talk about a "housewifization" process, will it empower people to improve their life situation? Such questions need to be posed – and answered.

Notes

1. I would like to thank Siri Gerrard, Lisbet Holtedahl, Kristi Anne Stølen and Mariken Vaa for valuable comments on earlier versions of this chapter. Susan Høivik made my English readable.
2. The empirical material was collected on two field trips to Costa Rica, 1986 and 1990. It is based on life story interviews with 29 women, semi-structured interviews with both men and women and participation in daily work on the farms. The majority of the respondents lived on farms in the central La Plancha area of the Coto Sur settlement in southern Costa Rica. I also spent some time living and working with a team preparing a development project for peasant women in the area. Odilia Matarrita assisted me in the field.
3. Such rural settlements are often referred to as "reformed sectors" in Costa Rica. They are designated areas where landless peasants have been granted land through a scheme organized by the state agency IDA (Instituto Desarrollo Agrario). For a more detailed discussion of the role of this policy in Costa Rica, see Seligson (1980) and Barahona (1980). For a survey of the situation of peasant women, see Madden (1985).
4. The Golfito Division of Costa Rica extending into Panamá (Chiriquí Land Co.) was the most important zone for banana production in all Central America from the Second World War to around 1975. At its peak in the 1960s around 12,000 hectares were devoted to banana cultivation, spread over a great number of farms (fincas). The last plantation closed down in 1984–85. Several explanations have been launched for the final withdrawal of United Brands: the market situation, a long drawn-out strike, an extra export tax, low productivity, and so on. For more details on the banana plantations and "La Compañía", see Lopez (1988), Ellis (1983), Burbach and Flynn (1980) and Hall (1984).
5. In the autumn of 1986 the payment was 150 colones per day (US$ 1 = approx. 60 col., 1986).
6. The investment in 1990 ran at about 1 million colones (the exchange rate was approximately 90 colones to US$ 1) for a 20 hectares farm. This is substantial for these households at this stage, having been used to earning 3,000–7,000 colones per month.
7. The project itself is planned to cover approximately 4,300 hectares of land. The settlement has an acreage of more than 18,000 hectares. This means that the majority of the peasants will be excluded from participation in the project. In turn, this will lead to differentiation between the two groups of farmers.
8. Until 1948 a father had the right by law to punish a child (Biesanz et al., 1981). Costa Rica now has a Family Code granting children born out of wedlock the same rights as all other children. The problem often arises in connection with pensions and inheritance and so on. See Rivera B. (1981) for a survey of women's legal rights in Costa Rica. For an overview see García and Gómez (1989).
9. See Arizpe and Aranda (1986), Medrano (1981), Achío and Mora (1988) and Deere and León (1987) for Latin American studies of the effects for women caused

by new agro-politics. Marginalization of people from rural areas seems to be a continuing process. For the current situation in Costa Rica, see Reuben (1989).

References

Achío, M. and Mora, P. 1988. La obrera florista y la subordinación de la mujer. *Revista de Ciencias Sociales* (Universidad de Costa Rica), No. 39, pp. 47–56.
Adams, J. H. 1988. The Decoupling of Farm and Household: Differential Consequences of Capitalist Development on Southern Illinois and Third World Family Farms. *Comparative Studies of Society and History*, pp. 453–482.
Arizpe, L. and Aranda, J. 1986. Women Workers in the Strawberry Agribusiness in Mexico. In E. Leacock *et al.* (eds), *Women's Work. Development and the Division of Labour by Gender*. Mass.: Bergin & Garvey.
Barahona, R. F. 1980. *Reforma Agraria y Poder Politico. El caso de Costa Rica*. San José: EDUCA.
Beneria, L. and Roldàn 1987. *The Crossroads of Class and Gender*. Chicago: University of Chicago Press.
Bennholdt-Thomsen, V. 1988. Why Do Housewives Continue to be Created in the Third World Too, and The Proletarian is Dead: Long Live the Housewife, both in Mies *et al.* (1988).
Biesanz, R., Biesanz, K. and Biesanz, M. 1982. *The Costa Ricans*. Englewood Cliffs: Prentice-Hall.
Boserup, E. 1970. *Women's Role in Economic Development*. London: George Allen and Unwin.
Bossen, L. H. 1984). *The Redivision of Labour. Women and Economic Choice in Four Guatemalan Communities*. Albany: State University of New York Press.
Burbach, R. and Flynn, P. 1980. *Agribusiness in the Americas*. New York: Monthly Review Press/NACLA.
Deere, C. D. and León, M. 1987. Introduction. In Deere and Leon (eds) (1987).
Deere, C. D. and León, M. (eds) 1987. *Rural Women and State Policy. Feminist Perspectives on Latin American Agricultural Development*. Boulder, Colorado: Westview Press.
Ellis, F. 1983. *Las Transnacionales del Banano en Centroamérica*. San José: EDUCA.
Ferro, C. and Quirós, A. M. 1988. *Mujer, realidad religiosa y comunicación*. San José: EDUCA.
García, A. I. and Gomáriz, E. (eds) 1989. *Mujeres Centroamericanas*. San José: Vol. II, FLACSO.
Hall, C. 1984. *Costa Rica, una interpretación geográfica con perspectiva histórica*. San José: Editorial Costa Rica.
Harris, O. 1981. Households as Natural Units. In Young, Wolkowitz & McCullagh (eds) (1981).
Long, N. 1984. Introduction. In Long (ed.) (1984).
Long, N. (ed.) 1984. *Family and Work in Rural Societies*. London: Tavistock Publ.
Lopez, J. R. 1988. *La Economía del Banano en Centroamérica*. San José: DEI.
Madden, L. 1985. El Agro Costarricense y la Situación de la Mujer Campesina: Recomendaciones de Pólíticas, Programas y Proyectos. Mimeo, Ponencia en el 45 Congreso Internacional de Americanistas, Bogotá.
Medrano, D. 1981. Efectos del proceso de cambio sobre la condición de la mujer rural: El caso de las obreras floristas de la agroindustria exportadora de flores de Sabana de Bogotá. Bogota: OIT.
Melhuus, M. and Borchgrevink, T. 1984. Husarbeid: tidsbinding av kvinner. In Rudie (ed.) (1984).

Mies, M. 1986. *Patriarchy and Accumulation on a World Scale. Women in the International Division of Labour*. London: Zed Books.

Mies, M., Bennholdt-Thomsen, V. and von Werlhof, C. 1988. *Women: The Last Colony*. London: Zed Books.

Moore, H. 1988. *Feminism and Anthropology*. Cambridge: Polity Press.

Oakley, A. 1974. *Woman's Work; The Housewife Past and Present*. New York: Pantheon Books.

Reuben S. W. (ed.), 1989. *Los Campesinos frente a la nueva decada*. San José: Editorial Porvenir.

Rivera B., T.E. 1981. *Evolución de los Derechos Politicos de la Mujer en Costa Rica*. San José: Ministerio de Cultura, Juventud y Deporte.

Rogers, B. 1980. *The Domestication of Women*. London: Tavistock.

Roldán, M. 1987. (a) Class, Gender and Asymmetrical Exchanges within Households and (b) The Marriage Contract: Renegotiation and Consciousness, both in Benería and Roldán 1987.

Rudie, I. 1984. Innledning. In I. Rudie, (ed.), *Myk start hard landing*. Oslo: Universitetsforlaget.

Seligson, M. 1980. *El campesino y el capitalismo agrario de Costa Rica*. San José: Editorial Costa Rica.

Skjønsberg, E. 1990. Kvinner og EF. Oslo: Utredning fra Norsk Kvinnesaksforening, Kvinnefronten, Kvinneuniversitetet.

Townsend, J. 1989. Gender and Generation in Land Settlement/Colonization. Paper presented to the 1989 Commonwealth Bureau Workshop on Gender and Development, Newcastle-upon-Tyne, England.

Valestrand, H. 1990. Somos Humildes – pero Decentes, Peasant Women in Coto Sur, Costa Rica. Institute of Social Sciences, University of Tromsø.

Whitehead, A. 1981. I'm hungry mum. In Young, Wolkowitz and McCullagh (eds) (1981).

Wilson, F. 1985. Women and Agricultural Change in Latin America. Some Concepts Guiding Research, *World Development*, Vol. 13, No. 9, pp. 1017–1035.

Young, K., Wolkowitz, C. and McCullagh, R. (eds) 1981. *Of Marriage and the Market*. London: CSE Books.

Part III
Politics and Institutional Change – an Introduction

This last section highlights the complex relationship between gender politics, implementation and outcomes in different institutional contexts.

The Malay women in Rudie's article live in a context of rapid economic change, through which a local way of life is more firmly integrated within large-scale market and political structures. The gender balance that previously characterized men and women as household members is becoming threatened as the domestic mode of production is crumbling and official development ideologies disregard female economic contributions in the family. Rudie presents the case of two female political leaders who are striving to make inroads for women into an expanding public field. She shows how domestic gender is inextricably interwoven with the ways in which gender penetrates public life and re-examines the very distinction between domestic and public domains introduced by Rosaldo (1974).

Gerrard analyses the impact of a small fisheries development project for women on the shores of Lake Victoria, Tanzania. Through an examination of the cooperation between men and women from the village and implementers from outside, Gerrard shows how local power relations, primarily based on gender and clan membership, are being challenged and negotiated. She depicts the planned intervention as an on-going socially constructed and negotiated process, not simply the execution of an already specified plan of action with expected outcomes. She demonstrates that policy implementation is not simply a top-down process, but that it is shaped by an interaction between the different actors involved. Through gender negotiations the tradeswomen acquired a new role as mediators between the local community and national and international development institutions. This role enhanced their position in relation to men. They became a source of inspiration for development, recognized by both men and women.

The last two articles in the volume deal with institutional change as a means of promoting equality and the emancipation of women. Berg and Gundersen analyse the impact on gender relations of the legal reform in post-revolutionary Mozambique, by examining cases presented to the popular tribunal in a neighbourhood in the outskirts of Maputo. The tribunals offer dispute settlement of conflicts that women and men experience in their daily lives. The establishment of the popular tribunals has opened women's access to the legal system, but when it comes to substantive law, the situation is quite complex. Principles of gender equality are often overruled by traditional norms, customs and pragmatism based on the lay judges' experience and knowledge of the local reality, which are characterized by male dominance and female subordination and poverty. Berg and Gundersen are critical of the introduction of formal gender equality in societies where social and cultural norms are based on difference. They suggest that *de jure* equality often conceals the fact that society is gendered and may thus confirm or even aggravate the situation of *de facto* discrimination. Berg and Gundersen also offer an alternative approach to legal transformation in such contexts.

In the final contribution, Lotherington and Flemmen discuss the gender negotiations currently taking place in the International Labour Organization as a consequence of the implementation of the ILO Plan of Action on Equal Opportunity for Men and Women. This plan of action not only represents a new approach to the planning and implementation of assistance, but also challenges gender notions and practices in the Labour Organization itself. Based on an assessment of the different actors' positions and strategies in the negotiations, they evaluate the probability of a policy change. Their conclusion is that the prospect of such change is poor in the short run. However, if a variety of strategies are used in a consistent way, the future for a gender-responsive policy in the ILO will be brighter.

These articles show that policy is transformed when it acquires a social meaning not set out in the original political statements. The outcome of interventions to improve the position of women comes as a result of the interactions, negotiations, and social and cognitive struggles that take place between different social actors, not just those present in face-to-face situations, also those who are absent but who nevertheless affect both actions and outcomes.

8
The Symbolism of Gender Politics: A Case of Malay Female Leadership

INGRID RUDIE

The following discussion of Malay local female leadership is an attempt at analytically sorting out different strands in the problem of change and continuity. In more specific terms, I shall argue that the leaders are ultimately striving to perpetuate domestic gender balance in a period of rapid economic development through which a local way of life is more firmly integrated in large-scale market and political structures. Gender balance is grounded in an essential economic equality between women and men as household members – an equality in resource control which, however, does not entail similarity of tasks. This equality enables women to meet a set of expectations in a wider network of kin and family, which in turn gives them wider social belonging and more alternatives for attachment than that of their nuclear families. In an earlier publication I argue that most Malay women are trying to perpetuate this position, but at the same time they are often left worse off relative to men because the domestic mode of production is crumbling and official development ideologies overlook female economic contributions in the family (Rudie 1989a). In the present chapter I shall concentrate on another aspect of the same complex of problems, trying to show how some leader figures are specifically trying to make passageways into an expanding public field. For domestic gender is inextricably interwoven with the ways in which gender penetrates public life – public both in the sense of high-level officialdom, and the most small-scale forms of local politics and ceremony.

These intentions leave us with two main questions of analysis and conceptualization. First, it becomes necessary to re-examine the definition of the public domain, as well the very distinction between domestic and public, and pay specific attention to the gender rules of politics and administration, and of market and ceremony. The second point is concerned with the perspective in which gender politics are to be seen. I will focus on its symbolic side, adopting a vew of "symbolic" which sees it as a way of *grasping* and *acting* the unspeakable rather than as an alternative language (Sperber, 1975; Strathern, 1988). Quoting Clay (1977), Strathern suggests that a symbolic expression is "the actualization rather than the representations of people's shared understandings", and continues: "This description accords with recent re-thinking of the nature of symbolic activity, in critiques of the supposition that we can understand symbols simply as expressive instruments of meaning" (Strathern, 1988, p. 174).

Later in the same book (p. 271) she holds that what are "symbolic constructs" from the analyst's point of view, are "recipes for social action" from the native point of view. In this line of thought symbolization can be handled as part of a spearhead discourse – a negotiation in acts rather than verbal argument about alternative ways of life.

The gender politics of the leaders are embedded in the symbolism of everyday life – only within this can they elaborate their complex roles which contain elements of teacher, model and social entrepreneur. It is an order that they share with the clients, who would not accept the label "client" if they were made familiar with it, but are rather "friends" in accordance with a local concept of ascribed, collective friendship (neighbour-friend). According to this wide definition friendship constitutes the social medium within which the "impersonal" market and bureaucratic goods can be delivered.

In order to set the stage for my actors, I will now describe briefly some features of the Malaysian political cultures, and the changing preconditions for gender balance on the local level.

I. Malaysia: The Old and the New Complexity

Malaysia is a multi-ethnic federation liberated from British colonial rule in 1957. During the Colonial period Chinese and Indians took part in the modern sectors of the economy, both as wage workers and as entrepreneurs, while the Malay community remained predominantly rural, and retained a social structure based on rank rather than class differences.

If Malays played a weak part in economic development until recently, they have been more important politically. They obtained political hegemony at Independence, and have since then retained this position. Malaysian politics are naturally heavily centred on development issues, and a number of impressive projects have appeared during the last 30 years. These are partly complete government enterprises for land development and community building, like the FELDA (Federal Land Development Agency) and related agencies; partly financing and counselling strategies aimed at building up private Malay entrepreneurship, like the MARA (Majlis Amanah Rakyat – Council of Trust for the Indigenous People); and partly more multifarious strategies for improving established communities. KEMAS (Kemajuan Masyarakat – Community Development Divison of the Ministry of National and Rural Development) is a ready example.

Development has to a large extent meant developing enterprise and differential skills among the Malays, and New Economic Policy (NEP) is explicitly geared towards this aim – towards breaking down the ethnic division of work in which Malays were primarily rural and of peasant status. The stress on recruiting Malays to new types of career implicitly leads to recruitment of a certain number of Malay women even though there are no special measures to secure the participation of women. But there are other trends in development ideologies which either plainly overlook women's productive role, or highlight reproductive work to such a degree as to boost up the formation of a specialized housewife identity (Rudie, 1989).

The Malaysian political structure must be characterized as centralized, and tightly intertwined with a heavy administration which rests on direct lines of command from Federal to State to District level. On the Federal level there are more than 20 Ministries, each with its various departments which are again further subdivided into branches with more specific tasks. To take an example, the Ministry of Agriculture includes four Departments, each consisting of different divisions. In addition, there are seven statutory bodies each of which takes care of a specific development activity or project. In this way all public issues seem to emanate in a very direct way from the Government. In contrast to this, local government as a democratically recruited institution is weakly developed, and the mere idea of it has been subject to considerable doubts and controversies since Independence (Norris, 1980).

The political system has been characterized as permeated by political patrimonialism. The dominant political parties probably derive part of their power from personal loyalties of a patron–client type, stretching from the top echelons down to the level of the local branches (Gale, 1981). A hierarchical administrative structure and political friendships also of a hierarchical nature are thus tightly intertwined, and the term "Government" is loaded with meaning.

In everyday speech it is a blanket term covering political establishment, administration and ultimate patron, all in one. My vantage point is local, but my focus will be on the extra restrictions facing women in a patrimonial system.

The personal element is part of the symbolism of political life, and makes the system move. This does not amount to saying that all favours go to close friends. It has a wider meaning than that, and is embedded in a communicative style: seeing a person face to face works better than just writing a letter. A pleasant manner is highly valued, and even the most brief and formal encounter is frequently lined with attentiveness of a more personal character. Malay society is of course not unique in stressing the personal element in market and bureaucratic encounters – this is done to a smaller or greater extent in all societies. But a high degree of person orientation in public matters combined with a high degree of gender segregation places particular restrictions on cross-gender cooperation.

II. Gender Balance in a Local Setting

My empirical case material is drawn from a cluster of villages in the central and most densely populated part of Kelantan. Kelantan has a few demographic, cultural and economic characteristics which may have affected gender relations in general and the productive roles of women in particular. The vicinity to Thailand has stimulated border trade, and with improved road connections to the rest of the Federation, the State's importance as a thoroughfare for goods has increased in recent years. The overwhelming majority of Malays in the population (93.3 per cent) has left room for Malay trading enterprise; in fact, male as well as female Malay traders in other states have often originated from Kelantan.

Field-work in this area was carried out in two periods widely separated in time: the first visit took place in 1965, and a new study was undertaken through three separate visits in 1986, 1987 and 1988. During the two decades between field-work the villages changed notably in terms of their economic structure. They used to be communities of small cultivators, where cultivation was often supplemented by other activities, mostly part time, but where access to land was the basis for security, and hence an ultimate goal. In this system women had a firm grip on the means of production and the exchange processes. They were landowners in their own right, they contributed heavily to agricultural production, and they were responsible for the marketing. Responsibility for marketing the products of the household provided the women with a basic skill for trading, which some of them cultivated further into a specialized full-time occupation. Trading as a female speciality was, and still is, a strong feature of Kelantan society. Women's identity as productive persons was very visible; the notion of women as essentially self-supporting was a central one.

At the same time there was a clear segregation between the sexes in public activities. Formal religious rules underlined the leadership of men, and when women moved outside their own homes, they had several taboos to observe. Still it would be misleading to say that the life space of women was restricted to the domestic sphere; they had a part to play in the public sphere of the village, they had decisive influence in matters of family politics and economy, and they had ritual and networking functions of major importance to the viability of household and community. This conveys the picture of a society permeated by a certain duality in rules and realities. Rules derived from religion underlined men's leadership and protector role, rules derived from custom in a wider sense underlined female solidarity and women's aptitude for cooperation between themselves.

Modern development in Kelantan is uneven compared to that in the western states of Malaysia (see Lie and Lund in this volume). It has mostly been focused on education and the creation of infrastructure, while industrial development is still weak. The local labour market at present offers a number of job opportunities for women with specific educational qualifications – in teaching, health service and clerical jobs, but practically no opportunities in unskilled industrial work – which would be the outlet for those who lack more specific educational qualifications, or have failed to acquire the traditional skills of trade. In contrast, there has been a steady increase in male opportunities in such occupations as transport services and construction work following public enterprise and the general growth of urban agglomerations. Male job opportunities are thus more evenly distributed to meet different levels of skill and education. It is this development in particular which has tipped the gender balance in the sense that women's importance as providers has become less prominent, relatively, than it used to be. This situation has placed its stamp on the local villages in different ways. A large number of the adult men commute to jobs in nearby towns. In this process gardening declines, and with it an important impetus for reproducing female trading skills. Many women are turned into "housewives" – in fact, a new word for "housewife" had become part of people's active vocabulary when I came back to the field in the 1980s.

III. Development and the Gendered Society

Despite formal equality in educational opportunities, and despite more varied modern job opportunities in certain regions on the west coast, Malaysia exhibits some of the classical features of female economic marginalization which have given rise to disenchantment about development among feminist researchers and politicians. Attention has been drawn to several instances of failure of development intentions in Malaysia to benefit the common people in general, and women in particular. Such failure has partly been attributed to a lack of correspondence between the understanding of urban planners and the real needs and qualifications of rural women in what Rokiah Talib characterizes as a "top–bottom policy orientation and implementation" (Talib, 1984). Others are more concerned with the "silence" and "shyness" of rural women in front of officialdom (e.g. Lockhead and Ramachandran, 1982), a feature which I also observed in numerous day-to-day situations during my own field-work. The problem can thus be described as a problem of practical and symbolic discontinuities between a local small-scale public sphere in which women have been securely positioned, and a large-scale one in which they are at a loss.

In village ceremonial women have cooperated in wider circles. They have been supportive of each other, and competitive (about prestige) at the same time. Market activities and ceremonial cooperation and competition have been the main activities through which networking and organizational skills have been developed. The leading question for my research in the late 1980s was what the women "could take along into modern society" of their traditional strength in household and community – a strength which was rooted in the extended family organization.

Thus the debate whether Malay and Malaysian society is "patriarchal" or not seems to be one in which it is possible to defend different positions. This same ambivalence seems to be present in Lenore Manderson's book on the history of the women's branch of UMNO (United Malay National Organization)[1] as her text also tends to convey a double argumentation. On the one hand, it draws a conventional picture of the "meek" and "shy" Malay women, village-bred and homebound. On the other hand, she claims that

Malay women were never without influence, not even in the political field (Manderson, 1980). To resolve what looks like contradiction and double evidence, we need an analytical perspective which can convey the complexity rather than decide between the "autonomy view" and the "patriarchy view". Female shyness, female autonomy and female political influence belong in different brackets of life, and are activated through different kinds of social relations. This is a problem of "fit" between different levels of socio-cultural integration, and the individual level must be included among these. We can then also add the precondition that all these levels must demonstrate the gendering of society, for it is not only persons that are gendered – social fields are also gendered. This is just a logical implication of the concept of gender itself. For gender is "cultural and social sex", and society is gendered to the degree that there are rules about the propriety for men and women to enter certain roles and fields of activity. When modern societies abolish some of these rules, this neutralizes gender in certain areas. This process is at the same time a process of individuation, and here lies, perhaps, a basic problem inherent to "gender and development". It becomes a problem if the individuation of men and women run at uneven paces, as they are then not able to circulate with the same efficiency in a society based on individual mobility and formal gender neutralization of positions (Rudie, 1984). Differences in "individuation" between men and women are a point on which a mass of research seems to converge, although in different analytical traditions, using different conceptual tools. Thus, Chodrow explored it in a psychiatric frame of reference early in the 1970s (Chodrow 1975). Ortner, in a presentation of practice analysis, suggests that the reproduction of gender relations in the family may be relatively untouched by processes taking place elsewhere in society (Ortner, 1984, pp. 156–157). Strathern's analysis of Melanesian world views draws attention to conceptions of the female body as able to contain the unborn child in the same way as the family contains the individual (Strathern, 1988).

The gendering of Malay sub-society takes different guises in different fields of interaction. Within the *household* the position of supporter or resource person can perhaps be characterized as gender neutral on one level of analysis (Rudie, 1971, 1984). The gender division of labour in the domestic mode of production was mild, and this carries over into the field of reproduction in a modern situation, as husbands frequently do a considerable amount of domestic chores in families where both spouses are in paid occupations. Close kinship has been women's organizational and emotional resource, but also to a degree men's. Up to the last few decades the extended family was a powerful and flexible base of organization which tended to encompass the marriage relation (Ortner, 1981). Sisters and parents could substitute husbands as partners in economic cooperation, and the marriage relation was brittle. Rank followed seniority rather than gender – only at points of articulation with religious and administrative institutions have men emerged as primary representatives of households.

Religion places men and women partly in gender-segregated spiritual authority structures, at the same time as the male authority structure takes precedence over the female. But *village ceremonial* in a wider sense does not repeat this pattern in an unambiguous way. In certain areas, such as marriage celebrations, women used to have distinct ceremonial collective responsibilities, complementary and juxtaposed to, rather than subordinated to, those of men. At present there is a contest going on between a principle of subordination and a principle of juxtaposition. (Rudie, 1988, 1990). Whatever the outcome of this contest, there is an organizational and practical core in women's ceremonial responsibilities which is still very much alive, and this is an important substratum of some of the activities which will be described below.

Trade and life at the market-place have been women's training ground in individuation, and their source of bargaining power in the family and community. It has nourished a type of competitive individualism which is reminiscent of modern society and stands in peculiar contrast to principles of loyalty and pre-established rank which are also present in society.

The bureaucracy, which has continued to develop and expand after independence, seems permeated by patrimonialism or patron-clientism. It is essentially a hierarchical structure which is hard to gender-neutralize, and hard to penetrate for women despite market training in self-sufficiency, and despite social skills obtained through exposure in market and ceremonial.

The gender-segregated society is not automatically, in logical terms, gender ranked. There is at least a theoretical possibility that the complementarity may be so deep as to preclude comparison. This opens up for different further possibilities. There may be parallel male and female hierarchies, or there may be male hierarchies, but not female ones. I will argue that the Malay situation is a more complex variety of the first possibility. Another clue to this problem can be found in Lenore Manderson's work. There have been different views among female UMNO leaders whether ambition should concentrate on competing for representation in the regular parliamentary assemblies, or on developing the female branch of the party as an organization taking care of special areas of interest. Arguments against the first choice were to the effect that women would be fearful or reluctant to compete directly against men (Manderson, 1980, pp. 71–77). This is a crucial observation which can give an insight into the gendering of society. The road to equalization is through a measure of gender neutralization, or at least rules which can regulate the relevance of gender in particular situations. Malay sub-society is hovering between different principles, and Manderson's record of the discussion around the structure of political competition shows an early incidence of negotiation between them.

On the basis of the description so far, I will now suggest a dynamic model of the gendering of Malay sub-society such as it seems to be working at the moment. The model builds on a distinction between domestic and extra-domestic fields of interaction, and is so far reminiscent of Rosaldo's (1974) model, according to which male dominance rests on a social practice in which men "inhabit" the public sphere, while women "inhabit" the domestic sphere. The meaning which I attribute to "domestic" and "public" (or extra-domestic) is, however, different, and more indebted to Marilyn Strathern's (1988) analysis of the gendering of Melanesian society. She draws a distinction between "same-sex" and "cross-sex" relationships, and argues that in Melanesia cross-sex relationships belong to the domestic field, while extra-domestic relationships are overwhelmingly same-sex. What is more, men more than women enter into such same-sex collectivities. These collectivities have two important qualities. First, they can be expanded to a larger scale just by expanding the network (while the domestic structure limits itself in this respect). Second, the same-sex collectivities are mediated, which means that they exist through and by tokens (gifts) between individuals, and this also opens up for symbolic debts and ranking. There are many differences between "primitive" Melanesian and "advanced" Malaysian society, but both have the same basic structure of gender segregation in the "public" and suspension of it in the "domestic" sector. The reluctance of Malay women to compete against men is founded on a conception of reality in which male and female hierarchies must be separate. For men and women to compete, new rules have to be made for cross-sex relationships, which also allow friendship and clientship. It is my belief that all societies have limits on this coordination of male and female, but some have it more than others. This points back to my earlier reflections on the importance of the personal element in social encounters: when the hierarchies are also cast in an idiom of personal loyalties or friendships, there are even more barriers against mixing male and female lines.

In the Malay gender structure, family and household make up a field in which men and women are tied together in primary relationships in which male and female rank orders are subsumed under the order of seniority, and blood or marriage ties take the danger out of cross-sex closeness. When women (and in principle also men) need a breakthrough between the gender-specific public collectivities, then it is most safely achieved through a cross-sex primary relationship as a mediating node. This is in fact how political hierarchies are built up: leaders in the female branches of political parties are recruited largely from among the wives of male leaders. This tends to permeate the structure from national to local level.

IV. Two Leader Styles on Local Level

My examples are Limah and Kamariah, who operate in two separate neighbourhoods. They are both in their fifties, both are firmly rooted in their neighbourhoods through kin ties and upbringing. Both are chairwomen of local women's branches of the UMNO party, both are concerned with teaching and developing skills and political consciousness in women. But in some other respects they are different. Kamariah's authority rests on a stock of esoteric knowledge and personal magic, while Limah's main asset is an unusual capacity for networking and initiating different activities. These differences are not only due to personal characteristics, but also mirror different structural positions.

In his book on Malay and Indonesian leadership Ahmad Kamar distinguishes between front leaders who initiate social behaviour, by virtue of prestige, power or position, and leaders who

> may also work from the middle and follow the needs of the people. A particular type is the opinion leader who guides from the "rear" and gives advice on the satisfaction of needs and the achievement of objectives. The "middle" and "rearguard" types of leaders are commonly found in rural societies, particularly in

South-East Asian countries. They may be referred to as informal leaders (Kamar, 1984, p. 2).

Leaders who are both rural and female may seem doubly determined to be middle and rearguard leaders. However, when we move focus down to local level and relativize our scale accordingly, the distinction between the prestigious and the non-prestigious becomes more blurred, as well as that between formal and informal. For both Limah and Kamariah have some support in formal roles if formal means the established bureaucracy, and at least Kamariah has a measure of what Kamar possibly means by "prestige", although I will prefer to describe it by going more closely into native concepts and the concrete social realities which surround them.

My leaders are "chairwomen" and "community developers", they are "examples" (*contoh*); they teach and organize. But they would be without any effect if they did not have a personal appeal to their followers. There are two elements in this appeal – loyalty and "magic". I will refrain from using the term "charisma", because that carries the notion of strong individuality detached from structural determinants. The personal appeal of these leaders *is* grounded in structural features of *some* sort, which may be either hierarchic or egalitarian. Hierarchy and egalitarianism are two modes of conceiving of relationships which run parallel through Malay society and have been commented upon and described in different ways. Shaharuddin Maaruf (1984) suggests that an overwhelmingly "feudal" political tradition coexists with egalitarianism at the village level. Jamieson (1984) refers to the same dichotomy as a Yang/Yin dichotomy, and argues that these principles are interlocked in a system which is basically the same all over Southeast Asia.

In everyday Malay conversation this dichotomy is echoed in the concepts *malu* and *biasa*. *Malu* means shy, self-conscious. You are shy in relation to the "public eye", or in front of certain people who have more power of sanction than others. You are more shy in relation to a village headman than a neighbour of equal standing. *Biasa* means strictly accustomed or familiar, and when applied to relationships, it carries a strong notion of feeling comfortable. You feel comfortable with someone with whom you are familiar. Familiarity equalizes a relation, and takes the danger out of a relation which may be unequal to begin with. A village woman may be shy in front of the headman's wife, who shares in her husband's prestige and thus stands higher than herself in the female hierarchy. She is somewhat more shy in front of the headman himself, who ranks in the male hierarchy, and even more in front of totally unfamiliar male "government persons".

When I asked my informants "who can lead? (guide, teach)", the answer was usually "someone towards whom people will feel shy, so that they follow their directions". Kamariah is a person who induces shyness. She is a traditional midwife of great renown and knowledge. "Traditional" means that there is a distinct stock of skills which have been handed over locally from one generation of practitioners to the next. Midwifery often passed from mother to daughter, and Kamariah's mother, still alive during my first fieldwork, was a legendary midwife who probably helped most of the local population now above the age of 30 into this world. Traditional midwives have been important figures in villages (Karim, 1984) and after Independence the health authorities have drawn on them as a resource. The hospital-trained health personnel have been encouraged to cooperate with them, and they have been offered courses in hygiene and nutrition, and furnished with vitamin pills to be distributed among expectant mothers. Kamariah has used these facilities, and she combines traditional lore taken over from her mother, modern hygiene acquired at hospital courses, and insights of a medical nature which seem very impressive as far as I can evaluate them, and which she has arrived at through her own experience and independent thought. Many of these insights have been clarified to her through dreams. Acquiring magical knowledge through dreams is a common experience in Malay culture, and traditional midwifery contained a distinct element of magical and ritual techniques. This syndrome turns her into a very "powerful" person on a ground which is rooted in traditional belief, at the same time as the factual content of her knowledge approaches that which is accepted in modern medicine. This is typical of her personal "kit" of skills and attitudes, which is a most appealing and striking mixture of the traditional and the modern.

In her active leader role she tends to talk principally about political issues which she finds important, and which to a large extent converge on her medical interest: the concerns of women and children are important to her, and she has a marked feminist approach to questions of marriage and family size. When others describe her activities, attention focuses on her teaching health care, and organizing political rallies in the village.

Her own personal manner is thoughtful, subject oriented, not very extrovert. Subject orientation and introversion are not very prominent qualities in the modal Malay "cultural personality", which is rather characterized by sociability and person orientation. But Kamariah is respected. She was mentioned whenever I asked who, among local women, would be able to lead or teach others. It had to be someone like her, it had to be a person who was capable of inducing a little bit of shyness (*malu*) in others. And other local women who are active supporters of UMNO describe themselves as her "assistants". But she is also a controversial person in the eyes of the most orthodox Muslims, particularly the few open supporters of PAS (the Islamic party) in the village.

Ability to organize may rest on respect or more egalitarian trust, but it also depends on an efficient access to different types of networks, and an ability to pass between different modes of relationships (such as the egalitarian and the hierarchical, the informal and the bureaucratic).

As mentioned earlier, the Malaysian administration rests on many agencies and sub-agencies which are repeated on all levels from the high administrative to the local, and this results in a seeming confusion of delegated roles and chairmanships. This is, however, radically simplified at local level because the incumbents invariably take on multiple roles (Amri Baharuddin, 1989). Friendship and multiple roles convert single-stranded relationships to multiple ones, and bring persons forward as "organizers of villages".

This has two main implications for gender – one which tends to place men and women leaders in similar positions, and one which underlines the difference between them. As far as similarity is concerned, both men and women leaders must meet essentially the same requirements for personal appeal and efficiency. Both can play on principles of equality or rank in their strategies.

But the friendship in which political favours are embedded is a single-gendered phenomenon outside the family circle. As a cross-gender phenomenon it is tied to the family. Therefore female leaders tend to be grounded in primary family relationships to men. Kamariah's limitations as a leader lie precisely here: in a certain paucity of network resources. Her kindred is not particularly large, and she has no really influential male relatives.

Limah is a different sort of person, and has a different type of network – a large and versatile one. Nobody mentions "shyness" in connection with her, nobody has the idea that she *orders* people. She is a pragmatist, and an organizer of a breathtaking amount of activity, but she does not discuss political principles. She helps people do things by partly doing it together with them within an idiom of traditional family-orientation, but her field of activity ranges across many conventional communication barriers. Although she does not discuss the theoretical aspects of politics, Limah has a very articulate view on her own calling and political role. In her youth she divorced a husband before she entered her present, lasting marriage ("I couldn't stay married to someone who did not understand the importance of my work"). Her *marriage pattern* is traditional, her *rationalization* is not. It was very normal for people of her generation, who entered arranged marriages at an early age, to go through one or two unsuccessful marriages before they finally settled down. But the reason given for breaking up was usually general unhappiness or family incompatibility. Her reason, personal commitment, was an unusual one.

The secret of her efficiency is precisely the multiple roles that were referred to above. Some of her roles are formal. Like Kamariah, she is also a local chairwoman of the Women's branch of UMNO. Moreover, she is chairwoman of the Women Farmers' Association, and employed as a KEMAS instructor. Other roles are "informal" or neighbourhood based: she is a skilled gardener, Koran instructor to neighbourhood children, and finally, and most important, she has a firm place in a large, localized kindred. Important male local leaders ranging from the headman downwards are her cousins of varying degrees.

Space does not allow a detailed description of the organization of the administrative and political bodies to which Limah is affiliated. Two things should be kept in mind, however, and that is the tight connection between the party apparatus and important Government agencies, which has been touched on above, and more specifically, the nature of KEMAS, of which I will now give a brief presentation.

KEMAS (Kemajuan Masyarakat – Community Development Division of the Ministry of National and Rural Development) is a large and widely ramifying federal agency which offers a variety of specific schemes for community improvement. KEMAS is a creation of UMNO. It was launched in 1966, and came to full development during the early 1970s, as a manifestation of the more comprehensive rethinking of development policies after the ethnic riots in 1969. The overall spirit and intentions of KEMAS are educational in the widest sense. It has a design for developing skills for virtually all areas of life. It runs public libraries on subdistrict level, and organizes religious classes for adults. It runs kindergartens in most rural subdistricts, with a heavy stress on the moral and intellectual development of preschool children. The rest of the educational activities are of two main types: "work-training groups", and home economics classes. The work training includes activities which can help generate income, such as sewing and embroidery, making artificial flowers (an immensely popular item in home decoration), basketry, motor mechanics, agriculture and animal husbandry. The home economics groups are meant to offer a full repertoire of "subjects" for good family living, such as family togetherness, health, resource management, nutrition and cleanliness, civic consciousness. In actual practice, the home economics groups tend to be interpreted as "cooking classes" by participants as well as instructors. The "cooking classes" together with some of the activities under the work-training programme have particularly attracted the younger jobless women, and have been seen by some as playing a considerable role in a process of "domestication" of women – in creating a modern, bourgeois housewife ideal. In this vein, Lockhead and Ramachandran (1982) deplore what they see as a lack of match between the village women's real economic responsibilities and the types of income-generating that are offered, and Hutheesing states: "... programs as shaped by KEMAS ... fulfill the needs of the young female who because of her education has largely become unproductive" (Hutheesing, undated.)

A problem which is recognized by KEMAS officials, as well as its critics, is a certain role clash at ground level between younger instructors who cast themselves in a role of teacher while they are meant to be more informal "community developers", and potential participants who avoid the offers on exactly these grounds. The success of KEMAS activities thus to a considerable extent depends on the local position, personal style and networking capacity of the instructors. Limah is a type of instructor and organizer who overcomes such problems. She has been directly attached to KEMAS for the last 15 years. Before the creation of KEMAS she attended the Women's Institute in the State Capital, another organization which has overlapped with UMNO both in membership and leadership (Manderson, 1980, p. 94).

Limah's day is packed with activities, and she describes herself as "never at rest" – but on the other hand she never seems tired or short of time. Her base for all the activities is the KEMAS sewing studio, located in a barren concrete building consisting of a large instruction room, a small "office" and an even smaller kitchen. Here she gives her daily six hours of relaxed instruction to women and young girls who are either learning, or just using the facilities for their own purposes. The location is ideal, it places her centrally in a physical as well as social sense.

Limah's allies are of three main types. First, there are women of her own background and age – rooted in traditional female skills, and with little or no formal education. She and they speak about each other as friends of old, "like sisters". They have all been broken in to the communal cooperation of the neighbourhood, and some of them are experienced traders. Their background is the traditional female training ground more than modern education.

Second, there are her younger protégées, the girls and younger housewives who come to her studio for sewing instruction, and who, through her, get in touch with other KEMAS initiatives. They are the young women who are at a loss getting a job under the new economic regime. They have a formal education of six to nine years' duration, and are women who have partly or completely lost the traditional producer role and failed to gain modern career success.

Third, one of Limah's main supporters in the administration is Rahmah, a young female officer from the local field station of the Department of Agriculture. She works as an instructor, mainly taking responsibility for women's projects. She has been educated at the Agricultural College in Serdang. She has a peasant background, and comes from a village very similar to Limah's. She is in her late twenties, and being still unmarried at that age, represents a new trend in building a life career. To Limah and her closest village friends her unmarried status gives her a junior position, daughter rather than younger sister. She, on her side, likens them to her own mother.

V. Two Food Projects

Together, Limah and the women surrounding her represent a cross-section of female roles and skills, and main types of adaptation. I will now go briefly through two projects which took place simultaneously in Limah's neighbourhood, and which exhibit the differences in person structures, communicative styles and ways of conceiving of relationships. The *sateh project* built on traditional skills in cooking and cooperation, the *soybean curd project* is an entirely new experiment both in content and organization.

Sateh is a famous Malay dish of small pieces of marinated meat, barbecued and served on skewers of palmleaf ribs. Various kinds of meat can be used, beef and chicken being the most popular. It is in high demand in restaurants, and quite expensive. Initiative to start chicken *sateh* production was taken by some local members of the Women's Agricultural Association, and as chairwoman and networker Limah took on the responsibility for initiating contacts with the appropriate body under the Agricultural Department. They deemed the assistance necessary to secure raw materials, transport and marketing. This is significant, because small-scale marketing is a skill which generations of Kelantan women have developed to a supreme art. This project, however, needed a different type of infrastructure. *Sateh* is a costly and perishable product, and without special facilities for refrigerated transport and storing, they would have had to limit themselves to small quantities for immediate sale and consumption.

This project involved several meetings, and three rounds of actual production. All the meetings that were necessary, as well as the rounds of actual production, took place at Limah's usual base, at the same time as sewing classes were on. The initial meeting was a mixture of formality and informality. It involved four categories of participants: the interested local women, Limah and the secretary of the local Agricultural Association, Rahmah and two junior officers from the Department of Agriculture, and a subcontractor. After formal greetings, a typed agenda was handed out, and the secretary read aloud a report on the recent activities of the association. After that the subcontractor got the floor, and spoke eloquently to the women about the problems of the *sateh* business, its risks and conditions. He also brought some *sateh* which was tasted. Then followed a very informal discussion about practical details to be settled. Time had to be found for production and transport, and there were several conditions to be met. Among other things, it had to fit in with the timetable of the schoolchildren. The subcontractor said jokingly: "Aren't you afraid the husband will be angry?" and one of the women retorted quickly: "the husbands sit around only": it is *our* time that is scarce and has to be given priority.

When the day of trial production arrived, five women got together in the morning. Rahmah from the field station brought the chickens on her motor bike, and production started immediately. The women worked swiftly and efficiently, they were now into a kind of cooperation which they all knew from long experience. Getting together to prepare large amounts of food is the backbone of women's ceremonial responsibility in villages, everyone knows what to do, and the conversation runs about other topics with which they are preoccupied. Limah did not actually take part in the production; she supervised the sewing class, kept an eye on the *sateh* production, and discussed prices and marketing with Rahmah, who was there most of the day, apparently to supervise and assist. When the women needed an additional container she was the one who set off on her motor bike to get one.

If there is a "boss" of production, however, it is the oldest woman in the team, who is addressed as "junior aunt" by the others. She is Limah's cousin, wife of a retired *penghulu* (headman on the lowest level of village subdivision)[2] and described to me as expert on *sateh*. She furnished me with running comments on the production, and on the kin network of the village. This is not because I had asked about it, but because the topic was important to her. The topic of family and kin is always brought up whenever Malays make new acquaintances. Her comments were in the vein of "Limah and I are cousins, we have always been together, we are like sisters" and "in this village we are all related, like siblings". I stress this point to draw attention to the dimension within which Limah builds up her trust. It is the local mode of "*biasa*" familiarity.

The first round of *sateh* production was not a very successful one, as the monetary return was rather a disappointment. The women found the reason partly in the quality of the raw materials: they had paid for too much weight in bones, the chickens had been skinny. It struck me that if they had gone to market themselves to buy the raw materials, they would have been extremely critical, and they would have haggled until they got good value for their money. This I told them. They agreed, but mentioned transportation problems. The deal with the Agricultural Development Agency was, of course, a package deal which included refrigeration and transportation of a larger quantity than could otherwise have been handled. On the other hand it meant that part of what the women were good at, handling the market situation as an open, face to face social game, was cut off from its continuation. What remained was the other side of their expertise: that of preparing the food and cooperating to that purpose. To women of the older generation, these activities bridge the gap between the domestic and the public: preparation of food is part of domestic work, while the cooperation is nourished by the ceremonial life of villages. But there are now also processes under way which are likely to destroy ceremonial cooperation, leaving cooking as a more privatized activity in the household. This happens partly because women in modern occupations are too busy to reciprocate, and hence avoid asking for the help of others. Partly, it happens because the younger women who have been formally educated have not acquired the same social "skills of the neighbourhood" that their mothers have. Finally, reinterpretations of relationships tend to realign traditional forms of reciprocity into new categories of "personal friendship" and "impersonal business", erecting barriers between them. The present case of cooperation, then, exhibits one stage on the process of transformation of female responsibilities: we saw above how the marketing skills of the women fell into disuse for practical reasons. They continue their ceremonially based cooperation, but may be the last generation who do this before cooking is fully "domesticated".

There was a tolerance of partial failure of this project, because the time spent in the work had no other income-generating alternative, and because Limah and Rahmah at least were perceived as on team with the women. Limah had been active in discussing the deal with the subcontractor, and information would flow back to him from her and Rahmah with the hope of improving the next attempt. There is not much to be improved except raw materials, but they agreed to continue for some time.

More or less simultaneously with the *sateh* project, there was another activity going on in another building nearby, where a group of local young women were learning to make soybean curd. This was not under Limah's direct responsibility, but as a KEMAS initiative it was definitely part of her area of interest and influence. Again, as the local community developer, she was the networker and inspirator, always on the lookout for new possibilities to start activity – this time "for those youngsters who have such difficulties finding a job these days". The other building is a large, two-room structure which has been used generally for cooking classes and other training purposes. It had been fitted with machinery and two large combined refrigerator/freezers. The soybeans were ground and mixed with water, the pulp was then strained, and the curd was finally spread in wooden frames, and left to congeal under light pressure. Everything around this enterprise was "new" in contrast to the traditional expertise and organization which characterized the *sateh* production. Soybean curd is not among the traditional local dishes, it belongs in a Chinese rather than Malay culinary tradition. Whereas the *sateh* producers built on their own expertise, the youngsters were taught to make their product by young Kemas instructors who commuted to the village from the headquarters in town. These are instructors of the "schoolteacher" type, both male and female, who have some knowledge that the others lack entirely, and mediate it in a formal and structured way. For the pupils, this is more like a continuation of the school situation in which they have been for nine years, so here we do not have the same role clash that characterizes the situations in which young community developers try to "teach" older people.

No definite arrangements had been made for continued production and marketing when my field-work ended. The direct involvement of Kemas is mostly on the training and developing side, while the continuation is left to people themselves, possibly with assistance from other government agencies. A possible follow-up route would be this: MARA (Majlis Amanah Rakyat – Council of Trust for the Indigenous People) could be approached for a loan for investments to start regular production. MARA also offers courses in business management on the most elementary as well as more advanced levels, and this might also be attractive for the youths, who lacked both formal business training and traditional market skills. Limah had no direct involvement in MARA, but her general knowledge and network would be sufficient to make the connection here as well. Further, for marketing purposes the Agricultural Department and its subcontractors might be a possible source of assistance in the same way as it had been with the *sateh* production. In that case, Limah's formal position in the Agricultural Association might again bring a possible soybean project under her direct responsibility.

Seen in isolation, these two particular projects are not very impressive as development undertakings: one is a financial disappointment in the first round, and the other one is not really a project, just a bit of skill which is likely to run into the sands unless some good coaching and networking can pull it along. If we look at the whole village over a longer time span, however, the picture changes into one of a higher level of activity and greater diversity than one usually finds in similar villages in the same area. Many initiatives have been started, some have failed, but the enterprising spirit remains on a high level, and Limah's versatility and organizing capacity is part of the explanation. One feature which particularly marks off this village, is the brisk continuation of gardening activities. Small-scale gardening is easily discontinued in similar villages when the impact of wage work reaches a certain level. Women's withdrawal from production when the men go to wage work is partly attributed to practical difficulties, partly motivated by a bourgeois ideal which is nourished from many sources in contemporary discourse, including the new Islamic rhetoric. In this village the women go on growing their gardens. Particularly good soil is part of the explanation, but not the whole. Equally important are the practical and ideological models of Limah and Rahmah. Together they make a very efficient pair. Limah is a gardener herself, she spends a couple of hours in the riverside fields every late afternoon in between sewing class and her evening Koran instruction. She represents, as it were, the older generation. Rahmah, as we have seen, goes to the villages and spends much time in direct contact with the gardeners. She is young, good-looking and well educated, and thus able to be an example to the younger women. At the same time she has a genuine respect for the older women of Limah's type, with whom she enters into a mother–daughter type of relationship. Rahmah and other officers claim that they concentrate much of their efforts on this village, and the reason is that activities are easily initiated there. There is a mutual reinforcement between local leadership and administrative involvement. This is no doubt due to favourable underlying network connections – I will revert to this below, with special reference to gender.

VI. Contrasts and Similarities

Contrasts and similarities run through this person gallery and their activities from top to bottom. The two leader figures both work for women's interests in a historical situation in which the economic structure and gender system are under a particularly rapid modification. They exhibit different styles, as one has her strength in esoteric knowledge and a "personal magic" which induces respect, one in closeness and an unusual amount of common knowledge. They are similar in so far as they both utilize their initial working skills in their development concerns: midwifery, gardening, religion, local knowledge. Their activities – particularly Limah's – reach out to women who seem very different – young and old, producers and housewives, "peasant" and "bourgeois", with formal education ranging from nil to nine years as a minimum. Part of Limah's activities builds on a side of women's skills and cooperation which seems about to crumble under the impact of modernization. At the bottom of all these likenesses and contrasts there is one big similarity: Kamariah with her principal concern for justice in marriage, and Limah with her proliferating practical activities are both basically trying to rescue women's important position as resource person in the family.

VII. Public and Domestic Gender

The development strategy of KEMAS is roughly two-pronged. They have their home economics programme which is aimed at enhancing the quality of family life, and they have their training programmes in income-generating activities. One of Limah's slogans is that she exerts all her energies in order to create "activities for women" – and she refers to the income-generating kind. She continues: "When the men have their activities, the women must also have theirs." This is a simple statement with very deep implications.

The field of her influence spans widely in the local community, as we saw, and the methods and the persons involved in the *sateh* project and the soybean project are very different. But in this difference there is a similarity: all her restless inventiveness in creating women's activities to match men's activities is nothing less than a strategy for perpetuating the balance of domestic gender. Women used to be as important economically as men were in households. Now there are trends in the production and employment patterns of society which threaten this position. There are a few modern women who are successful building working careers according to modern principles; these tend to perpetuate the traditional domestic equality with the husband. These are not the ones who need Limah's leadership, she is mostly concerned with those who remain behind in the primary sector, and those who are becoming "domesticated".

Public gender has a more complicated pattern, as there is one main change and two separate trends to take care of. For simplicity, let me first underline the main change such as it can be observed from the local vantage point. My zero point is the situation in the middle 1960s. At that time the village was less drawn into the large-scale political and administrative structures than it is today. Gender segregation in public situations was rather massive, and neither men nor women were much drawn into formal membership in organizations. The domestic gender balance was such as it has just been described, and the more sealed-off public gender balance was also in some respects a more balanced one. My reason for claiming this rests on the pattern of ceremonial life, which, with the weak articulation of local-level politics, was the one kind of activity most efficient in lending a measure of corporateness to neighbourhoods. In this men and women had different but complementary ritual roles. Of particular interest is the size of male and female collectivities. In purely religious officiating men's collectivities were always the largest. In marriage celebrations, women's responsibility was the staging of the largest ritual. When it comes to networking, women's networks were as wide-ranging as those of men, and for the practical purposes of family survival, at least equally efficient. As far as political and bureaucratic matters are concerned, however, male networks were more important, and this is still the case.

At present there are two trends to keep track of in public gender. First, the massive segregation has been broken down in many practical situations. Formal education and modern occupations have been important agents in this breaking-down process. The visible effect of it is that men and women mix more freely in public places. At the same time friendships and loyalties outside the family are still subject to strong gender restrictions. There are still limits to forming bonds between men and women. This places definite limitations on the form that cross-gender cooperation and alliances can take.

It is here that the mediating kinship enters. Kinship is a powerful vehicle for forming loyalties and getting access to scarce goods in general, and becomes particularly important for mediating between male and female collectivities in a society with strict rules on cross-sex contact. When male collectivities dominate in the public field, it will be more important for women than for men. If more women climb to important positions even in a segregated society – which is certainly possible in Malaysia – men may also need cross-sex nodes. These cross-sex nodes which imply friendship and informal loyalty, and a power of influencing, can only legitimately be found within kindreds.

This invites a further speculation of a more general character. The connection between modernization of societies and processes of individuation have been noticed often enough in social research (e.g. Dumont, 1986; Berman, 1982). Increased individuation and mobility imply neutralization of gender in more and more fields of interaction, and the importance of kinship yields to friendship formed on other bases. This means that cross-sex friendships are possible outside kinship and the domestic field. The logical final product of this process is a society in which there is no gender imbalance in the incumbence of public roles. This is a society in which gender – cultural sex – will seem to have lost much of its importance. But when gender is relegated to sexual coupling it becomes located in the core of individuals and personal relationships. It will then be even more easily conceptualized as "natural" – its culturality becomes harder to attack, and the question remains whether qualitative differences between all-male, all-female and male–female friendships will not continue to interfere with the working of the public system.

Notes

1 UMNO – United Malay National Organization – a political party which draws its support from the Malay population. It has been in government position within various coalitions since Independence, and despite internal problems, is without comparison Malaysia's most powerful political party.
2 In Kelantan some administrative titles differ from what is common elsewhere. The subdistrict headman is called *penggawa*, and his assistant headmen on lowest village level are *penghulu*. In other states in the Federation it is the subdistrict headman who is called *penghulu*, while the assistant headmen are called *ketua kampung*.

References

Amri Baharuddin, S. 1989. Formal Organizations in a Malay Administrative Village in Peninsular Malaysia: A critical Re-examination. Paper for the Conference on "Rural Southeast Asia in Transition", Nordic Association of Southeast Asian Studies, Lund, Sweden.
Berman, M. 1982. *All That Is Solid Melts Into Air. The Experience of Modernity.* London: Verso.
Chodrow, N. 1974. Family Structure and Feminine Personality. In M. Z. Rosaldo and L. Lamphere (eds): *Women, Culture and Society.* Stanford University Press.
Dumond, L. 1986. *Essays on Individualism. Modern Ideology in Anthropological Perspective.* Chicago/London: The University of Chicago Press.
Gale, B. 1981. *Politics and Public Enterprise in Malaysia.* Petaling Jaya, Malaysia; Eastern Universities Press Sdn. Bhd.
Hutheesing, O. (undated). Pros and Cons of a Government Programme. Penang, KANITA paper.
Kamar, A. 1984. *Malay and Indonesian Leadership in Perspective.* Petaling Jaya, Malaysia.
Karim, W. 1984. Malay Midwives and Witches. *Social Science and Medicine*, Vol. 18, pp. 159–166.
Lockhead, J. & Ramachandran, V. 1982. Income Generating Activities for Women: A Case Study of Malaysia. Penang: KANITA report, preliminary draft.
Maaruf, S. 1984. *Concept of a Hero in Malay Society.* Singapore and Petaling Jaya: Eastern Universities Press.
Manderson, L. 1980. *Women, Politics, and Change. The kaum Ibu UMNO, Malaysia 1945–1972.* Kuala Lumpur: Oxford University Press.
Norris, M. W. 1980. *Local Government in Peninsular Malaysia.* Farnborough: Gower.

Ortner, S. B. 1981. Gender and Sexuality in Hierarchical Societies: The Case of Polynesia and Some Comparative Implications. In S. B. Ortner, and H. Whitehead, (eds), *Sexual Meanings. The Cultural Construction of Gender and Sexuality*. Cambridge: Cambridge University Press.
Ortner, S. B. 1984. *Theory in Anthropology since the Sixties*. Comparative Studies in Society and History, Vol. 26, 126–166.
Rogers, B. 1980. *The Domestication of Women*. London/New York: Tavistock Publications.
Rosaldo, M. Z. and Lamphere, L. (eds) 1974. *Women, Culture and Society*. Stanford: Stanford University Press.
Rudie, I. 1971. Between Market and Neighbourhood. Unpublished manuscript, 330 pages.
Rudie, I. (ed.) 1984. *Myk start, hard landing. Om forvaltning av kjønnsidentitet i en endringsprosess*. Oslo: Universitetsforlaget.
Rudie, I. 1988. Malay Marriage Ritual as Field of Negotiation. In T. Bleie, V. Broch Due and I. Rudie (eds), *Gender: Symbols and Social Practices* (working title). Forthcoming.
Rudie, I. 1989a. Development Ideologies, Family Systems, and the Changing Roles of Malay Village Women. In M. Gravers, P. Wad, V. Brun and A. Kalland (eds), *Southeast Asia between Autocracy and Democracy*. Aarhus: Aarhus University Press.
Rudie, I. 1989b. Feltarbeid og tid. Dimensjoner i forståelse av endring. In *Norwegian Association for Development Research. Conference Papers*, University of Trondheim, pp. 203–218.
Rudie, I. 1990. Ceremonial, School and Market. On the Reproduction of Gender in East Coast Malay Culture. Report to NORAS. 270 pp. Limited circulation.
Sperber, D. 1975. *Rethinking Symbolism*. Cambridge: Cambridge University Press.
Strathern, M. 1988. *The Gender of the Gift. Problems with Women and Problems with Society in Melanesia*. Berkeley: University of California Press.
Talib, R. 1984. Developing the Rural Women. In Hing Ai Yun, Nik Safiah Karim and Rokiah Talib (eds), *Women in Malaysia*. Petaling Jaya: Pelanduk Publications.

9

Clans, Gender and Kilns

Examples from a fisheries development project in Sota village, Tanzania

SIRI GERRARD[1]

This chapter takes us to Sota, a multi-ethnic village on the shores of Lake Victoria in the Mara Region of Tanzania. It deals with co-operative ventures between female fish traders and representatives from the local and external fisheries bureaucracy and training institutions. The aim was to improve the traditional fish smoking technology as well as women's ways of organizing the processing and distribution of fish. Most of the events which constitute the material for this chapter took place in Sota, which is in fact one neighbourhood of a village, the others being Sidika and Kirengo. However, the entire village is also generally called Sota.[2] This chapter deals with the events in the period 1987 to late 1989.[3]

Since pre-colonial times, the peoples of Sota village, like other lakeshore peoples, have subsisted on agriculture, animal husbandry and fishing. There are also some private and public services which can be attributed to Sota's location near the Kenya/Tanzania border and its contacts with the external world in the colonial period as well as after independence.[4] The Lake Police are stationed in Sota, and the Natural Resources Division of Tarime District has a field station in the village. This station was concerned mainly with the fisheries and with a tree nursery.

Most employees in the public services come from various parts of the country and from several ethnic groups. The permanent inhabitants, however, belong to different clans of two patrilineal ethnic groups, the Nilotic Luo and the Bantu Kuria.[5] Sota village, and indeed the entire Nyancha Division of Tarime District, is situated within what was originally claimed to be the clanland of Warieri, a Kuria clan with a long history of intermarriage with the Luo (Wembah Rashid, 1989). The residential pattern in the community coincides roughly with ethnic, clan, lineage and family subgroups. These subgroups can be quite influential, especially when important issues are on the agenda, for example distribution of goods and services to the villagers. The basic loyalties and animosities embedded in the various aspects of local culture and social organization therefore constitute contextual factors of special interest to my analysis.

In the following, I will put special emphasis on women, men and their co-operative relations through a small fisheries development project and the ensuing discussions and activities. In particular I will focus on the way the local men and women and non-local men and women of the fisheries bureaucracy relate to such principles of social differentiation as gender, ethnicity, clanship or kin in defining goals, in forming groups and in distributing resources.

I. Analytical Perspectives

My basic assumption is that the outcome of development intervention is a product of interaction, negotiation and social and cognitive struggle between different social actors who represent different goals, interests and belief and are backed by different resources (Long, 1989, p. 223). The fisheries project in Sota can be analysed as an interface encounter, where interface is defined as

> a critical point of intersection or linkage between different social systems, fields or levels of social order where structural discontinuities, based upon differences of normative value and social interest are most likely to be found (Long, 1989, p. 2).

In particular I am concerned with how ethnicity, clan and gender relations affect the outcome of so-called "women oriented" development intervention. This chapter analyses the interaction between local female fish traders and fisheries officers, uncovering the dynamics and emergent character of this interaction (Long, 1989). I will explore how different ways of thinking about gender can provoke disagreements and discussions among the parties involved. Old gender notions and practices are challenged, negotiated and redefined (Rudie, 1984). One question to be raised as a result of the fisheries project in Sota is whether gender has gained a new significance or not.

Gender relations are also interwoven with other types of social relations. Thus, changes in the meaning of gender will have to be analysed in relation to other aspects of differentiation, particularly clan and ethnicity, which have a prominent place in Sota society. Clan and interclan relations to a large extent form the basis of property rules and rules for distribution of material resources. The development projects represent new ideas and practices regarding resource distribution. This challenges the meaning and significance of clans, which in turn are negotiated and perhaps reshaped.

Negotiation processes can be controversial, especially when, as in the Sota case, they involve institutions with established power and influence. Such institutions are, for example, clans, local political organizations or development agencies, each with their own various rules and regulations. Such institutions may also differ in terms of formality. Highly formal institutions have written rules and well defined working procedures and will often be more visible than clan or kinship. The norms and practices of the latter may be overlooked by external actors, although local actors will be well aware of and influenced by them. In some cases differences between institutions are so marked that they can be said to represent different cultures (Gerrard, 1975, 1983; Kets de Vries and Miller, 1985).

Controversies regarding social relations, rules and practices arise in all kinds of social contexts. However, they tend to become particularly visible in planned interventions, when development workers and local population have to work side by side. Too often, plans are simply thrust upon local populations because development workers do not acknowledge that their target group consists of knowledgeable and active subjects, with whom they can negotiate and develop a conceptual framework for the common effort (Goffman, 1974). Development workers too often consider local culture and organizations as obstacles to their work, rather than resources to be mobilized to the benefit of the project. This is one important reason why the outcome of their efforts is frequently disappointing.

On the basis of analysis of events in Sota, I hope to draw attention to the importance of gender in fisheries development in Tanzania (Bashemererwa *et al.*, 1986; Swantz, 1986; Gerrard, 1988; Wembah Rashid, 1989). I also hope to shed light on some of the problems involved in target-oriented development projects – particularly if one is to take the objective of people's participation seriously.

II. Conditions for Improving the Technology and Organization of Women's Fish Trade

1. *Women and Men: Ethnicity, Clans and Economy*

The Nilotic Luo people, Luo language and Luo customs are dominant around the north-eastern part of Lake Victoria. Clan and kinship structure marriage, economic partnership and political affiliations. Gender structures work. In farming, for instance, women do the hoeing, weeding and harvesting. They also provide their children and husbands with food, care and sometimes cash in the daily struggle to survive. Petty trade, especially fish trade, is the most usual source of cash income.

The husbands clear the land and sometimes help to plough and to harvest. Some husbands have a boat or work as fishermen on other people's boats. Men may also engage in casual paid work besides farming. Traditionally, cattle keeping has represented the most prestigious activity and source of wealth in Luo society. Thus, in a household, men and women share the responsibility for the livelihood of the family.

Men now face difficulties in meeting traditional expectations, because of the difficult state of the Tanzanian economy on all levels, and pressure on pasture lands in the region. Several households have been obliged to cull their herds. This has not been compensated for by fishing since there is a lack of equipment as well as capital. These difficulties have increased the burdens of the women in particular, due to their responsibilities for providing food. Women have responded by putting greater efforts into agriculture and the fish trade. Today there are about 70–80 female fishmongers in Sota, Kirengo and Sidika, representing about 15 percent of the adult women in the village (Gerrard, 1988). The majority live in Sota, but the number is fluctuating.

Fish trade is an individual activity. The women buy, preserve and sell the fish. Profits are often small, and are generally spent on commodities like flour, soap and oil. The women were well aware that they would not be able to compete in bigger markets and make a profit unless they could improve the quality of the fish which is preserved by smoking.

The intensity of trade varies with the financial situation of the family. Tradeswomen go to the landing sites early in the morning to buy fish, in competition with fishmongers from outside the village. When selling, they carry the fish on their heads in baskets and walk to the market eight kilometres away, usually cooking a meal for the family first.

Thus, the Sota population have tried to cope with a rather difficult economic situation through strategies often organized at the household level.

2. *Political and Administrative Conditions*

After independence, Tanzania developed a comprehensive political and administrative system at all levels. The highest political authority on the village level is the village assembly. The village council and its different committees constitute the executive body, responsible for day-to-day issues and for solving interpersonal conflicts or special types of problems (theft and so on) (Salomon, 1983).

The village chairman and the village secretary are also council members. Some of the duties of the chairman and the village secretary are to run the formal political life in the village between the meetings and represent the village at meetings in district and regional bodies. The smallest party unit is the tenhouse cell, but this level is not very active in Sota.

The only political party in Tanzania, Chama Cha Mapinduzi party (CCM), has a branch in Sota village. The various party organizations, among them the women's organization or Umoja wa Wanawake wa Tanzania (UWT), are also present. Some years ago the UWT ran a café, but from 1985 to 1987 the local branch was "dormant".

The important political positions have always been held by men in Sota. However, both men and women above 18 years of age can attend the village assembly, but men are in the majority as participants and speakers. Out of 25 councillors there are two women in Sota village.

The party, its various organizations and the Village Council with its subcommittees are intended to be the leading force in local development. The ideology of development, "maendeleo" in Swahili, is strong and much discussed. Questions of equality between men and women were rarely taken up, although some CCM leaders seemed to agree with the official Tanzanian equality policy when the topic arose in informal talks. But it is the day-to-day problems that absorb most of the people's time and resources.

Formal co-operatives or informal collective actions have been few, and short-lived. The same can be said about public development interventions. After Tanzania's independence, however, the national authorities earmarked Sota for an industrialized fisheries development project through a field station. Construction of a relatively expensive production hall, offices, a classroom, houses and motorboats were provided for. Unfortunately, this project never took off as the economy crumbled in the late 1970s and work had to be abandoned.

From that time until December 1989 three fisheries officers lived in Sota and had their office at the field station. In late 1989, however, the Fisheries Division moved to the ward centre,[6] about eight kilometres away.

The fisheries officers are supposed to initiate fisheries development programmes and projects and are responsible not only for Sota, Sidika and Kirengo, but for all villages in the division of Nyancha. They complain, however, that they are restricted in their activities because of lack of money and transportation. These days the local officers have to deal with theft of fishing equipment in the lake as well as letters of recommendation for fishermen who want to obtain loans to buy boats, new nets or engines, and so on. Once a week they collect fees at the weekly market at the ward centre.

The local fisheries officers report to the District Fisheries Officer and the Regional Fisheries Officer.[7] At the regional level the Regional Fisheries Officer, among others, has struggled hard to reopen a training centre, Mara Fisheries Development Centre (Mara FDC), which was built in the 1970s. The interest of fisheries development in the region is also demonstrated by the highest political and bureaucratic authorities, the Regional Commissioner (RC) and the Regional Development Director (RDD) (Gerrard, 1988). The Regional Commissioner has also expressed interest in women's development.[8]

Fisheries Division in the Ministry of Lands, Natural Resources and Tourism implements the national Tanzanian fisheries policies and is responsible for the training and research institutions. Mbegani Fisheries Development Centre (Mbegani FDC) is one of them. Mbegani FDC has received support from the Norwegian Development Co-operation (NORAD). Today Mbegani FDC is geared towards industrialized fisheries and administration, but also gives short courses to benefit both men and women in small-scale fisheries (Hersoug *et al.*, 1986; Johnsen, 1989; Falch, 1989). This is a bit controversial because the Fisheries Division at the national level, however, fears that emphasis on small-scale fisheries may delay industrialization in Tanzanian fisheries (Hempel, 1989).

Another national institution of interest is the Tanzania Fisheries Research Institute (TAFIRI) with subdivisions at various locations in Tanzania. They initiated biological and socio-economic research and opened a branch in Sota in 1988 in the buildings of the field station.

III. Improving Women's Small-scale Fish Trade

1. *Step One: Planning and Building a Fish Smoking Kiln*

The first measures for improving women's small-scale fish trade started in February and lasted until June 1987. The idea was to improve the smoking technology by building a kiln primarily for training purposes. A modern kiln was considered to be a necessary, although not a sufficient, measure to improve the quality of the fish and the women's work conditions.

Smoking is a traditional local method of fish preservation. Most women in lake villages have learned the technique from their mothers, mothers-in-law, female neighbours or friends. Even today, smoking methods are based on simple technology. Iron bars are placed across a hole in the ground which is filled with cow dung, occasionally with scarce firewood. The fish is put on the bars and covered with corrugated iron sheets. The quality, however, is not as good as it could be, because cow dung as fuel cannot produce the necessary heat, but it is available free of charge and is also more "sustainable" than firewood.

The plans matured through informal discussions involving some of the female fishmongers, local fisheries officers and myself. The training project was to start in Sota; if successful, it could then be replicated in Sidika and Kirengo.

In the project I was to provide for a sum of money corresponding to $300.[9] The fisheries officers were to contribute with their technical and co-ordinating skills, and the women with their work. The fisheries officers suggested building an Altona kiln. This type of kiln is made of brick with a roof of corrugated iron sheeting. Through the door in the front there is access to the smoking chamber where the fish is placed.

The project idea was launched one morning while the fish traders were waiting for the fishermen to arrive from the lake. The senior fisheries officer explained the ideas behind the training course and the smoking kiln. Some of the women had already been involved in developing the ideas, while others had not heard about them before. They quickly suggested and elected two representatives to a management committee. One of them, a Luo woman, was the wife of the village chairman at that time. The other, a Mrieri woman,[10] was a very active fishmonger. The meeting was short, with only a few women voicing any opinion. The committee consisted of three fisheries officers, two representatives of the women and myself.

Many partners were informed about the kiln plan. The village chairman and the village secretary were told, as were the District and the Regional Fisheries Officer and the leader of the regional training centre, Mara FDC. All supported the idea morally, although they complained about lack of resources to put into the project.

The village chairman and the secretary were invited to the first meeting of the management committee in order to secure contact with the village council. The chairman as well as the secretary supported the idea of a women's project, even arguing for the importance of improving women's possibilities in their village.

Major decisions to be made were how to organize the construction of the kiln and where to place it. My idea was that women who were interested in fish trade and fish processing should decide where to build the kiln and how to construct it. Nobody objected to this idea. Deciding where to build it proved to be not so simple, however. The fisheries officers proposed that it should be near the field station. The female committee members were somewhat sceptical of this, so the committee decided to let a bigger assembly of Sota women discuss the matter. That meeting was well attended. A few men, among them two of the fisheries officers, were also present.

Again the conflicting issue was where to build it. Of various places suggested, two alternatives were finally discussed. One was a plot across the road from where the village planned to build the new Party office. This site was also close to the homes of two of the most industrious fishmongers. The second alternative was at the field station. The first alternative won, by a few votes.

Two days later, a large number of women met and started making bricks. Working in high spirits, some of the women expressed great expectations; others said that they had no plans to start fish processing and trading, but they were afraid that they would miss out on something if they did not participate. It was at that stage that I began to realize that there were different and perhaps conflicting expectations and goals among the participants.

The next afternoon a lot of gossip began to circulate about the project. Some local men criticized the project since the entire village council had not participated in decisions concerning the kiln. Others claimed that the women elected to the management committee were "bad" women and that the site was not the best one. Obviously the kiln project was controversial.

The project came up for discussion at a meeting arranged in the village. This meeting was one of the first formal meetings called by the village chairman that year. Only two female representatives were present, both from Kirengo. The aim of the meeting was to form a co-operative to distribute seeds and farming tools at reasonable prices. Since representatives from all neighbourhoods of the village were present, the village chairman took the opportunity to inform about and discuss the kiln project at the end of the meeting. The debate was lively. The chairman explained his involvement in the project and expressed his support. Afterwards I was asked to present my opinion. I emphasized the training aspect and the argument put forward by the women that the kiln should be situated at a place where it could be looked after. Several speakers were active in the debate, but were not satisfied. Some said that this was a case for the village council and the councillors, not for women only. If kilns were to be built, it should be down at the landing site where they planned to build a centre for local and external fishermen. The Kirengo women present complained that the Sota women always got everything and asked me why I never came to their neighbourhood.

Even though the participants listened to me politely, their questions revealed that many disagreed. I felt that the interests and aspirations of the women were in conflict with most of the opinions at this meeting. One representative said that he could not allow his wife to go to a kiln close to the house of a certain man, who was a relative of hers. Because his wife was now married into his clan, it was inappropriate for his wife to go to work there. However, no concrete alternatives were proposed. The discussion came to nothing. Some weeks later the bricks were washed away in the rain and the project management committee was disbanded.

2. Step Two: Revitalizing the Women's Organization

One might think that this would be end of the kiln project. It continued, however, with a new phase, starting in June 1987 and lasted to September 1989.

The fisheries officers put a lot of energy into reviving the plan and proposed to build a kiln near their office at the field station. This time they started with borrowed ready-made bricks and planned to let the women produce new bricks later to replace the loan. One of the fisheries officers bought the necessary equipment and hired a bricklayer to build the kiln. The money was provided by me as agreed previously.

While the kiln was built at the fisheries field station, women's meetings were held in Sota, Kirengo and Sidika, arranged by the fisheries officers and myself. The purpose was to let the women elect their representative(s) to a seminar to be arranged at Mara FDC. The women also identified their plans and wishes for the future. Fish trade, improved agriculture, possibilities to learn to read and write, knitting and sewing were all mentioned. During these meetings, some of the old members of the UWT expressed the need to revitalize the UWT to work for women's development. The first step in this direction was to arrange a meeting to discuss development ventures and how to use my farewell gift of Tsh 10,000 ($150).

In July 1987, representatives from the UWT District branch were invited to participate in a local workshop on development work with women from the village. As a result of the workshop, a UWT fish trade group of some 20 members was founded. The intention was to use the kiln at the field station in order to earn money for the UWT. The interaction had changed in character, from being an interaction of fish trade women, fisheries officers and the researcher, into an effort at women's own organizing.

The seminar at Mara FDC which was financed by NORAD and arranged in co-operation with the Regional Fisheries Officer, the researchers and Mbegani FDC, focused on men's and women's roles in fisheries development. Here village men and women discussed the problems of the small-scale fisheries together with people from the Fisheries Division in Dar es Salaam, TAFIRI, people from the banks, from development institutions and development agencies. One of the results of the seminar was greater interest on the regional level as regards the role of women in fisheries.[11]

One of the participants at this regional seminar, the UWT secretary representing Sota, was also selected to participate in a longer fisheries training programme at Mara FDC together with two other women. Both male and female participants and some of the teachers (all men) reported that this was a new situation to which they had to adjust (Johnsen, 1989).

When the UWT secretary returned from the Mara FDC training course, bringing home three nets as initial capital for her own fishing, she put considerable effort into trying to get the UWT group to work. She was active in mobilizing women. The kiln was not used regularly in the daily smoking of fish, however. The women continued to use their familiar method of smoking and selling, working individually as before. The kiln was only used on special occasions when visitors came to study the women's project. The UWT organized fish traders used the UWT money to buy fish which they smoked and sold, returning the profits to the UWT.

In 1988 the field station, together with the buildings and the kiln, was handed over by Tarime District Council to Tanzania Fisheries Research Institute, TAFIRI. It had never been specified that this kiln was to be the property of the village. From now on the staff of

TAFIRI processed the fish and took it by car to the biggest market in the area, the Tarime market. They earned good money – just as the women had hoped to do. The women said to me later that the kiln, which they considered theirs, had been taken away from them. They had written letters to TAFIRI to complain, without getting an answer. Some of the women wanted TAFIRI to build a new kiln in Sidika or Kirengo to replace the one that had been "taken away".

Almost two years later, in 1989, Mbegani FDC, in co-operation with Mara FDC, arranged a new training course for women. The initiative was taken by two of Mbegani's female teachers and the Regional Fisheries Officer. Two of the students that were selected came from Sota and the third from Sidika. The one woman from Sidika was the wife of the new village chairman. The two women from Sota belonged to the most influential clan in the village.

At this course as well as at the previous one, the 15 participants learnt how to fish, how to produce and mend nets and how to smoke and preserve the fish to ensure good quality. They also learnt tree planting as well as simple bookkeeping. This was the first training course of its kind, arranged especially for women in this part of Tanzania. Both men and women acted as teachers. Initially some of the husbands objected to male teachers, especially at a residential course. The participants spent one month at the Mara FDC, one month in a village in another district in Mara Region, and one month in Shirati area. They also built a kiln and a cleaning table. Now the neighbourhood of Sota had its second kiln and its first cleaning table.

The local students of this course were now to go home and function as resource persons in fisheries development. New groups were started not only in Sota village but also in three of the surrounding villages.

3. Step Three: Support from Outside Increases the Interest for Women's Fish Trade Groups

As a result of the course, the already established fish trade group from 1987 was reorganized into several groups at the end of the course in August 1989. Also, the new groups were a part of the UWT, but with its own board. Members of these groups came from various clans, mainly in Sota, with a few from Sidika and Kirengo. In the very beginning they were supervised by the Mbegani female teacher, and one of the local fisheries officers was assigned to work with the groups of women. Five trade groups were formed with one leader and four to five members in each, in turn forming a subsection of the Sota UWT.

In economic terms, the new groups were based on the principle that members of one group started out with capital from the common UWT account. They bought fish, smoked it and sold it on the local market. They were then to pass their initial money on to the next group, while the surplus or profit was to revert to the common UWT account.

Some months later the Mbegani teachers, through NORAD, donated two bicycles and some seed money to the groups. One bicycle was placed in the home of the secretary of the fish trade group in Sota, and the other in the home of the leader of the UWT. There were, however, many reactions to this choice, because the women from Kirengo and Sidika felt entitled to use the bikes too.

In November Mbegani FDC sent three male students to the village for practical training. They started to build another kiln next to the newly built one. Again the work was based on a collective effort from the most active UWT members. The Mbegani students also brought along a special purse-seine net. The plan was that the women should learn to fish to secure raw material for smoking. They went fishing for two nights only, because of difficulties in obtaining ropes and because some husbands would not allow their wives to work together with men in the middle of the night.

The leaders of the trade groups, however, complained that the female fishmongers continued to work individually. Competition for fish was also harder than before because of an increase of male fish traders from outside. Some also mentioned that the fishermen were not willing to sell their fish at reasonable prices because they thought that the UWT groups was receiving outside financial support. The local women who had hoped that the new groups could ease their daily work complained that the whole system encouraged individual work outside the groups, since the workers did not get a share of the profit. They therefore kept on working as before in order to earn enough money for their families. Work in the groups was given low priority, even considered as a new burden. Most fish traders were still working on their own, using the same technology, and facing the same problems as before.

The difficulties of the groups were discussed at UWT meetings. The secretary of the fish trade groups explained the problems in terms of effort: some members worked, while others did not. She even suggested that new groups should base themselves on these criteria. The UWT secretary, who had experience and had been trained in this work, questioned this way of organizing. She also questioned the profit system. However, no clear conclusion in terms of a new policy or new formal guidelines was reached. These days the kilns are in minimal use.

The project has had side-effects, however, in the form of various private and collective initiatives undertaken among the women. Some of the Sota women tried to start their own private co-operative based on clan membership or close friendship outside the UWT. One woman built a little kiln on her own, explaining she intended to use it together with another woman. Others, including the secretary of the new fish trade groups, went to the regional centre to enquire about loans to buy fishing boats, enthusiastically supported by their husbands. Their plans were that their husbands could run the boats, while they would process and sell the fish. Such initiatives were not very popular among other UWT members who felt that the name of the UWT was being used for private purposes. In a Luo culture such enterprises between spouses are reported as a typical way of organizing Luo enterprises.

The women from Sidika and Kirengo continued to complain that the Sota women were getting everything. They had tried to get the kilns built in their neighbourhoods, but they were always in the minority when it came to the vote. As a result, Kirengo women founded their own group (with 30 members) without external assistance. They made their own rules and plans without any association with the UWT, because they feared that the Sota women again would end up with the profits. Their intention was to grow vegetables to earn enough to invest in the necessary equipment for an organized fish trade. They started without external support and argued against bank loans or waiting for government assistance.

Despite these problems and conflicts, men and women speak with pride about the kilns, the groups and about the visitors coming to Sota. The Regional Commissioner, Maria Nyerere, the wife of the former president of Tanzania, Julius Nyerere, and central UWT representatives have visited the village to look at the project. Some of these occasions were regular formal meetings while others had the character of parties, with beer and food, and with leaders of several villages and local branches of UWT present. Both ordinary men and women and representatives of the village council considered these meetings as an honour and a recognition, even though some did complain about the expenses. In this way, Sota is talked about as a place with fisheries activities also for women.

IV. Analysis: Clanship and Gender in Development Processes

Throughout the various stages of this process, I observed changes in local and external relations, in men's and women's understandings, their interests and their skills. Such changes meant new options and opportunities, as well as confrontations about traditional rights and duties of clans or family bonds and gender.

1. *Consolidating Clanship, Ethnicity and Neighbourhood*

During the first phase of the project, the strong reactions that were voiced, and the fact that the kiln was actually built at another location than initially agreed, illustrate the importance of clan aspect in social and communicative relations. The way local men and women spoke in terms of "good" and "bad" women also links in with clan relations. Individual actors tend to be judged and judge people in terms of clan membership, especially when the distribution of goods is in focus. There is always the fear that a family from another clan may get more than another family from one's own clan.

The importance of the clan became apparent also when the local women themselves were to select participants to attend the special women's training course. The women chosen all belonged to influential clans. The same criterion was used when other influential offices were filled: the women chosen to be leader and secretary of the special fish trade groups that were established in 1989 came from one of the most powerful clans. The same principles were applied with the bicycles, which were kept in the homes of the UWT leaders. Women who opposed this came from other clans and lived in other parts of the village.

Thus, interaction encounters between different actors from different levels of society point at the importance of clanship. In discussions, however, clan relations and clanship were not always referred to openly. Arguments of likes and dislikes, organizational position and educational training were often cited. Clanship and kinship as a principle in the distribution of surplus money or surplus goods have also been reported from studies in other Luo fishing communities, emphasizing the importance of the common demands and responsibilities to kin and clan (Jansen, 1973).

In some cases the clan aspect also concurred with ethnicity. The controversy about where to build the kiln can be interpreted as a choice not only between two plots and between two clans, but also between two ethnic groups, one belonging to the Bantu Warieri and one belonging to the Nilotic Luo. At the first women's meeting when the location was selected, the majority of those present were members or supporters of the Warieri. At the meeting called by the village chairman, however, most of the politicians came from the Luo group.

The ethnic aspect is also reflected in connection with an ongoing discussion about who were more skilled at fishing, the Luo or the Warieri. The Luo may feel threatened because they see the building of a kiln near the houses of Warieri people as a message of superiority in fisheries activities.

Not only the ethnic or clan identification, but also the "strict" neighbourhood aspect, is important to remember: women smoke their fish close to their own homes, and therefore want the kilns to be nearby. The question of location, when seen from the women's position, concerns efficiency and economic rationality. The women wanted at least one kiln near where they lived. This can be the reason why most women in Kirengo and Sidika felt that the Sota women had gained most from the project. It also explains why the Kirengo women later organized themselves without connections to the UWT groups. Seen in this perspective, the building of the kilns and the reorganization of the groups did little to change the latent conflicts between people from different parts of the village.

Indeed, the more assistance and goods offered from outside, the more visible did the aspects of clan, ethnicity and neighbourhood become. Clan differentiation and clan conflicts were actualized in the new context. Likewise there seems to be a correlation between power and clan. The largest clans are able to mobilize most voters in elections, they can generally manage to send at least some of their children to school and some of the families seem to have great numbers of cattle.

Men traditionally have had political power in the local community while women have been producers with their power related to the home sphere. If organized women's activities are seen as political in a community context, this may challenge the traditional pattern. The whole process of planning and constructing the new kilns turned into a negotiation process in which the power relations in the village were mirrored.

In the interaction described here, the interests of the ethnic group, clan and family were confronted with the interests of the external fisheries officers and myself. Some of the villagers managed to make their interests prevail over those of the public fisheries workers and party workers. Local men and women made use of the opportunity to re-establish local standards. A central development principle, promoted by external actors, that women should be the target group for development action without taking clan and kinship into consideration could easily fail. Likewise the external actors had limited influence because of their sporadic presence. The most influential among the local male and female actors were those who defined the interest in the longer run. Their experience with a clan-based organization system is of long standing and well developed. From their point of view this is the most rational way of organizing, as it permits them to maintain both the clan system and their own influence. In other words, we are dealing with a classic example of social interface where local actors turn new possibilities to the benefit of their own interests.

2. *Gender Negotiations: Men's Control over Women*

When the idea of building the kiln was first launched, organized co-operation was established between local fisheries officers and some of the Sota women. Neither the UWT as an organization nor the traditional decision-making bodies were mobilized. The planning of the kiln brought together the female fishmongers, local fisheries officers, myself and the village chairman and secretary. Our co-operation started smoothly with few open negotiations about common goals and values. No one questioned that this was to be a women's project.

However, when objections began to be voiced in the village, many women withdrew. This can be understood in the light of the different goals involved. The women's short-term goal of earning money was soon confronted with the goals of the fisheries officers and myself. What we were aiming at was to improve local technology and skills in order to create income opportunities for the longer-run perspective.

Politicians at the first formal meeting raised several questions about the project. Some were questioning the alliance and the persons involved, some the goals of the new co-operation. Some were questioning women as targets in development. Some of the politicians themselves wanted to build a fishing centre. These different goals represented different interests, but also different identities related to economic roles. Women identified themselves as "bread-winners" for their children, and saw the fisheries officers and the researcher as development agents. Both the fishery officers and myself saw ourselves in roles as planners and teachers and the women primarily as female small-scale fishmongers. The politicians stressed their position as legally elected representatives of the village council. They seemed to perceive the women as their own wives or as the wives of other husbands. They emphasized the work of controlling and implementing the development plans of the village towards certain priorities. Their strong reactions indicated that they saw activities in connection with the kiln as political and oppositional, since this project had not been taken up first in the village council.

The co-operation between the local women, fisheries officers and myself appeared as a breach of formal, accepted procedures. The contact with the village chairman and the secretary was not considered as sufficiently formal. Indirectly, the male politicians were saying that they would not accept political actions and organization outside the framework of formal procedures. Such breach of protocol was seen as a reason for becoming involved in the matter of the kiln. Their insistence on adhering to protocol can be a way of emphasizing the local importance of fulfilling the ideals of Tanzanian democracy. Outsiders – whether foreigners or public officials – had no right to question established democratic rules.

From the women's point of view, the formal procedures had been followed, since two women had been elected as their representatives. Here we see an example of male control of the negotiations between men and women: the men's definition of formality proved the stronger of the two. Even though the project was meant to reach a wide range of women, the men objected.

Open negotiations in the formal fora were negotiations between local men, for example between the elected politicians on the one hand and the village chairman and the village secretary on the other hand. Here the village chairman and the village secretary supported the local women, the fisheries officers and myself, our goals and ways of working. One reason for this can be that they were both familiar with the goals of Tanzania's equality policies. Local politicians, however, tended to cite other aspects in their arguments like following the goals formulated by the elected body. The conflict can be seen as a conflict between old and new, or traditional and modern structures and principles or rules. Existing roles and relations are thus challenged. The discussions led to a breakdown in the co-operation between female fish traders and fisheries officers.

When, through their organized activities, women tended to obtain more resources and thus challenge male control, such activities may be labelled "political", and the women, local fisheries officers and myself were "politicians". This then meant a challenge to the established patterns of power relations embedded in both the clan system and the new democracy and its bodies.

We could also cite other examples of male control. The working relations between non-local male teachers and local female students point up the interest of local men/husbands in controlling women and in maintaining the established rules of male/female positions and behaviour. Husbands realized that training courses would involve close contact between their wives and male strangers. This was difficult to accept for some; others, somewhat resignedly, accepted that new questions had arisen and required new answers. This should also be seen in connection with the traditional way of dealing with sexual relations between married men and women. Local standards of sexuality as defined by men seem to confirm that husbands may have lovers. At the same time, however, husbands expect their wives to stay completely faithful. Wives, however, were sceptical towards husbands' views. Some even expressed clearly that they could have a "friend" as long as this was kept secret.

These examples concern situations where men wanted to control women. The UWT context seemed initially to be a "private space" with female control and no direct male interference. Nor did the village men object when the fishmonger groups and the UWT started. Through this process of re-establishing the UWT, the women got new tasks, but also new resources. The local UWT regained acceptance locally and in the region. Here we should recall that the UWT is a recognized and established political organization in Tanzania. This makes it difficult to attack, and difficult for others to control. For their part, women developed new relations and new skills, thereby strengthening their position. Some of the women became active as leaders, arranging local meetings and participating in district and regional meetings with great success.

Later in the process, some men tried to gain influence by encouraging their wives to ask for loans and support. This indicated that women were "allowed" to control their own conditions up to a certain limit. In discussions in UWT fora, the women themselves raised the questions concerning principles of organization. The experienced UWT secretary argued for women's organization without taking the clan into consideration, but the practice of the others indicated that they felt clan principles should be applied in organizing the fish trade.

During the process conflicting relations between local women and men from outside occur. This was demonstrated through the matter of Tanzania Fisheries Research Institute. When the local women felt that they could not use the kiln whenever they wanted, some of them reacted strongly. To them it seemed as if it was their own property that had been taken from them. Negotiations with male representatives of the research station proved fruitless. The men said that there was nothing in the agreement between Tarime Council and TAFIRI to indicate that the kiln belonged to the UWT. In other words, they used lack of formality as their argument to support their view and continued to use the kiln in spite of the women's wishes. For the TAFIRI men, formal rights seemed to be more important than women's informal rights.

Against this background we can say that in the course of these interaction encounters, the women of Sota have acquired a position as middlemen or mediators between the local and national and the international levels of development institutions. In other words they can be looked upon as "vehicles of development". By means of women's projects, local men can demonstrate to the outside world that development is also in progress in their village. However, the men still want to have the final word. The fact that all this is going on also indicates political activity. In the end, the political aspect of the kiln case, the training and the UWT activity proved of greater consequence than the financial aspect.

3. *Has Gender Gained a New Significance?*

The initiative of the outside actors made gender visible and operative as a principle for organizing projects. Previously, local women had tried to apply gender through organizing the UWT, but they had little formal contact with the outside bureaucratic world. That had remained the preserve of the men. During the interaction they came to realize the interference of conflicting principles, like clanship and traditional gender concepts versus modern or Western ideas of gender equality. Although the co-operation between the women and the fisheries officers gave the various local initiatives a start, this did not seem sufficient to change individual fish trade work into lasting co-operative work. Local values and local hierarchies thus overruled the novel organizational guidelines which had been introduced by local as well as non-local fisheries officers and myself.

Another important effect of interaction was that the local men became more interested in women's activities. The women, for their part, offered visitors hospitality and hoped that their work could result in development of some kind. The fact that influential people had come to this village to visit and even had bought their smoked fish was very important in their eyes, and served to instil confidence in the local women. The women mentioned it as proof of the quality of their products, and both men and women used it as a sign of recognition. Thus, contact with prominent persons and prestigious agencies gave the women not only financial capital, but also symbolic capital, in the sense of winning for them prestige and support.

Men's acceptance can also be seen because some husbands supported their wives and recognized the benefits of allocating more resources to women. The husbands of some active women spoke of the possibilities of getting fishing nets and boats which they could administer to provide the women with sufficient fish to sell. Some men from Kirengo, for example, mentioned how unhappy they were about their women's lack of opportunities, and how their own village should have had such opportunities. Clearly, then, the men became more supportive when they could see possibilities for themselves.

It seems that using gender as a principle of organization can be accepted only after the relations between clan membership and gender are clarified. Male clan members have to realize that they can achieve development through female members and through women-oriented projects. Once this was accepted in Sota, the women became public persons who were representing the village to the outside world to a greater extent than before, although men still retained their influence.

Interaction between local women and external men faces challenges embedded in the ideologies and patterns of gender. However, women have an impact on values, interests and relations. This is clearly seen in the encounters where they promote their own interests.

This points up the importance of focusing on the gender aspect in dealing with social interface. The case of Sota shows that when we can understand the ramifications of the male–female dimension, we can better understand the character of situations involving social interface. Gender thus emerges as a central dimension in studying encounters of social interface.

V. Conclusions

In brief our findings can be summarized as follows. First, the individual female fishmongers in this project perceived and employed clanship and kinship identities as main criteria when planning and implementing project activities. Second, the agents of change attached to the women's fisheries project placed great importance on women's production and trade as an activity through which women could become mobilized for development. Women as a target group for development represented something new and therefore conflictual in this local setting.

Third, women who normally work within a household context can, when well organized and provided with external recognition and support, become a source of inspiration for development, recognized by both men and women in the village. However, this can be achieved only if and when the development efforts are seen as acceptable within the established systems.

Thus, we can agree that kilns and organizing groups proved to be minor things and relations with major far-reaching implications. The social processes and the various actors involved revealed and questioned traditional power relations, where clanship and gender emerged as the most important aspect being challenged and negotiated. The main gender patterns have not undergone immense changes. Nevertheless, gender can be said to have gained a new significance since women are "accepted" through long discussions, as development partners. Thus, the case of Sota represents a "classic" case of social interface.

Notes

1 The research project that forms the basis for this chapter is being carried out together with Dr John Wembah Rashid and Vivian Bashemererwa. We did our field-work separately in three villages of Tarime District, Tanzania.

This chapter was made possible through the financial support of the Norwegian Council for Applied Science (NORAS), Finnmark College, the Norwegian College of Fishery Science, University of Tromsø and the Norwegian Agency for Development Co-operation (NORAD).

Without the support of the inhabitants in the village of Sota, the fisheries officers on the local, district, regional and national levels, including Mara Fisheries Development Centre and Mbegani Fisheries Development Centre, this work could not have been done. In the process of writing, Inger Altern, Harald Eidheim, Ole Petter Gurholt, Lisbet Holtedahl, Susan Høivik, Jørgen Lindkvist, John Wembah Rashid, Sidsel Saugestad, Kristi Anne Stølen, Halldis Valestrand and Mariken Vaa have given inspiration and assistance. Heartfelt thanks to them all.

2 In the following I use the name of "Sota" when I focus on the smaller neighbourhood of Sota. When I focus on the whole village, I will use the term "the village of Sota" or "Sota village".

3 The material on which this study is based was collected during eight months in 1986–87 and one month in 1989 when I stayed in Mara region. The data have been collected through participant observation, interviews and informal talks. I accompanied the fishermen in their work and I listened to the long discussions at the landing sites where the fishermen and the fish traders meet. I visited the women's homes, observed their fish processing, their trade, their farming and their cooking. Often I would be invited for dinner. I also participated in formal meetings and in the first stages of the planning and building of the smoking kiln. In this way I learnt about the organization of work, which topics were important issues and also about values and priorities. In addition I obtained information about local contacts with the outside world, especially within the fisheries sector.

The research languages were English and Swahili. The fisheries officers and local men and women helped to translate when the local language, the Nilotic Luo language, was spoken.

I also interviewed 50 men and women who were engaged in catching and trading fish by means of a questionnaire. This provided with information about the division of labour and about people's views on development. I also paid several visits to the district and regional fisheries officers. Further I participated in arranging a seminar held by the Regional Fisheries Officer in 1987 in cooperation with Mara Fisheries Development Centre (Mara FDC) and Mbegani Fisheries Development Centre (Mbegani FDC) where men's and women's roles in fisheries development were discussed. The data from Mara Region were supplemented during a three months' stay in Dar es Salaam.

In Dar es Salaam I had interviews and informal talks with representatives of the Division of Fisheries in the Ministry of Land, Natural Resources and Tourism (its present name is Ministry of Tourism, Natural Resources and Environment). I also visited Mbegani Fisheries Development Centre outside Dar es Salaam and interviewed representatives of the Norwegian Agency for Development Cooperation working with fisheries and with women's issues.

4 A few notes on history might shed some light on Sota's relations to the external world. During the German colonial period, Shirati (as the geographical area was called) was an important border post, with Sota as its headquarters. Because of its proximity to the Kenya–German East Africa border and its natural harbour, it became a logical choice for a port. When Kenya, Tanganyika Territory and Uganda came under the British colonial umbrella, Sota became a port for East African Railways steamers, plying Lake Victoria with improved facilities.

With the breakup of the East African Community in 1977, lake steamer services were discontinued. Strained relations between Kenya and Tanzania necessitated the establishment of the Lake Police Patrol Post.

Simultaneously with these developments, the villagization programme of the mid-1970s was consolidating itself. One result was the establishment of a primary school which brought in teachers from many parts of Tanzania.

5 Clan and ethnic groups are well known concepts in social anthropology. A "clan" includes all members who consider themselves as descendants from a common ancestor. Clans are divided into lineages and families (Keesing, 1981).

Ethnicity provides a basis for social identification, social action and for political mobilization. Ethnic groups may be perceived in various ways according to race, culture, religion, language or place of origin. A unique combination of such items differentiates the ethnic community from the rest of society and provides the basis for self-consciousness among members of the ethnic community (Hulme and Turner, 1990, p. 378).

6 The Tanzanian administrative system consists of different levels: village, ward, division, district, region and nation. In this chapter Sota represents the village, Shirati the ward, Nyancha the division, Tarime the district, Mara the region and Tanzania the whole nation.
7 Until the mid-1980s the District Fisheries Officer and his employees were administrated by the Regional Fisheries Officer and the Division of Fisheries in the Ministry. In other words, they were employed by the Government. At present the District Fisheries Officer and his men are administrated by the District Council, which is also responsible for wages.
8 Personal interview, November 1989.
9 This money was private money.
10 Mrieri is the singular form of Warieri in Swahili.
11 A report from the seminar was produced by the Regional Fisheries Office (Wembah Rashid and Barnabas, 1988).

References

Bashemererwa, V. *et al.* 1986. *The Role of Women in Tanzania Fishing Societies.* Dar es Salaam: IDSWSG report, University of Dar es Salaam.
Falch, E. 1989. *Short Course – Training Program,* Unpublished report. Bagamoyo, Tanzania: Mbegani Fisheries Development Centre.
Gerrard, S. 1975. *Arbeidsliv og lokalsamfunn (Working life and local community).* MA Thesis, University of Tromsø, Tromsø (in Norwegian).
Gerrard, S. 1983. Kvinner i fiskeridistrikter: Fiskerinæringas bakkemannskap? In B. Hersoug (ed.) *Kan fiskerinæringa styres?* (Women in the Fishery Districts: The Foundation of the Fishery Industry. In B. Hersoug (ed.), *Can the Fishery Industry Be Governed?)* Oslo: Novus forlag (In Norwegian).
Gerrard, S. 1988. *Challenges of Fisheries Development, Training and Extension Work – Analysis and Recommendations Based on Examples from Men's and Women's Fisheries in Mara Region, Tanzania.* FDH report 1988 – 14, Alta, Norway.
Goffmann, E. 1974. *Frame Analysis.* New York: Harper & Row.
Hempel, E. 1989. The Tanzanian Fisheries Sector. Unpublished Paper, Dar es Salaam.
Hersoug, B. 1983. *Kan fiskerinæringa styres?* (Can the Fisheries Be Governed?). Oslo: Novus forlag.
Hersoug, B. *et al.* 1986. *The Evaluation Report of the Mbegani Fisheries Development Centre.* Oslo: Evaluation Report 4.86, NORAD.
Hulme, D. and Turner, M. 1990. *Sociology and Development: Theories, Policies and Practices.* London: Harvester Wheatsheaf.
Jansen, E. G. 1973. *The Fishing Population in the Kenyan Part of Lake Victoria.* Bergen: Institute of Social Anthropology, University of Bergen.
Johnsen, J. P. 1989. *Fiskeriutvikling: Et resultat av planlagt organisering og planløs tilpasning? (Fisheries Development: A Result of Planned Organization and Unplanned Adaption?* MA Thesis, Norwegian Fishery College, University of Tromsø, Tromsø (in Norwegian).
Keesing, R. M. 1981. *Cultural Anthropology – A Contemporary Perspective.* New York: Holt, Rinehart and Winston.
Kets de Vries, M. F. and Miller, D. 1985. *The Neurotic Organization.* San Francisco: Jossey-Bass.
Long, N. 1989. *Encounters at the Interface.* Wageningen, The Netherlands: Wageningse Sociologische Studies.
Rudie, I. 1984. Innledning. In Rudie (ed.), *Myk start hard landing.* Introduction. In I. Rudie (ed.), *(Smooth Start – Hard Landing).* Oslo: Norwegian University Press (in Norwegian).

Rudie, I. 1984. *Myk start hard landing (Smooth Start – Hard Landing)*. Oslo: Norwegian University Press (in Norwegian).
Salomon, R. 1983. Det politiske bildet (The Political Picture). *HODI*, 2–3, Oslo.
Swantz, M. L. 1986. *The Role of Women in Tanzanian Fishing Societies – A Study of the Socio-economic Context and the Situation of Women in Three Coastal Fishing Villages in Tanzania*. Oslo: Study commissioned by NORAD.
Wembah Rashid, J. A. R. 1989. *Women in the Fisheries Sector: The Case of Kirongwe Village, Tarime District, Tanzania*. Dar es Salaam, Tanzania/Alta, Norway: FDH report.
Wembah Rashid, J. A. R. and Barnabas, S. K. 1988. Resolutions of the Workshop on the Role of Women in the Fisheries Industry in Tarime District, Mara Region, Tanzania. In S. Gerrard (ed.), *Challenges of Fisheries Development, Training and Extension Services – Analysis and Recommendations Based on Examples from Men's and Women's Fisheries in Mara Region, Tanzania*. Alta: FDH report, 1988–14.

10

Legal Reform in Mozambique: Equality and Emancipation for Women through Popular Justice?

NINA BERG AND AASE GUNDERSEN

> Before independence we were not allowed to express an opinion about anything. Today we really feel we have the freedom to speak and the possibility of bringing out our conflicts, and that what we say will be listened to.
>
> Female judge, Luis Cabral Popular Tribunal

The Mozambican Constitution, adopted upon independence in 1975, declared that all citizens shall enjoy the same rights and be subject to the same duties "irrespective of colour, race, sex, ethnic origin, place of birth, religion . . ." (Art. 26). No exception was made for the use of traditional law regarding family life and land rights, as is common elsewhere in Africa. Among the fundamental objectives of the Republic listed in the Constitution was "the elimination of colonial and traditional structures of oppression and exploitation and the mentality that underlies them" (Art. 4). This was followed up by provisions aimed at destroying traditional structures which oppress women. Art. 17 stated that "the emancipation of women is one of the State's essential tasks", and proclaimed equal rights for women and men extending to political, economic, social and cultural spheres. The equal rights principle should further guide all legislative and executive action (Art. 29).

The Constitution can be seen as a political document, expressing the fundamental principles and values of the new state. Unity and equality were to lay the foundation for building the nation. Both represented radical change in a society full of diversity and with traditional norms which assign women and men to different spheres. To implement the new principles a thorough reform of the legal system was launched, introducing a unitary system of law based on Popular Justice. The term points to extensive participation of lay people in the creation and administration of law. A court hierarchy of popular tribunals was set up to replace the colonial as well as the customary legal institutions as the only courts recognized by the state. The legal significance of the Constitution in this context is that its principles shall guide the administration of law at all levels throughout the country.

Through legal reform the government has initiated a process of change, aimed at improving the position of women. The local popular tribunal is seen as an instrument for implementing the principles of equality and emancipation with effect for the everyday life of Mozambican women and men. The local popular tribunal is an institution in which ideals from political and administrative authorities, expressed through laws and policy formulations, meet the traditions, experiences and values of the people. The intention was that out of this interaction a transformation of the customary law and social norms would emerge, in line with constitutional principles.

This chapter will analyse the effect of the legal reform on the position of women. The principles of gender equality and emancipation are analysed at three levels: ideals, positive law and reality. The first refers to the phase in which new ideas are conceived and formulated as ideals on the political level. In the next stage the ideals are transformed into legally binding norms. Only when the legal norms are followed and respected will they have a significance for people in general. We will examine how the provisions are realized in a local popular tribunal, where legal and other factors interact in determining to what extent the ideals expressed through law become reality.

What follows is based on material gathered through recording and observing cases in the Popular Tribunal of Luis Cabral, a township (*bairro*) on the outskirts of Maputo with about 20,000 inhabitants,[1] during two periods of six weeks each in 1987 and 1988. The material comprises 50 cases, interviews with ten of the female litigants and with the ten elected judges. In 1987 election of judges for the tribunal was held, and we observed the final part of the election process. We also interviewed persons involved in the administration of justice or working with women's issues.[2]

Luis Cabral has a mixture of rural and urban features, where most people are involved in a monetary as well as a subsistence economy. A common feature is the migration of male labour to the mines of South Africa. Like the rest of southern Mozambique, the area is dominated by a patrilinear kinship system and patrilocal residence upon marriage. Traditionally, marriages in this area are polygamous, and the payment of brideprice (lobolo) is essential in contracting a marriage.

Mozambique has for the past decade experienced a situation of internal war. The warfare launched by Renamo[3] as part of South African destabilization policy has had the civilian population and the general infrastructure as main targets. New schools, health posts and tribunals have been attacked, increasing the difficulties of achieving results from the government's development policies. Women have in this situation suffered from sexual abuse and forced labour (Jeichande, 1990, p. 73). It is estimated that approximately 5.5 million people, or one-third of the population, are directly affected by the war. More than half of these are refugees in neighbouring countries or displaced within the country.[4]

For the rural population the war and repeated drought have reinforced the effects of mistaken agricultural policies during the first years of independence, when the family farming sector was neglected. The result has been an enormous influx of people to the major cities, especially Maputo. Two-thirds of the Mozambican people today live in absolute poverty (Hermele, 1990, p. 21). In the cities, unemployment, frequent devaluations, minimal rises in salaries and drastic cuts in the subsidized urban food ration are making survival precarious. It was in this context that the government, in cooperation with the IMF and the World Bank, introduced an Economic Rehabilitation Programme (PRE) in 1987. Criticism has been raised against it, focusing on the worsening economic conditions for the urban poor and the serious social impact of the programme (Brochmann and Ofstad, 1990). Attempts to overcome some of the negative effects were made when the programme entered into its second phase in 1990, renamed as an Economic and Social Rehabilitation Programme (PRES). The measures taken in the economic field represent a general political reorientation. A reform process, which includes a new Constitution, is under way.[5]

I. Creating the Ideals – the Historical and Political Context

1. *Unity, Equality and Popular Participation*

The Mozambican people had united in a liberation war against the colonial power despite ethnic, regional, religious and political differences. After independence internal differences constituted a threat to the new nation, and the government emphasized national unity as a political principle and nation-building as a fundamental objective for the state. The ideological foundation for the new state grew out of the struggle for independence. What had started as an armed struggle for national liberation had developed into a revolution (Egerö, 1987, p. 26). Well before its conversion from a liberation front to a ruling party, Frelimo[6] had chosen a Marxist-Leninist path. The declared aim of its political programme was to create a socialist society based on equality and people's power, free from "exploitation of man by man". Gender equality was one aspect of this, along with racial and tribal equality. The concept of "people's democracy" was to be founded on new structures of power based on popular participation. People's assemblies were established at national, provincial and local levels. A national People's Assembly was the legislative body and the highest organ of the state. The aim for the legal sector was to create a system of popular justice, where people's participation should be ensured not only in the legislative process, but also in the administration of justice.

2. Emancipation of Women

Women had participated in the liberation struggle side by side with men. The "Women's Detachment" to Frelimo was created in 1967, followed by the establishment of the Organization of Mozambican Women (Organização da Mulher Moçambicana – OMM) in 1973 as a "mass democratic organization" linked to Frelimo. The emancipation of women was defined as an integral part of the liberation struggle. In a famous speech to the opening conference of the OMM, Frelimo president Samora Machel stated: "The liberation of women is a fundamental necessity for the Revolution, the guarantee of its continuity and the precondition for its victory" (Machel, 1981, p. 20). A common view was that by breaking out of traditional gender roles to take part in the war, women had sown the first seeds of their liberation. The political line was followed up by the provisions about gender equality and emancipation of women in the new Constitution adopted upon independence.

At the political level, the question of the emancipation of women has been linked to their participation in what has been seen as the "principal task" (Hanlon, 1984, p. 158; Urdang, 1983, p. 17). During the liberation war this was fighting the enemy. After independence the principal task, according to Frelimo, has been the socialist transformation of society. Women have been urged to participate in production through wage labour and in cooperatives, and in the decision-making processes, whether in the leadership of cooperatives and communal villages, or as deputies to the people's assemblies and judges in the popular tribunals. Women were also called upon to fill positions in the Party organization, although mainly on the lower levels.

In line with the efforts to eliminate traditional structures of oppression and exploitation of women, campaigns were launched by the government against traditional customs and institutions that were considered discriminating to women, such as lobolo, polygamy, premature and forced marriages and initiation rites. Slogans like "down with lobolo", "down with polygamy" were repeated at political gatherings (Welch and Sachs, 1987, p. 379).

3. *Equality and Emancipation in Public and Private Domains*

At the level of party and government, equality between men and women is seen as part of the broader socialist concept of equality, which has been introduced without any specific analysis of gender issues. In this view, the primary contradiction is between women and the (capitalist) social order. Contradictions between women and men are recognized, but are seen as being of a secondary nature (Machel, 1981, p. 25).

With the emphasis on participation in production and decision-making, the notions of equality and emancipation, as put forward by the Mozambican authorities, have the male model as norm; women should be emancipated to be more like men. This approach overlooks the fact that women are already responsible for the majority of the country's agricultural production, namely the family farm labour, in addition to trading activities in the informal sector, extensive household tasks and child-rearing. The traditional sexual division of labour, especially in rural areas, leaves women with little time to assume additional duties in the name of equality and emancipation.

Introducing gender equality as a constitutional principle is far from sufficient in bringing about real change. And the question can be raised whether promotion of an equality ideal is the best way to improve the situation of women in Mozambique. The idea of gender equality is new and does not correspond to the reality of Mozambican women. As Arnfred notes, the traditional construction of gender identity did not rest on any notion of equality, but rather on ideas of complementarity between women and men and the separation of male and female spheres, whether this be in the sexual division of labour or in the concept of different capacities (Arnfred, 1988, p. 9).

The campaigns against traditions such as lobolo and polygamy acknowledged that the family patterns which still persist in much of the country constitute a major obstacle to the achievement of equality between men and women (Urdang, 1983, p. 27). This means that for a strategy of gender equality to succeed, it must also challenge the traditional gender roles inside the family.

However, the action for increasing women's public role has had positive results for many Mozambican women. Their participation in armed struggle and organized production or public duties bring women out of the home. For part of the time they are no longer under the direct authority of a husband or a male relative, and this gives them an identity independent of the family (Hanlon, 1984, p. 159). Participation in the political process gives women a decisive role which is often denied them in the home. Even more significant is the economic independence they can achieve as workers in a cooperative. Upon assuming a role in public life, a woman's image of herself, and subsequently the husband's image of her, may change. This can initiate a process of change in family relations leading to emancipation of the woman also in this respect. However, this is at best double-edged, as it may provoke conflicts in the family which eventually lead to a divorce (Urdang, 1989).

The failure to challenge male family authority and the almost total lack of measures to implement and follow up the ideals of equality and emancipation can lead to the question of whether there was, or is, true political will to carry out changes which could improve women's position. Even on the formal level, the commitment to equality in the political leadership can be questioned. A Nationality Law enacted on the same day as the Constitution deprived Mozambican women, but not men, of their citizenship when marrying foreigners. Despite the clear contradiction to the Constitution, the code remained unchanged until 1987. Implementation of gender policies has been left to the OMM, which as a Party organization has seen as its major role the political mobilization of women. The male-dominated party leadership also formulates the policies in this field, without being challenged seriously by the OMM. Gender issues have hardly been on the political agenda in

Mozambique, and when they have, they have had the character of mere rhetoric. Despite the policy of increasing women's participation in decision-making, the number of women in political or leading administrative positions is low (Casimiro *et al.*, 1990). In this context the establishment of the local popular tribunal could play an important role. Women are frequently found as elected judges in the local popular tribunals. It is a matter of policy that out of the 3-5 judges working collectively in a tribunal, at least one should be a woman (Welch, 1988, p. 44). In the entire court system there are approximately 9,000 elected judges, of which 15 per cent are women (Frelimo, 1989a, Chapter II, p. 20). For Mozambican women this means that for the first time they are allowed to participate in the administration of justice. Perhaps more important is that the local popular tribunal is an institution where conflicts in the family, typically disputes between husband and wife, are dealt with. Since the tribunals are to apply the guideline of equality and emancipation, this is an institution where these ideals can be put into operation also in relation to the private sphere.

II. From Ideal to Positive Law: Building a New Legal System

The principles of unity, equality and emancipation were brought into the Constitution of 1975. However, to give rise to positive rights for women, the principles have to be incorporated into the law enforceable in the courts. Introducing gender equality and women's emancipation as guiding principles required a transformation of customary law as well as the colonial law still in force. To achieve transformation towards a unitary application of law throughout the country, it was also considered necessary to build a new court system based on unity and popular participation. The courts are to liaise closely with political, social and state bodies (Law on Judicial Organization, Art. 6), thus ensuring a continuity between the phase of developing ideals on the political level in the Party, and the incorporation of these ideals into the law.

1. *Building a Unitary Court System*

Like many other African countries, Mozambique inherited a dual system of law upon independence. During the colonial era Portuguese law was the one in force for the settlers, while the "native" population was governed by the rules of their various traditional legal systems, as interpreted and applied by the Portuguese colonial administrator (Isaacman and Stephen, 1980, p. 13). As May points out, the question of how to deal with the inherited legal dualism caused a dilemma for the new African states. On one hand there was a need for a modern legal system to accommodate the social changes taking place. Their inclusion in the international community and subsequent subscription to universal values of human rights, as well as their own ideological commitment, also carried a desire to adapt the legal systems to new ideals. On the other hand was a call for the preservation of traditional African values after years of colonial rule and the desire to create a legal system which embodied them (May, 1987, p. 27). Most countries chose to continue a line of dualism and let customary law govern certain areas, typically family law and land law, while statutory law was adopted in other areas to meet the needs of a changing society.

In line with the political priorities outlined above, Mozambique chose to build up a unitary legal system to replace the colonial as well as the customary law. It was argued that dualism was not an option, since "customary law in [Mozambique] was actually so [...] mutilated by colonialism that at the time of independence it no longer existed as a formal and articulated set of norms applied by customary law courts" (Welch, 1988, p. 31). The Law on Judicial Organization was passed in 1978, establishing a court hierarchy of popular tribunals corresponding to the administrative levels of the locality, district and province, as well as a national Supreme Popular Tribunal.[7] Popular participation was ensured by election of lay judges to all levels of court. At the levels of the District, Province and the Supreme Popular Tribunal, the lay judges work with appointed professional judges.[8] The judicial function here is to be exercised according to the codes and other legal sources, and the lay judges are there to bring the people's sense of justice into the work of the courts.

At the local level the popular tribunal shall consist of elected lay judges only. The judges are to be elected by, and amongst, the people of the township or village over which the tribunal has jurisdiction. The local popular tribunals shall not apply codes or other formal sources of law as such. Their primary task is to mediate and seek reconciliation of the parties. Only if this cannot be achieved are they to pass judgments "in accordance with good sense and justice, and bearing in mind the principles that govern the building of a socialist society" (Law on Judicial Organization, Art. 38). Their jurisdiction is limited both in criminal and civil cases.

They cannot impose imprisonment, they can only deal with civil cases up to a certain monetary value, and they cannot grant divorce or make other decisions in relation to marriages that are officially registered. This still leaves them with the jurisdiction to deal with, and decide upon, marital conflicts for the vast majority of the people. It is estimated that less than 10 per cent of marriages are registered; the rest are established according to traditional ceremonies or are simply relationships of cohabitation (Relatório, 1988, p. 21).

The local popular tribunals draw on customary procedures for settlement of disputes, in the sense that conflicts are solved in the local community, in an informal manner and with participation of relatives and neighbours. And the wide discretion given to the judges to be exercised with "good sense and justice" makes for a concrete evaluation of the conflict in its full context, and thus resembles the customary guidelines for settling disputes. Whereas the normative basis for such a guideline was previously in customary law, the local popular tribunals are part of the state's court system, and as such they have to comply with the rules that are laid down for their function.

2. *Transforming the Substance of Law*

Creating new legal institutions is clearly not sufficient when the objective is a radical transformation of the law. The content of the laws needed to be evaluated and changed, and the long-term aim was to create a new, Mozambican body of laws. However, practical considerations required that most of the colonial law was also maintained after independence. The Constitution of 1975 has a provision to this effect, limited to former legislation which is not contrary to the Constitution (Art. 79). This vague guideline has not been sufficiently clarified by the courts and there is still some uncertainty as to which of the colonial laws are in force.

The difficulties in creating a unitary law based on the principles of gender equality and emancipation of women have been particularly evident in the area of family law. Family life and marriage patterns in Mozambique are characterized by a great diversity. Accounts tell that only in Nampula province no less than five major systems of marriage exist side by side; the traditional matrilineal system, the traditional patrilineal system, the Islamic system, Christian marriages and civil marriages, each of them with its own rules and regulations. Far from building on equality, the customary rules are based on the different status of women and men (Welch et al., 1985, p. 62).

A draft for a new national family law was put forward in 1980, prepared by the Ministry of Justice and the Faculty of Law at the University as part of a Family Law Project. Research was carried out in all provinces except one in 1979 and 1981, where material on the various systems of marriage that existed throughout the country was collected (Welch et al., 1985, p. 62). The proposed family law code attempted to reconcile the different marriage systems with the principles of unity and equality. It was realized that institutions such as lobolo and polygamy represented complex social and cultural phenomena, and could not be changed through slogans or legal action. The strategy of the law was neither to recognize nor to penalize, but rather to ignore the institutions (Welch and Sachs, 1987, p. 380).

The draft created controversy in the political bodies, and was redrawn for further preparation. The new report was completed in 1988, but at the time of writing the code is still not approved. However, due to the urgent need to replace the Portuguese family law which only regulated officially registered marriages, and to change the discriminatory rules of the customary law, parts of the draft were put into force as law by a Supreme Court of Appeal Directive[9] in 1982. Court practice following this has given Mozambican women a certain right to claim equality in questions of divorce, division of property, maintenance and custody of children. Building on a concept of "*de facto* union", the draft gives the formal courts competence to grant a couple the same legal rights and obligations after three years of cohabitation as they would have got in a registered marriage. However, no publicity was permitted about the directive which in fact brought about radical legal change, and few women know they have these rights (Hanlon, 1984, p. 165).

The directive applies in principle only to the levels of the court system which apply formal law, and not to the local popular tribunal. In some cases a woman would not see redress in a formal court of law as a strategy to solve her problem anyway, since it implies confrontation and antagonizing relationships rather than reconciliation and restoring harmony (Kasonde-Ng'andu, 1989, p. 32). The local popular tribunal offers an informal process of dispute settlement aimed at reconciliation, which bears certain similarities to customary legal institutions. However, customary law is not applied as such, and neither are other formal sources of law. Even if the provisions of the family law project do not have direct application, the same results can be reached using the "good sense and justice" guideline. Upon assuming their position, the elected judges shall be given briefings by the provincial tribunals as to the principles that are to guide their work, where the concept of gender equality is stressed.

With the wide discretionary power given to the lay judges, customary law will to a large extent subsist in the local popular tribunal. The intention is for its content to be transformed in line with the principles of equality and emancipation. Rules and customs that are discriminatory are not to be applied, but customary norms and values can be taken into consideration as long as they do not contradict the Constitution. The broad and vague guideline may thus lead to different applications of law in the various regions of the country depending on the local customs. The "good sense and justice" guideline is an interesting legal construction in that it opens for a legal pluralism to flourish within a unitary system of law. However, it may also lead to a diffuse situation where customary law functions "in disguise", making it difficult to obtain knowledge of its content and boundaries. The result must be some degree of uncertainty and unpredictability.

3. *Planned Legal Reform and Popular Justice – a Contradiction*

The idea behind popular justice is that the values of the people should determine the content of law. In the case of Mozambique, this ideal is combined with a strategy of using the law to promote radical social changes towards gender equality. This presents a contradiction, since the lay judges will often represent prevailing ideas and values about gender. The local popular tribunal may thus easily function more as a conservative than as a dynamic element in the process of planned social change. The intention of the government seems to be that in spite of being an instrument of change, the law should not be imposed from above. To change customs, attitudes and values requires a long-term, gradual transformation process. The courts are given a role in this process, beyond handling conflicts. They shall mobilize and "educate the citizens in voluntary and conscientious compliance with the laws" (Law on Judiciary Organization, Art. 2). The educative role is particularly stressed in the local popular tribunals. The idea is that the whole community shall contribute to and learn from the tribunal's work, thus ensuring a mutual influence on the content of the norms that govern people's daily lives.

For the tribunal to fulfil the purpose of bringing new ideals and principles into the community, it must be ensured that the elected judges are committed to these ideals. When the idea of popular participation in the administration of justice was introduced, the Central Committee of Frelimo stated that judges should be chosen "among elements of the Party, the Armed Forces and the Mass Democratic Organizations". The qualifications required of judges in the local popular tribunal are political competence, common sense and knowledge of the Frelimo political line (Welch, in Seminário, 1986, p. 8). In addition their life-style should set an example. For example, polygamists were not accepted. At a nomination approval meeting that we observed, a proposed male candidate was rejected because of alleged sexual promiscuity.

III. Ideals Meet Reality: Women's Emancipation and Equality in a Local Popular Tribunal

On a Saturday in June 1988 the Popular Tribunal of Luis Cabral is hearing the case of Ana and Jacinto. The couple is standing in front of the five judges, two men and three women.[10] Other people are sitting on a bench behind them. Some are relatives of the parties or other witnesses, others are waiting for their cases to come up. Ana is 44 years old, Jacinto is 36. Ana has appeared before the tribunal once already. Her first husband demanded a divorce after 25 years of marriage because of adultery. The tribunal called Jacinto, with whom Ana was having an affair, and asked if he was prepared to take care of her. He agreed, and the tribunal decided that from that day on Ana was under his protection and responsibility.[11]

Now Ana is complaining that he is breaking his promise. He does not support her, she does not get food or clothes from him and has to go to her relatives to eat. Jacinto already had a wife, and the two women do not get along well in the house. Ana found a house of her own, but Jacinto said he could not afford that. The judge president reminds him of the responsibility he accepted here in court:

> This woman has been married for 25 years. You took her away from her husband and therefore it is your responsibility to look after her. We advised you to consult your wife before taking Ana into your home. And we warned you that the price of food would

increase. The cost of living will continue to rise, and those of you who marry two wives, ten wives, you are going to suffer.

Jacinto is also criticized for not having fulfilled the duties of a new husband: he failed to present himself to her family, and he has not given her the *capulanas*[12] and other items that were to symbolize that she is now his wife. The tribunal advises him to call Ana and convince her that it is more practical for her to live in the house with him, his first wife and children. Then he has to reconfirm in writing that he accepts the responsibility for Ana.

1. Women's Access to the Law

The first prerequisite for legal measures to improve the lot of women is that they have access to the legal institutions. Under customary law, women could not appear before the courts, but always had to be represented by their male protector (Isaacman and Stephen, 1980, p. 7). In the popular tribunals every adult[13] can appear before the court in their own capacity. The formal access to the courts on an equal footing with men is perhaps the most significant change the legal reform has brought about for Mozambican women.

Formal access to the courts is, however, not sufficient to ensure women real access to employ the law. Other factors like costs, language and degree of formalism may hinder their real access to the courts. This has been taken into consideration in the local popular tribunal. There are no court fees. The hearings take place in the local language if the parties so wish and it is possible.[14] Furthermore, there is only a minimum of formal requirements. A complaint is presented orally, and presentation of written documentation is not required. The fact that the judges are ordinary people from the community, that the tribunal is located in the neighbourhood and that there is a short time span between the event and the process in the tribunal are features that in general increase people's access to the law (Ietswaart, 1982, p. 152; Abel, 1973). In addition, it can be assumed that the presence of women as judges to some extent makes it easier for women to approach the court.

The question is whether women, in coming to the popular tribunal, also have access to the law in a more substantial sense: does the law offer women solutions to their problems in line with their interests? The content of law is in the local popular tribunal left to the discretion of the judges. How the discretionary power is exercised determines how far the tribunal promotes the ideals of equality and emancipation. Thus, we must look into which principles guide the application of law, what types of norms the judges feel bound by, and to what extent women's interests and needs are taken into consideration. The point of departure will be taken in the conflicts that women experience, as we have observed them in the Popular Tribunal of Luis Cabral.[15]

2. Women's Conflicts as They Appear in the Tribunal

The case of Ana shows that the polygamous marriage still exists, and may cause problems for the women involved. Here the conflict concerned lack of maintenance for Ana as a second wife. The economic basis for polygamy is disappearing in the urban areas, and it seems that the custom is on the decline here. Thus, the Popular Tribunal of Luis Cabral has had to deal with cases where married men have entered into relationships with other women without assuming the responsibility of a husband. This leaves the woman in a weaker position than the second or third wife of a polygamous husband. In the case of Ana, the tribunal actually established a marriage between Ana and Jacinto, despite the fact that Jacinto already had a wife. Evidently this was to avoid Ana ending up in a position without protection from a man – her husband or her lover. They made Jacinto take the responsibility of a husband even though the couple never contracted a marriage according to any recognized form. What Ana wanted was the economic independence she had had in her first marriage, where she was the first wife and the family bread-winner. Ana's problem arose because she had an affair with another man. Her husband did not tolerate her adultery, despite the fact that he had several other wives and extra-marital affairs. Since Ana was considered the guilty party in the divorce case, she did not get any of the property, despite the fact that most of it had been bought with her income.

Several of the women who came to the tribunal experienced conflicts with their husbands because of their involvement in income-generating activities in the informal sector. Access to money and thereby a certain economic independence for a woman often leads to quarrels in the family. This was the case for Joana, a petty trader who spent 15 days in hospital after having been beaten up by her husband. When she moved out of the house, the husband complained before the court:

> The problem was that she didn't show me the money she made. She should have shown me, as her husband. She started to buy things and brought them home without telling me anything, without consulting me.

He accuses her of meeting other men when she is out selling, and of being involved in prostitution in her sister's house. Therefore, he has beaten her up several times. Joana replies:

> The first time he beat me up was when I refused to sell his fish and firewood, because I have my own work. I never get the money from the wood sales. He uses it to buy *tontonto* (a traditional alcoholic drink). I buy things to sell, I buy clothes and food, and I feed him. I never need money from him to go to the market. I maintain myself.

Joana now wants Manuel to take her back to her family who live in another province, to discuss a divorce. After attempting to reconcile the couple, the tribunal decides that Manuel should give her the money for the ticket, and that he should follow her later to resolve the problem there with her family. Women who wanted a divorce came to the tribunal and asked for a dissolution of the marriage. The reason could be battering, lack of maintenance, adultery or simply that the couple quarrelled all the time. If the tribunal found that the couple could not be reconciled, the judges granted a divorce, divided the common property and decided on the maintenance question. Women who were considered guiltless in the breakdown of the marriage often got a share of the property. However, the divisible property could frequently be rather insignificant, but what matters for the woman is to get somewhere to stay.

The case of Maria and José exemplifies this. Their case is referred to the tribunal by the police, after the couple had been fighting. They have been living together for six months. Before this, Maria was living with another man in his house, but he has gone to another province because he was ill. When Maria started an affair with José, the relatives of the other man threw her out of his house, and she went to live with José. He did not pay lobolo, but gave her brother some wine and a small sum of money to "show that he was having a relationship" with her. He has two other wives and several mistresses, and is characterized by the court as "a terrible womanizer". The couple fight all the time, and José accuses Maria of trying to poison him with traditional medicine. He does not want to live with her any more. The tribunal does not consider the couple to be married, but states that José, by paying the money and the wine, has indicated intention of marriage, and thus has a responsibility for Maria. Since he took her out of the house of her former husband, he is sentenced to build her a house of her own.

For some women divorce was the only solution they saw to their problems. However, it is not easy to be a single woman. Women who managed on their own without a man might become an object for harassment and persecution in the neighbourhood, as happened to Fernanda. Fernanda was chased out of her house by the *responsavels*[16] after some of her neighbours had accused her of bewitching them. Fernanda is a hard-working woman, with two fields where she grows peanuts and vegetables, in addition to her work in the cashew factory. She produces enough to provide well for herself and two nieces, whom she supports. The neighbours claimed that when they were asleep, she bewitched them to go and work in her fields. They started harassing her and reported to the *responsavels*, and eventually she was forced out of her house. Fernanda reported the matter to the police, and the case was taken to court. The local popular tribunal referred the case to the District Tribunal because of its seriousness. The case is heard in the neighbourhood in the presence of all the neighbours. The *responsavels* are charged with abuse of power and deprived of their positions. They are also sentenced to heavy fines and suspended imprisonment.

3. *Application of Law in the Local Popular Tribunal*

The application of law under the guideline of "good sense and justice" indicates what types of underlying norms are in force in the tribunal. Although customary law is not to be applied as such, we see that the Popular Tribunal of Luis Cabral often referred to traditions and customs as the norm for behaviour. Sometimes this concerned the traditional sexual division of labour, and the tribunal stressed that it is the responsibility of the woman to clean and cook for her husband. In other cases it could be a woman's sexual morals that were condemned. In the case of Maria, who had had two relationships with men before moving in with José, one of the judges said in their internal consultation: "She doesn't live a good life. She is practically a prostitute." Towards men, the tribunal emphasized their obligation to maintain the women and children, more than condemning their sexual promiscuity. Certain traditions were, however, clearly denounced by the tribunal. The case of Fernanda shows that the tribunal refused to deal with accusations of witchcraft. Likewise they would not accept claims that Maria tried to poison José with traditional medicines, without clear evidence.

The rules that determine rights and obligations attached to payment of lobolo are the parts of customary law which relate to the essential aspects of marriage. According to customs, once lobolo was paid by the groom, or rather by his family, they were in control of the woman's productive and reproductive capacity. Any offspring of the marriage, as well as the results of the wife's labour, belonged to the husband and his family. A woman could not obtain a divorce without the lobolo being restored, and in such a case the children and the property would remain with the husband. Upon the death of the husband the widow could be inherited by a relative of the diseased (Welch and Sachs, 1987, p. 369). Although it is difficult to say to what extent these rules were still in force at the time of independence, it is clear that many of them were, and still are practised (Urdang, 1989).

The Popular Tribunal of Luis Cabral followed up the official policy by ignoring these customary rules regarding lobolo in dealing with divorce cases. However, the case of Maria shows that payment of lobolo was taken into consideration by the tribunal. It had significance as evidence of marriage or of intention of marriage. The fact that lobolo is paid can thereby give women a certain protection, as it puts them in a position to claim the rights of a wife. With regards to polygamy, the tribunal seemed to accept the custom, but did warn men about the economic responsibility involved. In the case of Ana, the tribunal practically established a polygamous union. Also in the case of Maria, the relationship between José and her was recognized despite the fact that he was already married. The tribunal even criticized him for not paying the lobolo and marrying Maria properly. Thus, women of a polygamous marriage were given the same protection by the tribunal as they would have got in a monogamous union.

In modifying the customary norms, the judges sometimes referred to political or ideological norms of how a "good Mozambican" should behave. Sometimes direct references to Frelimo and "the new society" were given, often in a long monologue by the Judge President. He could refer to how the relationship between husband and wife had changed after Frelimo came into power, for example with regard to a husband's duty to maintain his wife and children after divorce.

In our case material there were hardly any direct references to the constitutional principle of equality between men and women. However, one could say that the equal right to divorce is an application of this principle. Women were granted a divorce for the same reasons as men, including adultery of their husband. There was in these cases no reference to the traditional right of a man to have more than one wife. When it came to division of property upon divorce, the equality norm was not practised. In the case of Ana, the tribunal applied a guilt principle and denied her any part of the common property because she was found to be the one who caused a divorce. This also occurred in other cases against women, but the same principle was not applied to men whose behaviour caused a marriage breakdown.

Rather than applying the principles of equality and emancipation, the tribunal seemed to try to protect the interests of women, as they saw them. This is clear in the cases of Ana and Maria, where the tribunal practically "invented" norms to cover the cases. All in all, it seemed to be a major concern for the tribunal to reach a pragmatic solution that they believed the parties could live with, rather than applying specific rules.

The examples also illustrate the close interaction between the local popular tribunal and other institutions of dispute settlement, both traditional and modern. The case of Joana shows how the family is still seen as the first instance for settling conflicts. Joana did not want a divorce by the tribunal. She wanted Manuel to take her to her family so they could discuss a divorce there, and this was the decision of the tribunal. Family conflicts are normally discussed with relatives, and also with the head of the block (*quarteirão*) before being presented to the tribunal. In the court hearings the people involved in the conflict resolution at other levels were drawn upon as witnesses. On the other hand, the case of Fernanda shows that the local popular tribunal referred a case of high complexity and seriousness to the next level in the court hierarchy, the district popular tribunal. However, the case was heard in Luis Cabral with the judges of the local popular tribunal assisting. Other cases were also referred to the district tribunal because of their complexity, even if the local popular tribunal had the competence to deal with them.

IV. What Improvements for Women Through Popular Justice?

We have traced the concepts of equality and emancipation from the phase of being introduced as political and ideological ideals, and seen how they were incorporated as bearing principles in the new legal system built up after independence. When looking at how the ideals have been realized in the Popular Tribunal of Luis Cabral, our aim has been to illustrate the implementation of these principles on a very concrete level. The effect of the legal reform on women's everyday life is demonstrated through the kind of conflicts women in this community experience and how the tribunal responds. A case-study like this does not give comprehensive descriptions of the legal position of women. Rather, the aim has been to raise questions in order to analyse problems and potentials of the local popular tribunal in realizing the ideals of equality and emancipation for women.

The legal reforms initiated after independence have led to improvements in the legal position of women, both *de jure* and *de facto*. One of the most significant changes is that women now have access to legal institutions which they previously did not have. The establishment of the local popular tribunal is particularly important in this respect, as it offers an informal process of dispute settlement of conflicts that people experience in their daily lives, and constraints to women's real opportunity to use the tribunals are minimized. Access to legal institutions is not merely a formal right; women do approach the tribunal to complain against their husbands, they are called to respond when a case is brought against them, and in both cases they are given the opportunity to present their own views. According to judges we interviewed in two local popular tribunals in Maputo, the majority of the cases here were brought by women. The establishment of these tribunals has thus also had an important effect in making women's conflicts more visible.

When it comes to substantive rights, it is more difficult to assess what women have gained through the reforms. In some respects their rights have clearly been improved. An example is the right to divorce without an obligation to restore the lobolo. Since the popular tribunal does not recognize any legal significance of lobolo, the woman's legal position in marriage and upon divorce is stronger than it was in customary law. We have seen that the Popular Tribunal of Luis Cabral granted women the right to parts of the common property, and that women got custody over small children. An ex-husband would often be obliged by the tribunal to pay maintenance to his children. However, families are not hindered from continuing practising the rules related to lobolo, but they do not give rise to any legal claims enforceable in the courts. This may result in many conflicts being kept and handled outside the tribunals. There is a danger in founding the law on ideals and values that are alien to the people, in that it can make the law inadequate and thus less accessible. A result may be that customary law continues to exist as a sub-system of law, outside the control of the government.

The question remains as to whether the popular tribunal actually applies the principles of equality and emancipation. It seems that when the application of the "good sense and justice" guideline differed from the content of customary law, it was on issues that have been actively debated at the political level, such as the recognition of lobolo and polygamy. Here the Popular Tribunal of Luis Cabral seemed to follow the political signals, which are reflected in the Family Law Project and generally addressed in the briefing to the elected judges upon taking office. Lobolo and polygamy were thus looked upon in their complexity, as issues which are relevant for establishing the facts and context of a conflict, but that do not give rise to legal claims. The popular tribunal looked for pragmatic solutions that give protection to women in such a situation, but did not grant men their customary rights as a result of lobolo having been paid.

That the popular tribunal did not build on an equality principle in its transformation of the customary law is evident in the cases where the woman was found to be the guilty party in a marriage breakdown. She got a divorce, but did not get the same right to parts of the common property as a man in the same situation. A woman might be found to have caused the divorce not only in cases of adultery, but also if she did not behave as "a proper wife", that is if she did not clean the house, cook food and perform the other duties of a wife and mother. Here the tribunal fell back on customary norms of behaviour rather than applying an equality principle.

Interviews with women who have had their cases tried by the tribunal show that they may find the result unjust and not in accordance with what to them is "good sense". On several occasions the interviews revealed that essential information about the conflicts was not presented to the tribunal. The reason could be that the woman did not have the confidence to speak out, that she felt she was not allowed to, or that she thought it would not have any impact on the tribunal's evaluation. This indicates that women's access to the law is not fully realized in the local popular tribunal, as its procedures and application of law might be experienced by women as disfavouring their interests.

The main institutional difference between the local popular tribunal and the customary legal institutions is that the position of a judge now follows from elections rather than status and power. Measures are taken to ensure that different groups are represented as judges, particularly that women are elected to the tribunals. In Luis Cabral this has been realized, and women here have thus assumed a role in public life which they did not have in the past. The participation of women as judges is meant to ensure that women's interests are articulated and considered in the popular tribunal. Despite the fact that the majority of the judges in the Popular Tribunal of Luis Cabral in 1988 were women, it seems that this has not had the impact intended in the law. The reason for this is complex, but some factors can be pointed out. The presiding judge was always a man and the male judges dominated the hearings. The Judge President tended to dominate the proceedings, and the other judges participated when called on by him to do so. The female judges were particularly encouraged to be involved in discussions of social or moral norms for behaviour, often in relation to women's roles. In such situations they often referred to tradition and customs, condemning behaviour that violated these. This can partly be explained by looking at the kind of women who are elected judges. They were all recruited from the local OMM and tended to be middle-aged or older women, who may have a conservative view on some of the changes taking place in the life-style of younger women.

Aside from recruiting female judges to all levels of the courts, the OMM has played a rather passive role in the legal sphere. The fact that all female judges have connections to the organization gives a potential for gathering these judges to seminars and discussions, and developing strategies for how the ideals of gender equality and emancipation for women can be realized in the popular tribunals. The women judges have a first-hand experience of what the problems and needs of the women throughout the country are. This could be utilized by the OMM to initiate debate and question the strategies that have been applied in relation to the women's issue. However, the OMM has been faithful to the ideals and policies of the Party, and has only to a limited extent seen as its role to be an agent for women's politics within the Party. The OMM has accepted the imperative that equality and emancipation should be brought about by increasing women's participation in public life, and has not really challenged traditional gender roles in the family. OMM has not participated actively in the reform process that has taken place over recent years, for example by raising the question of how economic reforms affect women or how women's interests should be integrated in the new Constitution. Other women's organizations have not existed. However, the situation might be in the course of changing. The recent political development makes for the establishment of new women's groups outside the Party, and separation of the OMM from the Party is being seriously discussed in line with the general debate on introducing a multi-party system.

In the draft for a new Constitution which is being discussed in Mozambique[17], the principle of gender equality remains unchanged, and is expressed like this: "Men and women shall be equal before the law in all spheres of political, economic, social and cultural life" (Frelimo, 1990). However, the commitment of the state towards the emancipation of women is reformulated in the proposed draft, which says: "The State shall promote and support the emancipation of women, and shall stimulate the growing role of women in society." It seems that the ideals thus have a more realistic formulation at the political and legal levels. The strategy followed up to now has been to use the law as an instrument for changing behaviour, without much support from other initiatives. Much research into the sociology of law indicates that law seldom assumes such a role. Aubert points to the major functions of law as being governance, conflict resolution, resource distribution and symbolic goal setting (Aubert, 1979, p. 29; 1989, p. 61). The legal strategy adopted by Mozambique with the aim of improving women's position cannot in a short term succeed as a means of governing behaviour. The main function of such a radical reform must therefore be in terms of symbolic goal setting.

In our view, true emancipation for women cannot be brought about by formal equality only, even if it leads to increased opportunities in public life and equal rights on fundamental issues like the right to divorce. The notion of equality must also challenge the relations inside the family, which are based on differences. Introducing formal equality in a society where social and cultural norms are based on differences can lead to what theoretical discussions in women's law describe as a situation of *"de jure* equality and *de facto* discrimination". This is the result when gender-neutral laws meet gender-specific realities (Dahl, 1987, p. 48). In some respects, taking the reality of Mozambican women as the point of departure, this may lead to doubts as to whether equality as such is possible or even desirable. Perhaps a better approach to the ideal of women's emancipation in this context would be a concept of equal worth, rather than equality.

The local popular tribunal has had an important effect in opening the legal system for women. Thus, women's conflicts are made visible. Along with the general development towards more freedom of expression and organization, this can bring women's issues on the agenda in a way which has previously not been seen. With support to research and networking among women, it can, hopefully, generate a debate in which Mozambican women themselves can discuss openly how to improve women's situation. Then they can define the ideals and the strategies to realize them, where law can play an important, and sufficient, role. That Mozambican women have their own ideas about these questions, that might differ from what is embodied in the official policy, is illustrated by this remark from an older woman, secretary of a local OMM group in Luis Cabral, when asked what liberation of women means to her:

> Life in a liberated family looks like this. When the woman falls ill, the man must be able to take a bucket and go to fetch water. The man must be able to wash the clothes, both his own clothes and those of his wife. The man must be able to cook because his wife is ill. And the other way around, the woman must be able to do these things for her husband.

Notes

1 According to figures given us by the Judge President of Luis Cabral Popular Tribunal in 1987.
2 The field-work was carried out in close cooperation with Alpheus Manghezi, who is a sociologist with long experience of Mozambique. He did simultaneous translations of the court hearings and during interviews. He functioned as an interpreter of language as well as of the Mozambican reality. We also received invaluable assistance as well as essential information about the Mozambican legal system from Gita Honwana Welch and Albie Sachs in the Department of Research and Legislation of the Ministry of Justice, and from the Judge President of Maputo City Court, Abdul Carimo.
3 Resistência Nacional Moçambicana (Mozambique National Resistance–MNR).

4 The figures are taken from an emergency appeal for 1990, worked out by the government in cooperation with UNDP and presented at a donor conference in New York in April 1990.
5 The reform process is bringing rapid changes, on the political as well as the legal level. This chapter was completed *primo* October 1990, and changes which have taken place after this could not be considered.
6 Initially FRELIMO was an abbreviation for "Frente de Libertação de Moçambique" – The Mozambican Liberation Front. The vanguard party established in 1977 took the name Frelimo.
7 Due to lack of resources and experience, the Supreme Popular Tribunal was not established until 1989. In the meantime a Supreme Court of Appeal assumed some of the tasks outlined for this court.
8 There are still not enough Mozambican lawyers to fill these positions. As a temporary measure, the District Popular Tribunals are administered by judges who have received a special six months training course by the Ministry of Justice.
9 Directiva No. 1/1982 de 27 de Fevereiro. Art. 7 of the Law on Judiciary Organization gives the Supreme Popular Tribunal the power to issue general and obligatory instructions and directives to the lower courts so as to ensure uniformity in procedure and in the application of law.
10 After the election in 1987, the tribunal had ten judges, out of which six were women. The tribunal functioned two days a week, and the work was divided so that two groups of five judges each worked one day a week.
11 The case of Ana and her first husband is not included in our case material. The information here was given to us by the Judge President as the case of Ana and Jacinto started.
12 The traditional piece of cloth that women wear.
13 There is no fixed legal age of majority in Mozambique (Francisco 1988, p. 24). However, the judges clearly use such a concept, for example by demanding that a parent appear in court with a child. The age at which a person is considered an adult and thus able to appear in court in his or her own capacity may vary depending on the type of case.
14 This may construct a problem in the capital with the mass invasion of people from all over the country, speaking different languages. Another tendency we observed was that men were often eager to speak Portuguese in court, thus showing signs of education and status. Most of the cases we observed were, however, dealt with in the local language.
15 The methodological approach of taking women as the starting-point and applying a perspective from below on law is described by Dahl (1987, p. 56). Its application in this project is discussed in Berg and Gundersen (1990).
16 There is no adequate translation of the term *responsavel*. It means persons who have responsibility for a certain function or over a specific area. In this context it refers to people holding administrative positions in the neighbourhood.
17 The draft for a new Constitution based on a multi-party system and a clear division of power was presented in January 1990. Throughout the country meetings were held with the population to discuss the draft, before a constitutional committee prepared the final proposal. The new Constitution is expected to be adopted by the People's Assembly in November 1990.

References

Abel, R. L. 1973, A Comparative Theory of Dispute Institutions in Society. *Law and Society Review*, Vol. 8, pp. 217–247.
Abel, R. L. (ed.) 1982. *The Politics of Informal Justice*, Vol. 2. New York: Academic Press.

Agência de Informação de Moçambique (AIM): *Mozambique News, 1981–1988,* from 1988 *Mozambique File,* monthly, Maputo.
Arnfred, S. 1988. Women in Mozambique: Gender Struggle and Gender Politics. *Review of African Political Economy,* No. 41, pp. 5–16.
Aubert, V. 1979. On Methods of Legal Influence. In Burmann and Harrell-Bond, (eds.) (1979) pp. 27–43.
Aubert, V. 1989. *Continuity and Development in Law and Society.* Oslo: Norwegian University Press.
Berg, N. and Gundersen, A. 1990. Methodological Issues in Women's Law: Research on the Popular Tribunal in Mozambique. In A. Armstrong (ed.) (1990).
Brochmann, G. and Ofstad, A. 1990. *Mozambique. Norwegian Assistance in a Context of Crisis.* Report R 1990:4, Chr. Michelsens Institute, Bergen.
Burmann, S. and Harrell-Bond, B. (eds.) 1979. *The Imposition of Law.* New York: Academic Press.
Casimiro, I. Loforte, A. and Pessoa Pinto, A. 1990. *Women in Mozambique.* Centre of African Studies/NORAD, Maputo.
Constitution of the People's Republic of Mozambique. 1980. Instituto Nacional do Livro e do Disco (INLD).
Dahl, T. S. 1987. *Women's Law. An Introduction to Feminist Jurisprudence.* Oslo: Norwegian University Press.
Egerö, B. 1987. *Mozambique: A Dream Undone – The Political Economy of Democracy 1975–1984.* Uppsala: Scandinavian Institute of African Studies.
Francisco, N. 1988, Women in the Context of Legal Reforms in Mozambique. *Working Papers in Women's Law,* no. 14, University of Oslo.
Frelimo 1989a, *For the Normalisation of Life.* Report of the Central Committee to the Fifth Congress of the Frelimo Party.
Frelimo 1989b. *Estatutos e Programa.*
Frelimo 1989c. *Directivas Económicas e Sociais.*
Frelimo 1990, *Draft Amended Constitution of the People's Republic of Mozambique.*
Hanlon, J. 1984. *Mozambique: The Revolution Under Fire.* London: Zed Books.
Hermele, K. 1990, *Mozambican Crossroads. Economics and Politics in the Era of Structural Adjustment.* Report R 1990:3, Chr. Michelsens Institute, Bergen.
Ietswaart, H. F. P. 1982, The Discourse of Summary Justice and the Discourse of Popular Justice: An Analysis of Legal Rhetoric in Argentina. In R. L. Abel, (ed.) (1982) pp. 149–179.
Isaacman, B. and Stephen, J. 1980. *Mozambique: Women, the Law and Agrarian Reform.* Adis Ababa: United Nations.
Jeichande, I. I. 1990. *Mulheres Deslocadas em Maputo, Zambézia e Inhambane (Mulher em Situação Difícil).* Trabalho de Consultoria Para OMM – UNICEF, Maputo.
Kasonde-Ng'andu, S. 1989. Cultural and Psycho-Social Aspects of the Law of Maintenance of Children: The Case of Zambia. *Working Papers in Women's Law,* no. 25, University of Oslo.
Machel, S. 1981. *Sowing the Seeds of the Revolution.* Harare: Zimbabwe Publishing House.
May, J. 1987, *Changing People, Changing Law.* Gweru: Mambo Press.
Organização da Mulher Moçambicana (OMM) 1980. Estatutos e Programa. Documentos da 3. Conferência da OMM, Maputo.
Perspectives on Research Methodology. *Working Paper No. 2 (1990).* Women and Law in Southern Africa Research Project, Harare.
Principles of Revolutionary Justice, State Papers and Party Proceedings, Series 2 (1979) Number 2, MAGIC, London.
Relatório da Comissão do M. J. Nomeada para Investigar e Fazer Recomendaçoes sobre a Reformulação do Projecto da Lei de Familia (Relatório)(1988), Maputo.

Seminário Sobre a Mulher e a Reconstrução Nacional em Moçambique. Relatório Final (1986), Universidade Eduardo Mondlane, Maputo.
Tempo, weekly magazine, Maputo.
Urdang, S. 1983. The Last Transition? Women and Development in Mozambique. *Review of African Political Economy*, No. 27/28, pp. 8–32.
Urdang, S. 1989. *And Still They Dance. Women, War and the Struggle for Change in Mozambique*. London: Earthscan Publications.
Welch, G. H. 1988. The New Legal System of Mozambique – the Uniform Principles of Popular Justice. In: Guest Lectures on Women and Law in Zimbabwe, Mozambique and Tanzania. *Working Papers in Women's Law*, No. 20, University of Oslo.
Welch, G. H. and Sachs, A. 1987. The Bride Price, the Revolution and the Liberation of Women, *International Journal of the Sociology of Law*, Vol. 15, pp. 369–391.
Welch, G. H., Dagnino, F. and Sachs, A. 1985, Transforming the Foundations for Family Law in the Course of the Mozambican Revolution. *Journal of Southern African Studies*, Vol. 12. No. 1, pp. 60–74.

11
Negotiating Gender

The Case of the International Labour Organization, ILO

ANN THERESE LOTHERINGTON AND ANNE BRITT FLEMMEN

The entire international development assistance system – i.e. the UN system, the governmental and the non-governmental organizations – is going through a process of change in a number of areas, among which environment and gender issues are of major importance. Efforts are made to integrate the new issues into the general development assistance activities of these organizations. In this chapter, we will explore policy changes within a UN body, the International Labour Organization (ILO),[1] and take a closer look at the ways in which the ILO implements its Women-in-Development (WID) policy.

When studying policy change, the ILO is of interest, not least because the organization has decided to change its policy, through the adoption of the "Resolution on Equal Opportunities and Equal Treatment for Men and Women in Employment" in 1985. This resolution states that in spite of the progress which has been registered for women workers over the last decade, the "majority of women workers continues to be concentrated in a limited range of occupations; doing work requiring low skills or earning low remuneration" (ILO, 1988a, p. 29). Efforts, therefore, have to be made to change the unequal opportunities and treatment for men and women in employment. Part of such efforts is to change the practice of the ILO itself, towards a more gender-responsive policy.

This resolution was supplemented by the "ILO Plan of Action on Equal Opportunity and Treatment of Men and Women in Employment" in 1987, to give effect to the resolution. The Plan of Action states that there is a need to "integrate women workers' question fully into the overall programme of the ILO" (ILO, 1988a, p. 86). The strategies to achieve this are discussed sector by sector in the document. Our interpretation of the ILO Plan of Action is that its implementation requires substantial changes to the ILO's policy.

Our intention here is to explain the process which is currently taking place in the ILO with regard to WID policy, that is within the technical assistance programme.[2] To do that, we have to know how extensive are changes that are required to implement the ILO Plan of Action. Further, we will have to explore the position of strength of the various negotiating parties in this process. We have found the work of Sabatier (1987), on policy change in organizations in general, helpful in developing our analytical tool.

According to Sabatier changes may occur on a number of levels in an organization. He classifies the changes on the basis of how substantial they are, from the more "superficial" ones, aiming at changing what he calls "Secondary Aspects" to the more profound changes in what he calls "Near Core" and "Deep Core". Deep Core refers to the fundamental normative and ontological axioms which define a person's or an organization's underlying philosophy. Changing Deep Core is demanding, but if achieved, the change will remain sustainable.

Near Core refers to basic strategies and positions for reaching deep core beliefs in the policy area in question, expressed through policy statements (what an organization wants to do) and plans of action (how they want to do it). It is an explicit, shared interpretation of the problems within the area in question. To achieve fundamental changes of Near Core is also demanding. However, changes in Near Core often come about by adding new aspects, rather than replacing all aspects of Near Core. These additions are easier to effectuate than replacements, because they do not require total change of political positions. Competing interpretations of the problems within the area in question may coexist.

Secondary Aspects comprise a multitude of instrumental decisions and information searches necessary to implement the Near Core in the specific policy area. These are rules and routines for the execution of policy statements. Of the three levels, this is the easiest to change, because changes here are of a more practical nature. One will, however, also meet resistance against efforts at changing everyday working routines.

When we refer to the ILO's "policy", we shall understand a combination or coalescence of all these three levels. The policy is a consistent relationship between deep core beliefs, near core statements and practical instruments of Secondary Aspects. Deep core beliefs, or an organization's underlying philosophy, can only be grasped through an understanding of its various practices. Policy can, therefore, in other words be expressed as a consistency between what the organization says it will do and what the organization does in practice. Independent of each other, changes may occur at all three levels, but for a change to be called a "policy change" a new consistency between Deep Core, Near Core and Secondary Aspects must be developed.

In the case of the ILO, we shall understand the adoption of the "Resolution on Equal Opportunities and Equal Treatment for Men and Women in Employment" in 1985 as a policy statement added to Near Core. It can be seen as a statement about what the ILO wants to do with regard to women workers. The ILO Plan of Action is also an addition to Near Core and it can be seen as a plan for how the ILO intends to implement the Resolution mentioned above. In our analysis, therefore, we shall concentrate the discussion around the implementation of the ILO Plan of Action.

The adoption of the two documents does not represent a "policy change". Whether a policy change will take place as a result of a successful *implementation* of the ILO Plan of Action depends on how fundamentally different the WID policy is, compared to the regular technical assistance. If the WID policy can be implemented as an addition to the regular policy, we cannot speak of a policy change. However, if regular technical assistance will be an obstacle to the implementation of the WID policy, a policy change may be necessary. Our intention is, therefore, to examine the ILO's WID policy regarding to what extent its implementation requires extensive changes.

Our unit of analysis is the process of committing the intentions of the ILO Plan of Action into practice. Such processes of change in organizations are always associated with resistance. The opposition will increase, the closer the changes come towards Deep Core (Sabatier, 1987). There will be resistance to the implementation of the Plan of Action, in spite of the ILO's decision to change itself. Negotiations, therefore, take place between supporters and opponents of the WID policy. We shall call the process "gender negotiations", because it is concerned with gender relevance in the ILO. At the most basic level, the negotiations concern the right to define reality; and further, about using this perception of reality in policy statements and practical action. The gender negotiations reflect a formal or informal debate among women and men, crossing borders of "objective truths" about what women and men may or may not do. Everybody joins in the debate, consciously or unconsciously (Rudie, 1984).

In our analysis, we shall identify various actors and discuss their position in the gender negotiations. We shall further analyse the negotiations from the supporters' point of view and discuss their negotiating strategies. This analysis will provide an insight into the prospects for a successful implementation of the ILO Plan of Action, and whether a successful implementation requires a "policy change" in the ILO.

The data on which this study is based have been collected during two visits to the ILO in Geneva. On the first visit, in November 1989, we collected documentation on the ILO's general policies and on its work on WID policy. In addition, we interviewed a number of the central personnel about the implementation of the ILO's WID policy. On our second visit, in May 1990, we interviewed several categories of ILO personnel: policy-makers and executives; superior personnel, lower rank and general service staff; opponents and supporters of the WID policy; women and men.

I. The ILO

The ILO was established in 1919 as an organization for international cooperation on issues concerning economic life. It became one of the specialized agencies of the United Nations system after the Second World War. The ILO's responsibility is regulation of economic life and social security for workers worldwide, and its overall aim is to promote this in three main ways; first, by developing international standards for economic and social matters (standard setting), second, by improving workers' living and working conditions through general international cooperation, and third, by undertaking technical programmes in the fields of employment, training, social security, conditions of work, industrial relations and labour administration. Standard setting and the technical assistance programme are the two areas of primary interest to us.

The ILO is different from other UN bodies, because its decision-making bodies consist of three parties: national governments, trade unions and employers' organizations. The three parties are independent of each other and participate on an equal footing. It is called the "tripartite system". Nearly all ILO bodies are organized according to this system.

The standard-setting activities consist of adopting conventions and recommendations. A convention is an international standard for regulating conditions of work, economic relations and social policies of the member states. It is adopted at the annual International Labour Conference on a tripartite basis. A convention must be ratified by a member state before it becomes binding for that state. When a country ratifies a convention, it is obliged to bring its laws and practices into conformity with the convention. Recommendations are formulated as supplements to conventions, or as instruments independent of conventions. They cannot become binding. The ILO's Conventions and Recommendations constitute the International Labour Code. At the end of 1990 the total number of adopted conventions and recommendations were respectively 171 and 178.

The ILO supervises closely how member states implement ratified conventions. The member states are obligated to report to the ILO at regular intervals about the implementation of the ratified conventions. These reports must also be sent to employers' and workers' organizations which may give feedback to the ILO about how member states are implementing these conventions (Vihma, 1988). Governments' reports and other available information are examined by the Committee of Experts on the Application of Conventions and Recommendations, a body of independent legal and technical experts. The Committee's report, containing comments, criticism and suggestions for corrective action, is submitted to the International Labour Conference. The system of sanctions the ILO can use is limited, but criticism by the ILO is generally considered serious and well founded. The member States, therefore, do what they can to avoid criticism and to implement any necessary changes (ILO Info, 1987).

From its establishment in 1919, the ILO has adopted conventions and recommendations giving special attention to women workers. Over time, there has been a change in types of standards relevant to women, from preventive conventions for women workers, to conventions giving women and men equal rights and equal opportunities. We shall list some examples. In 1919, Convention no. 3, the Maternity Protection Convention, was adopted. This convention had been ratified by 28 of the 150 member States of the ILO at the end of 1990. Convention no. 100, on Equal Remuneration, was adopted in 1951. This is one of the most widely ratified conventions, with 111 ratifications. The Discrimination (Employment and Occupation) Convention (No. 111), a more comprehensive standard when it comes to women's rights, was adopted in 1958. This convention addresses the overall problem of discrimination, both in public and private sectors, on the grounds of race, colour, sex, religion, political opinion, national extraction or social origin (ILO,

1988a, p. 3). This convention has been ratified by 111 member States of the ILO.

From the modest start of the ILO's technical assistance programme (Technical Co-operation Programme in ILO terms) in the 1950s, the ILO has made efforts to apply international labour standards through the programme. The technical assistance programme is the ILO's

> major instrument for translating into practice its preoccupation with the social aspects of development. It is the means through which the ILO assists governments, employers, workers (and local communities) to create the conditions necessary for productive, gainful, healthy and safe employment [...] Technical co-operation and the promotion of international labour standards are interlinked and mutually supportive activities for furthering the ILO's mandate to work for social and economic progress (Working for Development, undated, pp. 1, 2).

The technical assistance programme now constitutes around 30–40 per cent of the ILO's total expenditures. Its tripartite structure enables the ILO to draw on the combined experience of workers' and employers' organizations together with governments.

According to the ILO's overall aims and its conventions, the technical assistance programme *should* be directed as much to women as to men. However, a need has developed for an action programme to promote women's rights in economic life in general and in the ILO's technical assistance programme in particular. Since the Nairobi Conference in 1985, concern for women's issues has increased both among ILO staff and among the member States. In 1985 an assessment of ILO operational activities concerning women illustrated this need (ILO, 1988a). During the Governing Body meeting in November 1987, the "ILO Plan of Action on Equality of Opportunity and Treatment of Men and Women in Employment", prepared by the International Labour Office (the ILO secretariat), was adopted. This is a comprehensive document, discussing problems that have to be dealt with, the aims of the ILO's future work, and strategies to attain these goals.

The overall aims of the ILO Plan of Action are as follows:

(1) to identify measures and implement them with a view to changing social attitudes towards women and furthering under-

standing of the complex relationship between the full implementation of equality in employment-related issues and the achievement of economic progress, social justice and peace for all mankind;
(2) to promote implementation of legislative and policy measures aimed at the elimination of all forms of discrimination against women and thereby encourage economic and social development to which women can equally contribute and of which they can equally enjoy the benefits;
(3) to highlight further the actual economic and social contribution of women workers, including unremunerated activities, through statistical concepts, data collection and research methods to reflect the scope of women's activities as producers of goods and services, especially in the informal sector in both the rural and urban areas;
(4) to integrate women workers' questions fully into the overall programme of the ILO and ensure that women's issues feature adequately in research, information dissemination and technical co-operation activities. While recourse to women-specific activities may be necessary within this overall policy, these will only be undertaken to respond to special needs or requirements (ILO 1988a, p. 86).

The Plan of Action states that the responsibility for changing women's situation in the developing countries rests with the countries themselves. What the ILO as an organization (i.e. with member States and the secretariat) can do is to adopt new, or emphasize existing, conventions, recommendations, resolutions, declarations and so on concerning women workers. What the Office (the secretariat) can do is primarily "to strengthen the ILO assistance to governments and employers, and workers' organisations in developing policies to promote equality" (ILO, 1988a, p. 86). However, the Office can also effect changes within itself and the way in which it executes its policy, so as to increase its influence on the legislation and the general policies of its member States. By changing its own practice towards gender equality, the Office may provide an example on what attitudes governments ought to take towards women. Then, it will be up to the member States themselves to internalize the new attitudes, a process the ILO cannot influence directly. In order to stress the sincerity of the new attitudes towards women's issues, the Organization may draw attention to countries not following up the conventions on discrimination, equal pay, equal opportunity and treatment for men and women workers, and so on, provided the countries in question have ratified these conventions.

If we look at the overall aims of the ILO Plan of Action, we find them consistent with what is within the ILO's power to change. It is stated that they are to "integrate women workers' questions *fully into the overall program of the ILO* and ensure that women's issues feature adequately in research, information dissemination and technical co-operation activities". Further, they shall "identify measures and implement them *with a view to changing social attitudes towards women* ..." (ILO, 1988a, p. 86) (our emphases). The adoption of this document was of great importance to the Office's promotion of a gender perspective on the work of the ILO. It was a confirmation of the Resolution from 1985 and a formal acceptance of the work done by the Office on women workers' questions. The member states gave the Office "permission" to continue the efforts at changing the ILO's activities towards gender equality.

In the following, we shall discuss the process of change as it applies to technical assistance, as this was the point of departure for our interviews in the ILO. Due to the interlinking of different aspects of the ILO's activities, it may, however, in some contexts be impossible to treat technical assistance separately from other activities.

II. Discrepancy Between Old and New Policy

How demanding and time consuming the implementation of the WID policy will be depends *inter alia* on the discrepancy between the old and the new policy. The more the old policy must give way to the new, the more obstacles there will be to change, because changes close to or at deep core level are then required. In what follows, we shall discuss the discrepancy between the ILO's regular technical assistance policy (the old) and its WID policy (the new).

When interviewing the ILO personnel, we explicitly asked whether the WID policy could be perceived as contrary to the ILO's general aims as previously established. Conceivably, focusing on women may be experienced as discriminatory to men. At the time when our field work was conducted – nobody thought this a real problem (but most of the respondents knew someone who had this concern!). Looking at the ILO's overall aims and the aims of the WID policy, we find that, after all, they are quite similar. The ILO shall improve working and living conditions, increase employment possibilities and implement basic human rights. The aim of the WID policy is that this should also apply to women. The major discrepancy at the goal level is that the new policy puts emphasis on ensuring that women are taken into account, but this is probably not a minor difference. Overall aims and practical day-to-day work are not the same issue. To succeed with the implementation of a new policy, there is a need for special efforts to attain coalescence between statements at near core level and practical day-to-day work at secondary-aspects level.

We have found that the ILO promotes the implementation of the WID policy in four different ways. In the ILO staff, there may be disagreement with our way of classifying WID projects, but to us this classification has proved fruitful: "Women-specific projects", "women component", "integration of women" and "mainstreaming". All of them are challenging to existing ways of thinking and working in the ILO, although to a varying extent. We use the term "WID policy" as including all four approaches, although it currently has turned out that this term is in a process of change. The first time we conducted interviews in the ILO, "WID policy" was used the way we do here. Six months later, the term implied "women-specific projects" to a number of people. Until now, we have not found a more adequate term than "WID policy" for all four approaches.

Women-specific projects comprise projects designed exclusively for the benefit of women (ILO, 1988a, p. 176). They are supplementary to the regular policy. The projects are self-contained, either focusing on and aiming at improving particular working conditions for women, or aiming at conveying knowledge and courage to change one's own life situation – what we would call empowerment (Morgen and Bookman, 1988). The women-specific projects are small and few in number. The Plan of Action states that "these will only be undertaken to respond to special needs or requirements" (ILO, 1988a, p. 86). The discrepancy between these projects and the regular policy may be large, but that difference is not very relevant to their implementation, as they are an *addition* to regular policy. If funds are available, only minor adjustments are needed in regular policy to implement the women-specific projects. The strength of their advocates will, however, be of major importance when it comes to which role the women-specific projects will play within the ILO's technical assistance in the future. Opposition to the women-specific projects is, namely, based both on resistance to the "preferential treatment" of women and to treating women "in isolation", separately from men. The objections to them are, therefore, of a principled nature.

Projects with a *women's component* comprise projects which either provide separate resources for activities aimed at women or specifically mention women as beneficiaries (ILO, 1988a, p. 176). Efforts are made to make part of the project relevant to women, but the women component usually enters the project after the regular part of the project has been planned. The point is that women will not benefit from the project if no resources are allocated particularly to them. There are no requirements for changes in the content of the regular project. They can be implemented with minor changes in the daily routines. This approach is mostly used as a way to orient already planned male-dominated projects more towards benefiting women. The resistance against them is similar to that of the women-specific projects. Of total project expenditure, these two kinds of projects constitutes about two per cent (ILO 1988a:178). The majority of the ILO's technical assistance staff is, therefore, rarely occupied or confronted with these projects.

To integrate women workers' questions fully into the programme of the ILO is the overall aim of the ILO Plan of Action. There are two main strategies for fulfilment of this objective. One is to give women the opportunity to participate and benefit from the technical assistance programme as it appears today, what we will call "integration of women". The other is to change the technical assistance programme, so that it initially will benefit women as well as men. That is to give the programme a gender profile, or what we will call "mainstreaming" of the technical assistance programme. "Integration" and "mainstreaming" are terms used by ILO personnel but it has been difficult to grasp their own interpretation of their content. The following is, therefore, our interpretation based on general WID-documents and discussions with ILO and other UN personnel.

The point with *integration of women* is to include women on an equal footing with men in all projects. Adjustments, rather than basic changes in the characteristics of the project will occur. The technical assistance programme as such will remain largely unaltered. That is, the programme will cover the same sectors as now, and the same focus as now will dominate. Efforts are, however, made to increase women's participation in the training courses and employment and other activities. It is a question of numerical equality.

Integration of women implies that *all* staff members have to take women into consideration and start perceiving the target population as gendered. They must find ways to increase women's participation in their projects. They must find out whether gender differences are relevant to their projects. Beyond that, there is no substantial discrepancy between the new and the old policy. This is, however, a change large enough to cause conflicts and to be met with resistance from the personnel: it represents additional work, and the work-load is already heavy; it implies a new way of working and thinking that they are not used to; they don't know how to do it; they find women's participation irrelevant; or they are against women's increased participation for one reason or another.

Mainstreaming implies a reevaluation of current policy. Enquiries will have to be made as to what types of projects will benefit women as well as men. An examination of the technical assistance policy will have to be made. What kind of development is promoted today, and does it respond to the wishes and needs of women? It should not be taken for granted that women and men have common interests. Mainstreaming presupposes that any programme or any project is initiated with the awareness that we live in a gendered world, and that the concept of gender is relational, pointing at male-female relations in production and reproduction. This implies that changes for women consequently require changes for men. The norm for mainstream-planning is gender responsiveness, and it should be performed by regular staff. In addition, gender must be a constituent category in implementation and evaluation of technical assistance.

A fundamental rethinking of this nature may shake the foundations of current policy, as the aim is to make certain that any activity allows for the fact that the world is gendered, and that women and men may differ in their views on what is desirable development. "Malestreaming" rather than mainstreaming has characterized previous practices, it is argued. If this is a correct observation, the process of mainstreaming means a process of fundamental changes of current technical assistance. In that case, there is a major discrepancy between old and new policy and a larger part of the old must give way to the new if the implementation is to succeed. According to our terminology, mainstreaming means that gender responsibility of the technical assistance programme will replace current practice, rather than being something added to the ILO's Near Core. A successful implementation of this WID policy approach will, therefore, imply a "policy change" in the ILO's technical assistance programme.

By studying the text of the overall aims of the ILO Plan of Action, supported by other documents and discussions in the ILO, we find that the principal goal is mainstreaming. The other three approaches are considered as well, but mostly as elements in the strategy to realize mainstreaming. Some of our informants gave the impression that they consider efforts to obtain gender orientation as a historical process: starting at a stage where "malestreaming" predominates, and then seeing the process of implementing the WID policy as commencing with women-specific projects, running through a period of ensuring the women component and integration, and finally reaching complete mainstreaming. Others were more doubtful:

> The first reaction was, that to make the situation right, we have to put in more women. We have to do more for women, women-specific projects, women-specific research etc. And suddenly some women started to ask: Hey, isn't that another form of discrimination? Aren't you kind of making it even worse by doing this? And then everybody started using the word mainstreaming. I just wonder whether someone really knows exactly what it means in every situation. [. . .] I just don't know whether we are ready for only mainstreaming . . . .

III. How Extensive are the Changes Required to Implement the WID Policy?

We shall take a closer look at the various levels of change in the ILO and try to understand at which level the different WID approaches require efforts to be implemented. This will give an impression of the prospects for policy change in the ILO.

Changes occurring merely at the executive level are called "Secondary Aspects". These include administrative routines, budget allocations, professional dispositions and interpretations/revisions of norms (Sabatier, 1987). In the ILO, changes of this nature are expressed through project implementation. Examples of changes of this nature in the ILO may be increased cross-sectoral cooperation, allocation of funds to WID-relevant projects, or increases in manpower at the disposal of the supporters of the WID policy. An alternative to this is a more active use of the ILO's instruments –

that is, the ILO's conventions and recommendations. This can be done by formally paying attention to the countries breaking conventions they have ratified.

To implement "women-specific" projects, "women components" in projects or to "integrate women" into current policy, requires changes in Secondary Aspects. These changes may be accomplished without substantial alterations; they are technical changes. It is mostly a question of utilizing current rules and routines. Changes in Secondary Aspects are feasible on a short-time basis: "It took about three years, I think, to begin to see the impact of what I would call negotiations", as one of our informants expressed it. Sabatier (1987) suggests a transitional period of 4–5 years in general as realistic for changes of this nature. However, no "policy change" is taking place in the organization, in spite of the Secondary Aspects being changed, because the fundamental characteristics of the work of the organization still exist.

The second level of change is "Near Core", which include the basic strategies and policy positions of the Organization. It is an explicit, shared interpretation of the problems within the area in question. The Near Core is expressed through policy statements – that is, overall aims and the strategies to achieve them.

The WID policy supporters' attempts at getting the gender issue on the agenda meant in fact a questioning of the Near Core of the ILO. Their interpretation of economic and social life included an understanding of gender relations and their impact on development, which previously only to a minor extent had been a part of the ILO's Near Core. The understanding of gender relations constituted a new interpretation of the development process. The first phase of the process towards a change in Near Core culminated in the adoption of the 1985 Resolution and the ILO Plan of Action in 1987. So far, this is an addition to, rather than a replacement of, other policy statements. The Near Core is not changed. Simultaneously, there is no longer *one shared* interpretation of the ILO's work area within technical assistance. This creates a turbulent and confusing situation for the personnel. One of our respondents said that, "*We* need to have some very clear objectives as to what we want to achieve. We need to have *one* Office policy, we need to have *one* Office standard. We cannot have many ILO voices talking." In the present situation, at least two interpretations of the problem within the area in question coexist.

The mainstreaming process is an attempt at changing Near Core so that the basic strategies and policy positions in the ILO will be gender responsive. These kinds of changes are, in general, considered very difficult, because it is a question of changing political positions, in contrast to the technical changes of Secondary Aspects (Sabatier, 1987). We find no reason to believe that this is different for the WID policy. One of the supporters of the WID policy finds it to be so difficult that she resignedly concludes that it is feasible to relate to Secondary Aspects only: "We have to look upon WID as a technical issue. It is a technical issue."

However, if changes at near core level succeed, changes in Secondary Aspects will be the consequence, and a "policy change" has taken place. On the other hand, changes in Secondary Aspects do not automatically lead to changes in Near Core. A near core change does not, however, secure a lasting change in the ILO. It will have to be reviewed regularly. One of our informants expressed it this way: "You may always need somebody somewhere to keep an eye out – just constant!" The reason for this, she said, is "that what we are dealing with is very deep cultural values and attitudes. It will take us a long time to change those attitudes." And changes in fundamental attitudes of this nature take us to the third level of change – "Deep Core".

Deep Core, or fundamental, normative belief systems are basic ideological values and norms. Deep Core concerns perspectives, values and world view in general; philosophy of life, basic views on people and society, and the relationship between them. Deep Core is the basic attitudes on which Near Core is developed. It may be more or less conscious and more or less explicit. An example of deep core attitudes might be to view society as balanced and harmonious, as opposed to being characterized by disparities and conflicts; believing that individuals may create their own life on their own terms, or that external social phenomena like exploitation and oppression have deprived some people of the possibilities that others possess.

In our context, ILO personnel perceiving the relationship between genders as harmonious have a Deep Core which is inconsistent with the intentions of WID policy. They may be of the opinion that division of labour between genders is a "natural" consequence of biological functions, and consequently, that a change of this relationship will be against nature.

Another type of attitude is characterized by technical assistance personnel who disapprove of the subordination of women in the Third World. They react negatively when men in the Third World refuse to allow their wives or daughters to participate in the ILO's development projects. Personnel with such attitudes may be gender sensitive and responsible as far as technical assistance projects are concerned, but hold the opinion that the situation of women in the ILO is somewhat different. They will say that there exists no male power which could prevent women from a career within the ILO's bureaucracy. If female ILO staff qualify, they have the same opportunities as male colleagues. This type of personnel will have an (at least implicit) attitude that the rules are different for different women. Women in the Third World are one thing; they may be oppressed. Something quite different is the woman in the office next door. They will say that she has the same opportunities as her male colleagues.

A third category of the ILO's personnel perceive that there is a superior/subordinate relationship between the genders, expressed through power and dominance. This may create conflicts between the interests and priorities of women and men in the Third World as well as in the ILO.

The organization as such does also have a Deep Core.[3] This constitutes an aggregate of Deep Core of the personnel and the ideological foundations on which the structure of the organization is based. A dominant group of the staff will, through a commonly shared Deep Core, shape an ideology and create an atmosphere which will constitute part of the Deep Core of the organization. It is thus difficult to imagine a "policy change" without replacing a majority of this dominant group of the staff (Sabatier, 1987). In our context, this implies both an increase in the number of gender sensitized personnel, and that they occupy strategic positions in the organization. However, replacement of personnel will not be enough to change the Deep Core of an organization. The personnel work within an organizational structure builds up to serve a certain policy. In spite of replacement of personnel, such a structure will remain, and Deep Core will be disturbed but not substantially changed. A new policy may be in conflict with the old structure and require a new one if its implementation is to be successful. In such cases Deep Core must be substantially changed.

The ILO's Deep Core consists of the ideological foundation of the hierarchical and bureaucratic structure, the ideas of tripartism and the aggregate of the Deep Core of the staff. The bureaucratic structure is common to all UN organizations, and its ideological foundation is a belief in superior/subordinate systems and a sector perspective as well-functioning and suitable organizing principles. On the other hand, the ideas of tripartism are unique for the ILO compared to other organizations. This Deep Core has functioned for the execution of previous policy, but will it also serve the WID policy? Are gender relations perceived as relevant? Is, perhaps, the structure of the organization an expression of current gender ideology (superiority/subordination)?

> As both a structure and a process, bureaucracy must be located within its social context; in our society, that is a context in which social relations between classes and sexes are fundamentally unequal. Bureaucracy as the "scientific organization of inequality", serves as a *filter for these other forms of domination*, projecting them into an institutional arena that both rationalizes and maintains them (Ferguson, 1984, pp. 7, 8) (our emphasis).

In our view, the tripartite structure expresses the ILO's recognition of class-based domination in economic life, and the Organization's attempt at neutralizing the "filtering function" of the bureaucratic structure. We have found no similar attempts at neutralizing the "filtering function" of the ILO's bureaucratic structure when it comes to gender inequality. The structure is rather patriarchal.

> Relations among members of a bureaucracy are impersonal and rule-governed. [. . .] Thus managers who break these rules and seek to humanize, perhaps even democratize, relations within their offices are posing a fundamental threat to the organization; even if their offices function effectively, they are subverting the hierarchy, undermining the official value system, attaching the organizationally defined identity of other managers, and propagating relationships within the organization that are antithetical to the legitimated ones. Small wonder that managers who do attempt such reforms are seldom rewarded and often punished (Ferguson, 1984, p. 12).[4]

Mainstreaming presupposes "policy change". If one succeeds in altering the Deep Core of the ILO in line with the intentions of the WID policy, then Near Core and Secondary Aspects will also be changed, and, no doubt, a "policy change" will have occurred. A long step will also have been taken if the "policy change" takes place at near core level, but maintaining the change will be more demanding as long as there is not a consistency between Deep Core and

Near Core in the Organization. The changes must be looked after to prevent a relapse. "One of my jobs is to sit up here as a bird or a watch-dog, and bark occasionally", said one of our informants. It is necessary to "bark" every time the consistency is violated.

If we compare mainstreaming with the other ways of implementing WID policy – that is, "women-specific", "women component" and "integration of women" – these three do not presuppose "policy change". They are operational within Secondary Aspects and, therefore, more easily implemented than mainstreaming.

IV. Negotiating Gender in the ILO

Gender negotiations take place in at least two different areas of the ILO which are of interest to us. First, there is the debate on gender relevance in the technical assistance programme. It is, for instance, argued that women's activities influence economic development, and that this has to be taken into account, if one wants to succeed. In other words, women are made to appear as relevant and important actors in the general development process. Further, it is argued that in a number of contexts, women as a group are in a disadvantaged position *vis-à-vis* men as a group, for instance in education and employment. Therefore, if the ILO's aims are to be achieved, there is a need for compensatory programmes aiming at women as a group – an affirmative action. This argument underlines the importance of being a woman or a man when it comes to one's quality of life.

The second area of gender negotiations in the ILO is a debate on the relevance of gender in personnel management policy. In 1989 women constituted 20 per cent of the professional staff in the ILO. This was an increase from 17.4 per cent in 1985. The issue is, therefore, the importance of gender in recruitment, selection and career promotion in the ILO. It is argued that women tend to be recruited at lower levels than men, and that they tend to be promoted less rapidly. Women have a longer way to go than their male colleagues in order to reach higher level positions, if they ever reach these positions. In 1989 nearly half of the professional male staff (44.5 per cent) were found in the higher grades (P5 and above), while 13.5 per cent of the professional female staff were at this level (Inter-Agency Equal Opportunities Group, 1989). To express it differently, women's share of the higher grade posts was 6.3 per cent in 1989, while their share of the lower grade posts was 29.8 per cent.

Studying the figures of recruitment to the ILO, the prospects for an increase in women's share of the posts at the higher grades seem to be not too good. In 1989 12 women and 32 men were appointed into the Professional category (P1–P4) and above (P5–D2). Of these, three women (25 per cent) and 16 men (50 per cent) were appointed in the higher category, while none of the men and four of the women (30 per cent) were appointed at the P1 and P2 levels (ILO, 1990f).[5] It is, therefore, also argued that the ILO makes little effort to increase the supply of good female candidates, or to recruit a larger number of those who actually apply for vacancies. This may indicate a discrepancy between the ILO's perception of women in the Third World vs. its own female staff, which may be an expression of the Deep Core of the ILO.

In a discussion on the personnel issue, one of our male respondents said that he would not like to have a female superior: "You know it's a sort of feeling that you have. You cannot overcome those traditional patterns of things back in the past." He demonstrated how his private Deep Core was determining his attitudes towards female superiors in the ILO. On the other hand, others argue that women may be even better leaders than men, and that in some areas they have different experiences, which would benefit the organization.

> I think that women are better planners. I've always asked myself the question; why? But when I see a man being unable even to make priorities between telephone calls . . . . I just shake my head. They are not as able to do that as women, because organizing a day in the house, which may include bringing the children to school, combining that with a doctor's appointment for one of the kids, seeing one of the teachers, taking the car to the garage, plus getting the house clean and the shopping done . . . . This will give you a competence that can be transposed into working situations. I've seen secretaries (female) being much more efficient in organizing their work; this is first, this is second etc., than some men who just stand there and say: "Oh God! What do I do first!!"

The argument is that by admitting more women in general, and more women leaders in particular, the ILO will become a more efficient organization.

The negotiations about gender relevance in the technical assistance programme and in the personnel management policy are interconnected. Both concern the organization's gender attitudes, but in the ILO they are preferably discussed separately. Here, we will mainly discuss negotiations on the technical assistance programme, referring to personnel management whenever relevant for this issue. In the words of one informant, the interconnection may be like this: "The fact that we are so few women, that the departments are male dominated and headed by men, gives too little space for gender orientation. They can do as they always have done without any form of gender specification of their programme ..." Another interconnection may be that the personnel management policy is an expression of the Deep Core of the ILO, and that these deep core attitudes will determine, or at least influence, the implementation of the WID policy.

1. *Who Negotiates?*

On the basis of the interviews we carried out in the ILO, we found that it is possible to map the negotiating parties along two dimensions. One dimension is the goals of the WID policy expressed in the ILO Plan of Action. We find both supporters and opponents to these goals. The other dimension concerns the implementation of the WID policy. We find supporters and opponents to implementation as well as to goals.

		WID policy goals	
		For	Against
Implementation of WID policy	For	Innovators	Loyal Bureaucrats
	Against	Hesitators	Hard-headers

Figure 1. Negotiating parties of the gender negotiations.

Who among the ILO personnel will be present, in which category, at any given time, will vary. To succeed in changing policy, a minimum critical mass of the staff will have to be among the *innovators*, who are the active supporters of the WID policy. If the majority of the personnel is among the *loyal bureaucrats*, it is possible to effect changes in Secondary Aspects only. The status quo will be maintained if the majority of the staff is among the *hesitators* or the *hard-headers*, as we find the opponents to the implementation here.

The scenario may, however, be considerably altered, as it is not only a question of proportions. It is also of importance who is occupying central positions on the different levels of the Organization. An essential part of the negotiation game is to increase the number of innovators and loyal bureaucrats at the expense of the hesitators and hard-headers, and simultaneously increase the innovators' share of central positions in the ILO. In the following we shall characterize the four negotiating parties, and concentrate on actors in the Office (the secretariat), even though they all also have important supporters outside the Office.

The Innovators. The innovators are the WID policy supporters. They have been active in putting and keeping gender-responsive technical assistance policy on the agenda, and they are active in its implementation. We label them innovators, as they have contributed to a policy which in practice differs from the existing one, so much that substantial changes within the organization are necessary if the policy is to be implemented (Leonard-Barton, 1988). In other words, we see the WID policy as an innovation in the area of technical assistance.

The innovators are mainly women, but according to our informants, an increasing number of men are joining. The innovators are located at all levels in the organization, but the majority is at middle and lower professional levels, where we find the major part of the female staff. Compared to their male colleagues, the female staff are more often employed at middle and lower levels in the organization. The innovators consist of sub-groups with divergent views. These groups may even strongly disagree on which of the four WID policy approaches they wish to emphasize. This may be a problem when talking about changes at deep core level, but not necessarily on near core level. We will not elaborate on this nuance, however. We have to deal with the innovators as a uniform set of actors, with the limits this implies.

The Loyal Bureaucrats. It may seem strange to oppose a goal, and at the same time work for the implementation of it. However, this part of the ILO staff represents what we will call the "loyal bureaucrats". They have their own ideas about the world that surrounds them, but they let this affect their professional life only to a minor extent. Or to express it differently, they do not let their private Deep Core determine their professional life. They wish to execute their work professionally, and in line with the policy and signals from their superiors. They are the "ideal bureaucrats" in Max Weber's sense.

With the knowledge we have today about how bureaucracies function (see, for example, Hernes, 1978 and March and Olsen, 1989), the category may appear empirically empty. That is, however, not the case. We have representatives of this category included in our interviews. They are usually found at a middle or lower level of the organization, and all of our respondents in this category were men.

The loyal bureaucrats may turn into efficient supporters of the innovators. The innovators must ascertain that they are equipped with tools enabling them to exercise a new gender orientation. In practice, this implies that the loyal bureaucrats have to be made aware of the effects of the gender orientation on their own work; how to proceed, what to emphasize, and so on. They must also be assisted in arguing as to why they do this. When the loyal bureaucrats are proficient at implementing the WID policy, and argue as to why they do so, they may act as examples: this is possible, even without enthusiasm for the cause itself. The point is that Secondary Aspects have to be changed so that the loyal bureaucrats may have adequate tools to implement the WID policy.

The Hesitators. The hesitators will be found at all levels of the organization. First, there are those who consider the aims proper *per se*, but for one reason or another, find it impossible to support the implementation of the new policy. They may be encountering resistance in the country where they are working on projects, they may lack expertise for the implementation of projects, they may feel that they are losing prestige by working with women workers' questions – or perhaps they have altogether different reasons. This group of hesitators may as well be women as men.

In this category we also find those who only pay lip-service to gender orientation. These are the ones talking warmly about the WID policy, but who do little or nothing about it in practice. They are mostly men and often placed at a higher level in the organization.

We have also met a third type of hesitator in the ILO: those who appear to be supportive to the WID policy, but who still "live in the reality" that what women need is protection (the ILO's earliest work for women). This is in contrast to perceiving women as active participants in economic life, which is the view of the ILO Plan of Action. This is, they believe that the ILO Plan of Action concerns increasing the protection of female workers. They do not directly oppose the implementation of the Plan of Action, but it seems as if they work to implement something which is not the ILO Plan of Action. Also, these hesitators will normally be men, and they may be found at all levels of the organization.

Among all these types of hesitators, the innovators may find allies. To a certain extent, technical problems stop the hesitators; they do not know what to do and how to make their work gender responsive. The issue is, therefore, to make it possible in a practical way to overcome the technical barriers; Secondary Aspects have to be changed.

The hesitators may be moved to join both the innovators and the loyal bureaucrats. However, one has to be aware of the fact that the hesitators may just as well tip to the hard-headers. If the consequences of the Plan of Action for their own work are made clear to them, or if the goals are better illuminated, they may end up in total resistance. In this case they may be confronted with their own gender attitudes (their own Deep Core), and they may see a connection they dislike between this and the WID policy.

The Hard-headers. To reach the hard-headers may prove difficult, as they are frequently silent resisters to the WID policy. It is not accepted to be a "sworn" opponent, as, formally, gender orientation is now one of the ILO's policy statements. Many of those who cannot accept this new policy choose to work along the same lines as they have always done. By ignoring the gender perspective, they avoid having to relate to what they find problematic; namely, relating themselves to gender as a factor in technical assistance. Their strategy is revealed only if their superiors are sufficiently concerned with the WID policy to engage in exposing them.

When infrequently, one encounters the articulate opponents, one gets an insight into how difficult it will be to overcome their opposition. They are not easily persuaded. They are individuals that, for one reason or another, feel threatened by the new ideas. They may relate the whole debate on gender orientation to their personal attitude to women. Their Deep Core does not "allow" them to execute a gendered policy. They constitute a political, or even an ideological, problem. The hard-headers are (nearly) always men.

The hard-headers will fight against a change in the ILO's policy as a prolongation of their own, private gender battle. More than negotiating tactics are needed to make them implement the WID policy. If the innovators can use means that are strong enough, they may be moved into the category of loyal bureaucrats. One such measure may be to prevent the opponents from an internal career promotion, if they do not implement the WID policy. According to one of the innovators, the WID policy "must be part of a job description. Something you measure achievement against, something you measure performance against, that it is one of your duties." If that is achieved, the hard-headers cannot ignore the WID policy if they wish a career promotion in the ILO.

If we shall categorize the ILO personnel according to the four categories, we have to know more exactly what the staff do in practice. As it is not acceptable to be against the WID policy in the official debate in the ILO, it is of little use to ask people about their position. It is, therefore, difficult to know whether people are hesitators paying lip-service to gender orientation or whether they are real innovators. However, as the process of change has turned out to be difficult and efforts are needed to make the staff gender responsive in their work, our assumption is that the hesitators and the hard-headers still dominate in the ILO. The innovators must, therefore, direct their negotiations at altering this domination.

2. How Do They Negotiate?

We shall now take a closer look at the strategies of the innovators. How do they act in order to make the variety of opposition become allies? First of all, the innovators have to take the gender ideologies held by ILO staff into consideration and understand the fact that everybody has personal feelings about gender, simply because we are women and men. To quote one innovator: "Everybody thinks they know something about women, because they know women." The innovators try to "de-sexualize" the WID policy. They want the ILO personnel to think abstractly about "women", rather than relating the policy to some women they know. Their intention is to make the opponents' Deep Core non-determining for their behaviour in the organization. The term "professionalize" is also used to describe this process. The resisters must learn that the WID policy is part of their profession and that it is something they have to relate to in their work, to do a good job. Professionalizing is reflected in the innovators' strategies in different ways.

We have found that the innovators use three main strategies: how they behave; how they prepare the ground, making it possible to implement the ILO Plan of Action; and how they argue.

Behaviour. Among the ILO staff, there is a feminist fear which finds several expressions. One of the loyal bureaucrats said about his implementation of the WID policy: "We do not, of course, do it to make women more revolutionary or feminist!!", and laughed, as if that were obvious. These are attitudes the innovators have to take into account, irrespective of the reason for the feminist fear. They must avoid provocative behaviour. One of the innovators put it this way:

> To enter as an aggressive feminist with solid historical facts as arguments – guarantees that you lose. You understand that very quickly. It doesn't work. That you are able to argue is important, yes, but the arguments must pop up only when the discussion is well underway, and not be thrown out at the beginning.

The opponents will only reveal their distrust of women's issues if the innovators "act in a feminist way in the negotiations", as the innovators express it themselves. The opponents' view of "feminist behaviour" is in fact a traditional male way of behaviour, being aggressive, pushing and arguing. Such a behaviour is perceived as a threat to their idea of womanhood. In some contexts, the (female) innovators play on their femininity as part of the strategy. By their behaviour, they show the opponents that it is possible to remain feminine and still work for the WID policy. They make themselves and the WID policy non-provocative by showing that they are no threat to the resisters' ideas about "women". This is perceived as necessary. Paradoxically, this strategy supports the opponents' ideas of gender, their Deep Core. That is, this strategy will not contribute to changing the opponents' Deep Core or to de-sexualize the issue, which is also seen as necessary. A problem may be that: "Feminists may bend so far backward to avoid conflict or even avoid criticism for being feminist that their efforts are ineffective or perpetuate female subordination" (Staudt, 1990, p. 17).

Practical Preparations. The practical preparations to facilitate the implementation of the WID policy take different forms. To give concrete, practical solutions is one of them:

> I give the experts some solutions that they can use in their fieldwork, and then ask them to report back. This is the way I work with people out in the field, but this is of course dependent on the preparatory work I have carried out within the Office, to make the ILO staff put me on the briefing list of the experts. I spend a lot of time on this preparatory work.

Another innovator said that "it is important to have connections with the desk officers, the people who actually do the daily work, so that they come and use you. Now this has been a very slow, and I would say frustrating and painful, process, but now I begin to see results."

A more formal way of providing knowledge has been an effort to create an information base on gender issues in the ILO. It contains documentation of what the range of obstacles and problems confronting women are and, therefore, what areas the WID policy should concentrate on. Personnel feeling inadequate in the face of the WID policy, the loyal bureaucrats and some of the hesitators welcome this opportunity. One of the innovators said that "one important resource to them was the advisory services and the knowledge-base on gender issues. And it's something they reach out for and use." This strategy is consequently a way in which the innovators try to function as an internal base of expertise, preferably only for a period of time, till the knowledge is widely disseminated. Such a strategy may also have its disadvantages. One of the innovators stopped doing it because she felt it became possible for others to disclaim responsibility for WID issues.

Funding is another means that can be used in a practical preparation strategy. Many of the innovators consider extra funding for projects to be a motivating factor: "I found that I needed funding to be able to give incentives. We are talking about overworked people. Working with gender orientation was perhaps also more interesting, because I could use green-apple temptations like that." The "green apples" are provided by the gender-responsive donors. One example is the Norwegian "women's grant", which was established as "an innovative instrument of policy; an instrument designed for the specific purpose of providing rapid and flexible support to WID activities" (Lexow, 1989, p. 2). It was "seed money" to promote gender-orientated activities. The innovators could use them as extra funding, if the projects were redesigned so as to favour women.

Argumentation. There are different ways in which to argue gender orientation. Some of the innovators choose an indirect argumentation, mainly playing on the fact that the WID policy will be beneficial not only to women:

> because when we change the conditions of women we change the conditions for men. When you for instance get better protection of reproductive functions, it's for men! If you get better services for taking care of children it is to the benefit of the whole society. So, I think that this is how we could promote women's interests, not saying that it's because they're women.

Others are preoccupied with the idea that the personnel themselves will experience the benefit of utilizing the women perspective. When the innovators argue how the gender orientation may be implemented, the technical departments may react negatively and feel that external personnel enter their professional arena. To avoid this problem, the innovators try and make the opponent feel that the need is their own: "I often put words into their mouth, but the point is to make them believe it is their idea." Another said that

> you can't order people to do things, you have to demonstrate the need. And if they don't want to do it then they don't have to. Good will doesn't always work, but the worst is then to get dictatorial about it, because then you get a real backlash.

This is also a question of professionalizing the staff. The intention is to show that if they draw on a gender perspective, the probability of succeeding in achieving the ILO's general aims will increase. They have to learn that the WID policy is the ILO's policy.

An example of confronting the opponent's arguments goes like this:

> When you talk about technical assistance, and ask for a more gender-specified programme, you have to endure "yes, but how and why, and it won't work because the recipient country itself is not conscious about the gender orientation". But this is not correct, because it is something they assume. The key word is assumptions. They assume in East, West, North and South the

most unbelievable things. Assume, assume, assume! They say things in such a self-assured way! But when I start arguing and say that it actually isn't true, that the recipient country in question has women officers, that they have ratified such and such – then I have to use the ILO language – then they become very surprised. Then we can start talking about practical ways of orienting their programmes towards women.

In this way, the innovators use facts and information about women's conditions as "evidence" in the debate on whether gender orientation is possible. This is a tactic frequently used when the opponent is a hesitator. The innovators answer the hesitation with reference to the hesitator's own way of arguing.

The ILO has a well-developed system for influencing the policy of member States. It is argued that these formal channels in the Organization should be utilized more efficiently by the WID supporters, for instance by using the standards they already have:

> We need to do more work in this Office, to be quite frank with you, we need to build on our mandate for equality. The ILO is the only UN agency that makes these standards, and has the mechanisms for monitoring and supervising them. And we are in fact trying to influence laws. We have standards, they are very good standards. We need to know how they affect women, and we need to promote that side far more than we have done in the past.

This is an argument for the fact that the technical means in the ILO (the standards) also apply to women, and that it is within the mandate of the ILO to utilize them in favour of women. This argument is also most often directed towards Secondary Aspects. It is the implementation level where the activities appear. The innovators seem to find it difficult to enter into negotiations beyond Secondary Aspects. A number of them indicate that changes at near core and deep core levels prove extremely difficult and, at best, very time consuming.

As the innovators, relatively speaking, are more often employed at middle or lower levels in the hierarchy in the Office, one can understand that their main efforts are directed to opponents at the same or at a lower level than themselves. It is far more difficult to negotiate "upwards" in the hierarchy. One strategy to go beyond this problem is, however, to cooperate with external actors, like for example gender-responsive member States. The delegates to the

Governing Body may then confront the top management in the Office with the progress of the implementation of the ILO's WID policy. This is a strategy to create external pressure to push "policy change".

We may so far conclude that the negotiation strategies are mainly directed at changing Secondary Aspects. The negotiations *may*, however, also influence Near Core, and even Deep Core. The innovators feel that to succeed is a long and strenuous process, irrespective of the level on which the change is meant to take place. One informant said that

> it has taken us five years to come where we are now, but I'm not at all certain if it can be done more quickly. There is still resistance. The process is highly frustrating. You're constantly alone in the battle. You're always on the defensive.

Quite a few confess that the negotiations can be rather tough at times. One talks about the importance of having external allies to be able to cope: "I'm working to create better cooperation between the UN organizations. All female contacts within all of the UN system are my sisters and solidarity supporters. We talk about survival. It is very lonely to promote the WID policy."

V. Understanding the Process?

Is it, on the basis of the discussion on the previous pages, possible to understand the process of change currently taking place in the ILO, and to foresee the success of the negotiations? In what follows, we shall sum up our discussions and answer these questions.

First, we said that the more an old policy must give way to a new one, the more resistance there will be to change, because a major discrepancy between old and new policy requires changes at near core or deep core levels. How much of the regular ILO policy must give way to implement the WID policy depends on which of the WID approaches one uses as a basis for analysis. To a certain extent, all of them require changes, but the "women-specific", "women's component" and "integration of women" approaches are more easily adapted to the regular policy than is the "mainstreaming" approach. The first three approaches require changes in Secondary Aspects, while "mainstreaming" presupposes change in Near Core or, if it shall be sustainable, in Deep Core. Consequently, only the implementation of the mainstream approach will result in a "policy change" in the ILO. The degree of resistance towards the WID policy will increase, the closer the implementation comes to "policy change".

Our second discussion attempted to understand what the negotiations are actually about. It is negotiations about gender relevance in two main areas of the ILO: the technical assistance programme and the personnel management policy. These two areas are interconnected as they express the Deep Core when it comes to attitudes towards gender, but even the innovators dislike bringing in the two areas of gender relevance simultaneously. As far as we understand, this is because gender relevance in the technical assistance programme may be interpreted as being about how to make the programme more efficient. In other words, women can be viewed as un-utilized resources in the development process or instruments to make projects more efficient, rather than questioning why women are in a subordinate position in economic and social life. An "efficiency" view does only to a minor extent challenge deep core attitudes about gender. On the other hand, gender relevance in the personnel management policy is about a fundamental view of the relations between women and men, which is founded in Deep Core. Asking for gender equity in the personnel management policy is, therefore, a major challenge to Deep Core.

In the discussion of the negotiating parties, our assumption was that the hesitators and the hard-headers still dominate the ILO staff. The innovators' negotiation strategies are, consequently, attempts at decreasing this dominance. The main goal is that the majority of the staff will become real innovators, that is, a change of attitudes in the staff. Changing attitudes is, however, much more demanding than changing behaviour. The negotiation strategy is, therefore, mainly directed towards a change of behaviour – that is, to move the resisters to the group of loyal bureaucrats. One of the innovators said that, "I don't bother what they think, my concern is what they do!". When the hesitators are the opponents, the main goal is to move them to the group of innovators, but they may also join the loyal bureaucrats. The innovators must, however, be aware of the risk that the hesitators may become hard-headers. The hard-headers will never become innovators, but hopefully they can be moved to the group of loyal bureaucrats.

This way of thinking is, however, based on a zero-sum game, where the staff is a stable mass, and the point of the negotiations is to change the behaviour, or at best, the attitudes of its members. Another way of decreasing the dominance of the resisters is to replace them with innovators or loyal bureaucrats. In this context, replacement means securing that the posts of resisters, who for one or another reason leave the ILO, are filled with WID supporters. This strategy is less used by the innovators, because they are rarely in positions that give them authority to influence the recruitment policy.

To conclude, the gender negotiations in the ILO are mainly directed at gender relevance in the technical assistance programme. In this area, ILO seems to be willing to change itself. The innovators begin to see results of their efforts. These results are expressed as changes in Secondary Aspects. The efforts at changing the resisters' behaviour are also connected to changes in Secondary Aspects. Loyal bureaucrats do not have to change their near core attitudes or deep core beliefs to act in favour of the WID policy.

To us, the innovators' strategy seems fairly consistent as far as changes in Secondary Aspects are concerned. If the innovators are allowed to continue their work as they have done until now, the prospects for real changes in Secondary Aspects are quite good. In Secondary Aspects we find the technical barriers to implementation. They are the main barriers for the hesitators, and they are possible to overcome. That is, "women-specific" projects, projects with a "women component" and even "integration of women" in current practices, may be the result of the gender negotiations.

However, according to our interpretation, the aim of the ILO Plan of Action is "mainstreaming" and, hence, "policy change". The prospects for a successful implementation of the "mainstreaming" approach are not as good as that of changes in Secondary Aspects, at least not in the short run. "Policy change" requires changes in Near Core, which means that a new, explicit, shared understanding of the problems must be developed. A shared interpretation of gender relations, based on equity, must be the foundation of a new Near Core. Development interventions should, according to such a new understanding, take the different situations for women and men as their point of departure. To effectuate this change, a rethinking of development is required. It is necessary to view economy as an instrument of human development, rather than viewing people as instruments of economic development. To a certain extent, such discussions are taking place in the ILO, but they do not (yet) represent a new Near Core.

A new Near Core of the ILO should, in our opinion, focus on the connection between gender relevance in the technical assistance programme and in personnel management policy. The relationship between the genders is at the present time a superior/subordinate one, expressing power and dominance. This creates a relationship of conflict between women and men in the Third World as well as in the ILO. The expression of this conflicting relationship will, however, vary from place to place and over time. A new understanding of the issue in question requires more than a new behaviour of the staff; it requires new ways of thinking. The political positions of Near Core must be changed. Political barriers must be overcome.

People *may* change political positions and attitudes, and the political barriers *may* be overcome. A stronger focus on change in political positions and attitudes in the negotiations is one possible strategy but, as we have seen, the innovators find such a strategy difficult. Some may change political position through logical argument, but for a majority the connection between near core attitudes and deep core beliefs remains strong.

Changing deep core beliefs is almost impossible. It is a question of identity, values and ideological barriers. An additional strategy is, therefore, to conduct the negotiations on the personnel issue, as it is necessary to increase the innovators' share of strategic positions and to replace opponents with supporters of the WID policy. In addition, an open focus on personnel management policy is necessary, in order to put the connection between gender relevance in the technical assistance programme and the personnel management policy on the agenda. As mentioned earlier, focusing on the personnel management policy in the negotiations is less used as a strategy by the innovators. At the moment, the innovators are not occupying positions which make such a strategy viable. Another important factor making it nearly impossible is that such a strategy may be perceived as if the female staff of the ILO negotiate to their own advantage, at least as long as the innovators are mainly women. The innovators feel uncomfortable by doing it. It is easier, then, to speak for women in the Third World. With an increase in the number of male innovators, the negotiations may turn in a mainstreaming direction. No one can accuse men of acting to their own advantage when negotiating gender in the personnel management policy.

Another element making mainstreaming difficult is the basis of the organizational structure of the ILO, which is part of its Deep Core. The ideological foundation of the hierarchical and bureaucratic structure (superior/subordinate relationships, sectoral approach) is opposed to the principles of the WID policy (equality, comprehensive and relational thinking). To us, it has been a paradox that none of the innovators was concerned about the issue of bureaucracy. That may of course have changed now. According to our view, a bureaucracy may be perceived

> as a type of social system, one in which certain social acts are established and maintained, certain social objects are valued, certain languages are spoken, certain types of behaviour are required, and certain motivations are encouraged. The norms and rules dominant in bureaucracy, as in any social system, are generally those that support the requirements of bureaucratic self-maintenance (Ferguson, 1984, p. 9).

Some of the barriers towards a "policy change" may, therefore, be found in this part of the Organization's Deep Core.

We do not say that "policy change" is impossible within this bureaucratic structure, but that the structure will, counteract rather than support implementation of the WID policy. Is it, then, a desirable strategy to work for a change of the Deep Core of the ILO, i.e. to work against bureaucracy and hierarchy as organizing principles? It may be a waste of the innovators' time and resources to direct the efforts *only* towards a structural change, because "bureaucracies are with us for our lifetimes and probably for many generations to follow" (Staudt, 1990, p. 7). As part of the innovators' comprehensive strategy towards a "policy change", however, questioning the Deep Core philosophy of the ILO is necessary. The system criticism must be a part of the overall strategy of the innovators as long as mainstreaming is the goal. If a change is to have any chance of coming about, everybody must contribute to altering the system from their own positions. But, to avoid being punished by the bureaucracy when doing it, i.e. to be denied career promotion, to be deprived of interesting working tasks or reasonable working conditions, such a strategy must be a collective action among the innovators. Collective action is a way of empowering the female staff of the ILO.

A way to get around the problem of Deep Core beliefs is, however, to redefine the "women-specific" projects, so that they can become a more appreciated part of the strategy. As these projects only require changes in Secondary Aspects, they may be implemented without too much resistance and within a short-term perspective. "Women-specific" projects can be used to empower women in the Third World, so that they themselves can collectively "define the problem, identify solutions, and act to ameliorate disadvantageous situations. Change comes from the bottom up, from women who have been excluded from channels leading to centers of power" (Gallin et al., 1989, p. 7). Embedded in this strategy is that empowered women in the Third World can, themselves, demand changes of the ILO's practices in the direction of the Third World women's own interests. Empowered women can, through an improvement of their own situation in economic and social life, contribute to increasing the external pressure for changes in the ILO. Empowerment is, thus, an additional strategy which may be necessary, outside as well as inside the ILO. Our conclusion is, therefore, that the prospects for a "policy change" coming about in the ILO are poor in a short time perspective. However, by utilizing a *variety of strategies* in a consistent way, the future for a gender responsive policy in the ILO is more optimistic.

Notes

1 It is necessary to emphasize that we only use the ILO as one example of several in analysing this process. From the rest of our empirical material, we have seen the same tendencies as we have here elaborated on with respect to the ILO. That counts for other international organizations, and for national and local bureaucracies in Norway.
2 This chapter is part of a research project called "Barriers to Implementation of Women Oriented Assistance in International Organizations". The aim for that project is to identify barriers, and assist in the struggle to overcome them.
3 The autonomy of organizations is an ongoing discussion within political science. See, for example, March and Olsen (1989) and Staudt (1990).
4 The problems of gender and bureaucracy will be discussed as a separate issue in a forthcoming paper.
5 For a more thorough discussion of the personnel issue, see Pietilä 1990, Annex 3.

References

Acker, J. 1990. Hierarchies, Jobs, Bodies: A Theory of Gendered Organizations. *Gender and Society*, Vol. 4, No. 2.
Bookman, A. and Morgen, S. (eds.) 1988. *Women and the Politics of Empowerment*, Philadelphia: Temple University Press.
Ferguson, K. E. 1984. *The Feminist Case against Bureaucracy*, Philadelphia. Temple University Press.
Gallin, R. S., Arnoff, M. and Ferguson, A. (eds.) 1989. *The Women and International Development Annual*, Vol. 1, Westview Press.
Hernes, G. 1978. *Forhandligsøkonomi og blandingsadministrasion*. (The Negotiated Economy and Mixed Administration). Bergen/Oslo/Tromsø: Universitetsforlaget.
ILO Info 1987. *Norge og ILO*, (Norway and the ILO), FN-sambandet i Norge.
ILO 1988a. *Women Workers: Selected ILO Documents*, Second edition. Geneva: International Labour Office.
ILO 1988b. *Director-General's Programme and Budget Proposals for 1990–91*, GB.242/PFA/3/1, Geneva, December.

ILO 1988c. *Composition and Structure of the Staff*, GB.239/PFA/9/13, Geneva, February–March.
ILO 1988d. *Integration of Women's Interests in Project Design: Application of ILO General Guidelines and UNDP Project Review Form*, ILO Circular, No. 44, 29.08.88.
ILO 1988e. *1988 Programming Guidelines for Multi-bilateral Projects*.
ILO 1988f. *Chart of Ratifications of International Labour Conventions*.
ILO 1989a. *The ILO Multi-bilateral Programme – 1988 Performance Report*.
ILO 1989b. *Participation of Women in ILO's Technical Cooperation Programme – Status as of June 1989*.
ILO 1990a. *Mainstreaming. Lessons Learned on Women's Role in Selected ILO Mainstream Projects*, Geneva: ILO (draft copy).
ILO 1990b. *A Compendium on Women's Participation in Selected ILO Technical Cooperation Projects*, Geneva: ILO.
ILO 1990c. *The ILO Multi-bilateral Programme – 1989 Performance Report*.
ILO 1990d. *Programme and Budget Proposal for 1992–93*, Programme, Financial and Administrative Committee, GB.245/PFA/3/1, 245th Session.
ILO 1990e. *ILO Activities for Equality of Opportunity and Treatment of Men and Women in Employment*, Committee on Discrimination, GB.246/CD/4/4, 246 Session.
ILO 1990f. *Composition and Structure of the Staff*, Geneva, February–March.
ILO 1990g. *A List of Ongoing Women-Specific Projects Within ILO's Technical Cooperation Programme*, Geneva: ILO, PROMOTEC.
ILO 1990h. *ILO Experiences in Making Women Visible in Selected Mainstream Projects in the Southern African Region* Geneva: ILO.
Inter-Agency Equal Opportunities Group 1989 *Women in International Organisations*, A Presentation for International Women's Day, 8 March 1989. (This group is an informal group of female staff from 17 Geneva-based International organizations.)
KAD (1989): *ILO – Ajourført oversikt over det totale antall konvensjoner og rekommendasjoner ILO har vedtatt og norske ratifkasjoner og tiltredelser*. (Total ILO Conventions and Recommendations and Norwegian Ratifications). Kommunal- og arbeidsdepartementet, Oslo.
Kardam, N. 1989. Women and Development Agencies. In R. S. Gallin *et al.* (eds) (1989).
Leonard-Barton 1988. Implementation as Mutual Adaptation of Technology and Organization. *Research Policy*, Vol. 17.
Lexow, J. and McNeill, D. 1989. *The Women's Grant*. Evaluation Report 2:89, Royal Norwegian Ministry of Development Cooperation.
March, J. D. and Olsen, J. P. 1989. *Rediscovering Institutions*, New York: The Free Press.
Martin, P. Y. 1990. Rethinking Feminist Organizations. *Gender and Society*, Vol. 4, No. 2.
Morgen, S. and Bookman, A. 1988. Rethinking Women and Politics: An Introductory Essay. In Bookman and Morgen (eds) (1988).
Pietilä, H. and Ingrid Eide 1990. *United Nations and Advancement of Women*. The Nordic UN Project, Report No. 16, Stockholm.
Rudie, I. (ed.) 1984 *Myk start – hard landing*, (Soft Start – Hard Landing). Oslo/Bergen/Stavanger/Tromsø: Universitetsforlaget.
Sabatier, P. A. 1987. Knowledge, Policy-Oriented Learning, and Policy Change. *Knowledge: Creation, Diffusion, Utilization*, Vol. 8, No. 4, June.
Staudt, K. (ed.) 1990. *Women, International Development, and Politics*, Philadelphia: Temple University Press.
Utenriksdepartementet 1990. *Oppfølging av kvinnespørsmål i multilaterale bistandsorganisasjoner*, (Norway's Follow-up of Women's Issues in the UN Organizations) Oslo.

Vihma, J. 1988. *Internationella arbeitsorganisationen – ILO*, Stockholm: Norstedts Förlag. (A descriptive book about the ILO.)

Weber, M. 1979. *Makt og byråkrati* (Power and Bureaucracy), Oslo: Gyldendal Norsk Forlag.

Working for Development (undated): *The Technical Cooperation Programme of the ILO*, Geneva: ILO

Contributors

NINA BERG holds a cand. jur. degree from the University of Oslo (1987), where she is presently a research fellow at the Institute of Women's Law, Department of Public and International Law. She has carried out fieldwork in Mozambique and her research interests include Women's Law and International Human Rights.

ANNE BRITT FLEMMEN is presently a Ph.D. student at the University of Tromsø. She obtained her cand. polit. degree in development geography at the University of Trondheim in 1988 and worked at the Foundation of Applied Research at the University of Tromsø (FORUT) from 1988 to 1991. Her main research interests are gender, regional development projects and women's activity space.

SIRI GERRARD holds a mag. art. degree from the University of Tromsø (1975, ethnography/social anthropology). Today, she is a senior lecturer in the social sciences at the Norwegian College of Fishery Science, University of Tromsø. She has conducted fieldwork in fisheries communities in Finnmark, Northern Norway and the Mara Region of Tanzania. Her studies have focused on gender, fishery culture and fisheries development.

AASE GUNDERSEN holds a cand. jur. degree from the University of Oslo (1987), where she is presently a research fellow at the Institute of Women's Law, Department of Public and International Law. She has carried out fieldwork in Mozambique. Her research interests are Women's Law and International Human Rights.

GERD HOLMBOE-OTTESEN holds an M.S. degree in nutrition from the Massachusetts Institute of Technology in Boston, USA (1979). At present she is a senior research fellow at the Centre for Development and the Environment, University of Oslo. She has been working on issues related to agrarian change and implications for nutrition and is currently finishing a dissertation (Ph.D.) on this topic. She has carried out fieldwork in Ecuador, Sri Lanka, Tanzania and Botswana, and has written several articles on gender issues related to household food security and child nutrition.

AN-MAGRITT JENSEN has a cand. polit. degree (criminology) from the University of Oslo (1975) and is presently a senior research fellow at the Norwegian Institute for Urban and Regional Research. Her field of specialization is demography, and she is now working on (a) the relationship between female employment and fertility in Norway, (b) children's family experiences in Norway in relation to changes in family composition, and (c) fertility development in Kenya.

MERETE LIE holds a mag. art. degree in social anthropology from the University of Oslo (1975). At present, she is a senior research fellow at the Institute for Social Research in Industry (SINTEF) in Trondheim. Her main research interests are gender, technology and work focusing on the effects of new technology on the sexual division of labour and the definition of skills in Norwegian enterprises. During the period 1986–90 she was responsible for a project on women in Norwegian industry in Malaysia. Currently, she is studying the link between technology and gender identity.

ANN THERESE LOTHERINGTON is a research fellow at the Foundation of Applied Research at the University of Tromsø (FORUT). She obtained her cand. polit. degree in Political Science at the University of Oslo in 1986 and has since been doing applied research within the areas of national and international public policy. Her main research interests are gender, politics and organization.

RAGNHILD LUND obtained her cand. philol. degree (human geography) from the University of Bergen (1979) and is currently senior lecturer at the Department of Geography, University of Trondheim. Her work has mainly been in the field of agrarian problems and gender issues, and she has field experience from Sri Lanka, Thailand and Malaysia. She has conducted consultancies in Asia and Africa. During the period 1986–90 she was responsible for the project on women in Norwegian industry in Malaysia. Currently, she is working in human resources development in Sri Lanka.

ASTRID NYPAN obtained her mag. art. degree (1958) in sociology from the University of Oslo, where she is now a senior lecturer in the Department of Sociology. She has worked as a consultant to various UN and bilateral aid agencies and has been a research fellow at the University of Ghana and senior research fellow at the University of Dar es Salaam. She has carried out research in Africa on market trade (Ghana); rural development, diffusion of innovations and leadership; youth, education and occupational aspirations (Tanzania).

INGRID RUDIE obtained her mag. art. degree in social anthropology at the University of Oslo in 1962, where she is presently lecturer in social anthropology. She has carried out fieldwork in Norway and Malaysia, and her current research interests include the person and the reproduction of culture, with special reference to gender and modernization.

KRISTI ANNE STØLEN holds a mag. art. degree in social anthropology from the University of Oslo (1976), where she is currently a senior research fellow at the Centre for Development and the Environment. She is presently working on a project entitled "Economy, ideology and gender relations in Latin American rural societies" and has previously researched on agrarian movements, socio-economic change and gender relations among immigrant farmers in Argentina, on gender and agricultural transformation among Andean peasants (Ecuador), and on agricultural change in Northern Zambia.

MARIKEN VAA obtained her mag. art. degree in sociology from the University of Oslo in 1967. She is at present a senior research fellow at the Institute for Social Research in Oslo. She has done fieldwork in East and West Africa as well as in Norway. Her fields of interest are urbanization and migration, development theory and technologies for basic needs.

HALLDIS VALESTRAND obtained her cand. polit. degree from the University of Bergen (1978, human geography). She has done fieldwork in Norway and in Latin America and is currently working as a research fellow at the Department of Social Science, Section for Community Studies and Planning, University of Tromsø. Her research interests focus on gender and regional development, feminist theory and development studies.

MARGARETA WANDEL obtained her cand. real. degree in nutritional physiology at the University of Oslo in 1980, and is now a senior research fellow at the National Institute for Consumer Research, Oslo. She has been working on issues related to agrarian change and implications for nutrition and is presently finishing a Ph.D. dissertation on this topic. She has written several articles from field research in Sri Lanka and Tanzania dealing with gender issues, household food security and child nutrition.